A TALE

OF

TWO SCREWS

Bob Richards & Steve Shepherd

A Tale of Two Screws

By Bob Richards and Steve Shepherd

Foreword

This book is about the joint memories of two prison officers, Bob (the chair) Richards and Steve (Shep) Shepherd who joined the Prison Service at different times and served at different prisons until they met in the visits department at HMP Belmarsh. We aim to share our experiences and stories from our service. You may find some of it shocking and we hope you find some of it funny if you have a dark sense of humour, this is not a book about prison procedures or how a prison runs but about how prison officers and prisoners build a working relationship. We hope it gives an insight into the interaction between prisoners and prison officers every day.

Some names have been changed, some nick names have been used and the names of some staff that are sadly no longer with us have been used. The case details of certain prisoners are taken from previously published accounts readily available to the public on the internet through sites like Murderpedia, Wikipedia and newspaper articles.

Contents

Bob (the chair) Richards

1. Applying For The Job

I joined the Prison Service basically because I was earning £9,000 a year as a security guard in a shopping centre and myself and my partner were buying our first house and we were looking to start a family, that meant I had to earn on my own what we were earning as a couple. I had seen an advert in the local job centre for about six months advertising the Prison Service the advert said London recruitment which meant I would be posted to a London prison and the starting wage was just over £10,000 rising to £15,000 when something called "Fresh Start" happened.

I applied for the Prison service in February of 1987 and was called for an entrance exam at a place called Cleland House in London in April that year. They sent me an example of the test I would have to take, I had never seen anything like it, and so I attended on the day and awaited the test.

Apart from the observation element which consisted of a drawing of a cell and I had to note down things like a bar missing at the window and a radio on the table, there was the English test which if you were any good at crosswords wouldn't be a problem.

But then there was a series of tests which consisted of predicting the next sequence "i.e." two small squares two large squares two small triangles what comes next? Although this seems simple it was not long before the sequences made no sense at all, and I couldn't see any logical sequence.

I ticked anything because I thought I may pick up the odd point by luck if I did and we had been told to finish the test instead of leaving blank spaces.

There were about forty of us at Cleland House that day taking the test, and we were all in the same room while the test went on. At the end of it, about 12 or 15 of us were called out of the room and I thought well that's it the one's that had passed were the ones left in the room.

To my surprise, the woman that called us out told all of us not to look so glum as we had passed and were being taken to have our medicals, and if all was well with that we would have our interviews. The medical consisted of providing a urine sample, and then I was asked about my weight, I could have lied as they never weighed me and then I had an eye test. All of this was fine so I was called into another room for my interview with three people sitting on the board. I was asked various questions, some about if I would treat a black prisoner any differently to a white one.

I had no trouble with this as in my view all prisoners were scum this may sound harsh but I had spent the last seven years dealing with shop lifters, assaults and the local criminals, I have lost count of the fights I had in the centre and because of that my views were somewhat biased so I would treat them all the same. I was asked what I would do if I got involved in a fight with prisoners, it was at this point I thought I had messed up and would not get the job. I answered that I had been in numerous fights in my security job and that up until that point in time I had never lost, as soon as I said it I thought I had come across as treating the question flippantly and they would think I was too aggressive or lacked self-control.

I needn't have worried as the interview carried on and at the end; they said they would be in touch if I were successful. I went home and told my partner I was not confident, but we would have to wait and see. The following day a letter arrived and I thought it would say sorry I had not been successful because I had expected to wait at least a couple of weeks for a reply, to my amazement I had been accepted and they wanted me to start in May.

I then thought I would get knocked back because I had to write to them accepting the position but asking if they would postpone the start date because I was getting married on the 27th June and I didn't want to come home from the college on Friday, get married on Saturday and then return to college on Sunday. They were good enough to postpone my start date until the 20th of July when I was to report to Wandsworth Prison to start my training.

As it turned out this delay would be advantageous as a family friend who was a bookkeeper had a client who was also joining the service at the same time and so I contacted him and arranged for him to pick me up and travel to HMP Wandsworth on the first morning.

2. Starting at HMP Wandsworth

As it turned out I had to miss my first day because I had to attend court because of a fight that had happened in the shopping centre. So on the 21st of July Nic picked me up to travel to Wandsworth, I was not the smallest of guys at 5'11 and over sixteen stone when Nic turned up I could see he was about 6'2 and about the same weight, what difference does this make you may ask but Nic drove a Hillman Imp car and we both had to squash into the front seats.

We only got about four miles up the road when the car broke down, luckily Nic had a friend who lived close by and so he nursed the car to his friends and borrowed his car. We arrived late at Wandsworth so we had to explain why and I had to explain why I had missed my first day.

I have already mentioned Fresh Start but Nic and I didn't know really what it was, but the officers at Wandsworth were quite militant and because they thought we had started on Fresh Start already there were big discussions about whether they would let us through the gate.

(The prison Service had been drastically understaffed, and prisons ran on officers working overtime. This was called the "V" scheme Officers would often not take annual leave because they would go onto basic pay for that period, and they were earning high wages doing overtime. Fresh Start would put a stop to that and increase the basic pay rate. This meant a lot of officers could lose thousands of pounds as they would work as many hours as possible on overtime rates.

The POA (Prison Officers Association) was not happy with this, it also meant working a 48 hour week reducing in increments over five years to a 39 hour week with no overtime because it was part of a large recruitment drive) for me this was fine I had come from a job earning £9,000 a year and over a five-week rota I worked two 84 hour weeks a 60 hour week a 48 hour week and a week off. For me, it meant a shorter working week more time off and a £6,000 pay rise, happy days the flip side of that was my first experience of Wandsworth was nearly being refused entry.

We were called NEPO's then (New entrant prison officers) the training was twelve weeks, three at Wandsworth and nine for me and Nic at Newbold Revel an old manor house near Rugby. The three weeks at Wandsworth consisted of reporting to the training department every morning to be given tasks for the day. This might consist of being told to go onto whatever wing and reporting to P.O (Principal Officer) whoever, who would tell us to go and see officer whoever on one of the landings and observe what went on. Wandsworth ran on a seniority basis and so the P.O probably wouldn't take his head out of his newspaper and would just wave his arm in the general direction of whatever officer we would have to go and see. That officer would just say stand over there out of the way and if there is an alarm bell just get back against the wall and don't interfere.

We were told that whatever area we had been sent to we had to record how many sand buckets, fire hoses or extinguishers and locations along with alarm bells. Everywhere we went we were met with the same seniority crap if you didn't have at least five years in you weren't worth talking to. Even the prisoners had an attitude; we went to see the bath house and the laundry and the officer in charge said to one of the prisoners tell these new staff about the laundry and the prisoner replied "I'll talk to them when they are real screws" because at that time we were walking around in civvies with a cap badge pinned to our jackets.

I thought to myself I will see you when I come back here, we then went to see how reception worked and even in there I was standing leaning on the reception desk and one of the reception orderly's told me not to lean on the desk. This attitude was beginning to piss me off; we went to the security department and the S.O (Senior Officer) said you won't get on security until you have at least five years in. By contrast, we had a visit to HMP Brixton which was a remand prison as opposed to Wandsworth being a convicted prison. Basically from the beginning of our tour the P.Os, S.Os and officers were completely different asking us what we wanted to know and helping us in any way they could.

This made me think this is the prison I am putting in for. Back at Wandsworth we went to the Segregation Unit and watched Adjudications, I was surprised that the officers escorting the prisoner on report stood facing the prisoner eyeballing him and we were told if the prisoner got agitated or made a move they would be removed. We had a visit to Inner London Crown Court which was run by Brixton staff as were all London courts.

We had gym sessions at Wandsworth and the first time we entered the gym I think all of us were surprised, the prisoners in there were huge and by this I mean muscular. An officer who would go onto be the World's strongest man was a PEI there and he was huge as well, I asked why the prisoners were allowed to get so big and he said the lads in the gym at that time were members of Wandsworth's power lifting team and they would go around the country competing. I asked if their size ever cause a problem if they had to be restrained, he answered that they wanted to be in the gym so much they would never play up or that privilege would be taken away.

Our three weeks at Wandsworth came to an end and we were going off to Newbold Revel near Rugby for the last nine weeks of training. Our training at Newbold consisted of regular runs to improve our fitness, C&R (control & restraint) rolling around the Dojo in very ill-fitting Gi's (Judo suits) this included cell removals, handcuffing and the different types of cuffs used (ratchet and escort, closeting chains) cell searching as well as rub down searches and strip searches. Classroom work covering report writing, prison rules, adjudication process, IPS (inter personal skills) and racial discrimination. We also did lessons on how to use a personal radio and the procedures relating to this and of course key security and how to unlock and lock cell doors, prison officers are not just Neanderthal turn keys there is a lot to learn and you are tested on all elements through the training process.

3. Newbold Revel

Newbold Revel is an 18th-century country house in the village of Stretton-under-Fosse, Warwickshire, England. It is now used by HM Prison Service as a training college and is Grade II listed. Newbold is quite an imposing place surrounded by beautiful grounds, especially as I started there in August 1987 and the weather was warm and sunny.

I was placed in 'I' Section there were twenty-one of us in the section from all walks of life, ranging from four ex-military; the owner of a hair salon, myself from a security background and several others, there was a range of ages as well from their early twenties to mid-forties.

We would be taught to march as a section; this was to help instil discipline and teamwork. In my section, there was a Marine drill instructor, an Army drill instructor and a Navy drill instructor. This wasn't too bad but we would all take turns marching the section onto the parade ground every morning, I didn't have any experience of marching but when it was my turn to march the section to the parade ground the one thing the P.O tutor said was I had a good voice for it. The problem came when the Navy drill instructor was in charge, the Navy in comparison to the Army and Marines swagger more than march. Even worse when the Navy guy was part of the section he was always in front of me and that made it hard to keep instep as he was swaggering along. The training was based on teaching us to work as a team, if we were running as part of the P.E lessons the faster ones among us were encouraged to hold back and encourage the slower ones like me.

It wasn't long before we had our first test to see if we were gelling as a section, Race Relations was part of the lesson plans for the nine weeks we were to be there. We had a black lad (I can't remember his name) in the section and one day the P.O tutor came into class and over several minutes started to pick on this lad and the rest of us were looking at each other and then we asked the P.O to stop and told him he was out of order the way he was talking to this lad. The P.O smiled and said that's the end of your Race Relations training for the rest of the course, the P.O had been speaking with the lad outside of the class and told him what he wanted to do to gauge our reaction. We had jumped in to defend the black lad and so the P.O got the reaction he wanted and the lad was chuffed because we had defended him.

I was born and raised in Kent but according to those from "up North" I was a cockney and so in roll play, I would be cast as a gobby Chelsea football thug. I never realised that not only were we being taught what was needed for the job but we were being evaluated all the time as well, we had a roll play and I was an officer rub-down searching prisoners coming off visits.

This time the other one of our two P.O tutors was playing a prisoner and was not being very cooperative during the search and was getting in my face trying to intimidate me, I stepped into him and told him to back off and do as he was told, the P.O complied but when the roll play was over he said I came across as too aggressive, I explained that I wasn't being aggressive but I was letting him know I couldn't be intimidated he grinned but said: "don't be too aggressive".

IPS (inter personal skills) was the psychological part of our training, we were given a couple of tests during this phase of training as well. We had a Governor tutor who did this training and on this day we had just settled in class when he handed us some papers and said let's see how good you are at reading people's feelings and emotions.

On these papers were numerous facial pictures of people and multiple choice answers underneath, our task was to guess what feelings or emotions they were experiencing from the photos. We all gave our answers and the Governor said right let's consult the book and see how you have done, a few minutes later he came back and said go and get yourselves a coffee because you have got them all right and you have just ruined my lesson.

On another occasion, he told us to draw a dot on a piece of paper and then we would step into the middle of the class and have someone walk toward us from the front, back and both sides. When we felt uncomfortable we had to tell them to stop and plot their position on the piece of paper. We then drew a circle linking the dots and that was our personal space, when it was my time I let the people from all directions walk into me, the Governor said this was not possible. I said to him he had not taken into account that I worked previously as security in a busy shopping centre with hundreds of people all around me all day and so I could not afford to have personal space or that would impact my job, he didn't like it but he had to concede.

The first weekend on the course was a duty weekend; the idea of this was to get those that had come from Monday to Friday jobs used to the idea of working weekends. That first weekend was eventful for me I phoned my wife every night, on the Friday of the first week I phoned to find out she had written the car off luckily she had not been hurt. On Saturday night I phoned her to be told she was pregnant and so my career started.

I enjoyed the training especially the Control & Restraint (C&R) this is a method of controlling violent or refractory prisoners through pain compliance. Pain is applied until compliance is achieved and then the pain is eased off. Perhaps it was because I had limited experience of martial arts but I picked it up quite quickly. We had an ex-psychiatric nurse in the section that for some reason we called Psycho, we got on well and when we had progressed to the point of being taught to do cell removals Psycho said he wanted me to be shield man on the team that came in for him.

We kitted up and were waiting at the cell door, back then the practice cell was as you'd expect a concrete box with a cell window a metal cell door, there was no bed in there but there was broken wooden cell furniture all over the floor.

Psycho who was playing the prisoner was in his tracksuit and he had a 3ft lump of tree branch as his weapon, there was no protection for the prisoner but the team were in full PPE (helmet, gloves, overalls, knee/shin guards) the cell door was opened and the three of us with me on the shield entered, as soon as we went in Psycho was hitting the shield with all he could muster. My job was to protect the team until we could get the weapon away from him and restrain him, as I stepped forward I began to slide.

He had laid the broken cell cupboard pieces on top of each other and they were sliding all over the place, I knew if I didn't do something fast the team was going to end up in a crumpled heap on the floor and he would have won. I pushed forward and hit Psycho with the shield and he went down like a sack of shit, we jumped on him and I threw the shield behind me and someone grabbed the tree branch and threw that out of the cell. In the confusion I ended up controlling one of his arms (as shield man I should ideally take control of his head) we put him in wrist locks and manoeuvred him out of the cell, we searched him and then let him go so the instructors could critique how we had done. It was then that Psycho called me a bastard as he had blood running down his face, when I had hit with the shield one of the bolts that hold the handles on must have caught him on his head and cut it, I told him he to be careful what he wished for. He saw the funny side of it and we were fine, the instructors said we had controlled him well when we had him but I needed to pay a bit more attention to what is on the floor as they had seen me start to slide on the furniture and they said prisoners flood their cells to make it slippery or put other substances on the floor.

We were also one of the last courses at Newbold to be taught MUFTI which stood for (Minimum Use of Force Tactical Intervention). This was an archaic system, where the Mufti teams would charge any barricade which had been erected in front of them and batter anyone who came in range with long riot sticks. The unit would advance on the blow of a whistle and withdraw at the blow of a whistle; they would peel off to the side and run backwards as the next unit charged. Of course, when you have a unit of adrenalin-filled screws who have just been battering people who had been throwing things at them running backwards the inevitable happens, someone trips over and then you end up with twelve screws in a pile on the floor or possibly more if the next unit were quicker than you. Those behind the barricade were throwing six-inch lumps of hosepipe at us as we approached, we had plastic shields that weighed quite a bit, but the problem was if you held the shield high enough to protect your head you would get hit in the nuts and if you lowered the shield you got hit in the head. Yes, we wore helmets but in a real situation prisoners could be throwing anything at you, I dread to think what we looked like dressed in Brown boiler suits with gauntlets that resembled wicket keepers gloves, a right motley crew but it was a laugh.

An incident during our final MUFTI test nearly got the whole section thrown off the course the day before our passing out parade. We had been out the night before and got ratted, one of the lads was tea total and wanted to be a PEI, we got him so pissed he couldn't stand. Anyway he was in no fit state to take part in the MUFTI test and so we asked the instructors if he could sit it out as he felt unwell, they agreed and off we went charging the barricade.

While this lad was sitting there trying to recover the Principal of the college came and stood next to him, this lad couldn't hold it in and leaned over and puked on the Principals shoes. The whole section was ordered back to our class room where our governor tutor threatened to throw us all off the course then and there.

Everyone was crapping themselves, after coming so far and there was a chance we would be sacked the day before we passed out. But in the end, the tutor calmed down after some intervention from the two P.O tutors. I think the cost of nine weeks of training also played a part in the decision. We were told this incident wouldn't appear on our final reports from the college, the following day we packed our gear ready to leave after the passing out parade.

We also had a sit down with our P.O tutors for them to tell us how we had done and wish us well, and then we had an individual meeting with our Governor tutor who went over our final report which would be going to our establishments. I had a good overall report which highlighted my ability in C&R and our PE instructor wrote "Officer Richards will never be an Olympic athlete but he gives 110%", I was happy with this and the governor said I had a good course but I need to learn to step back and not be the first one to volunteer all the time, especially for the rough stuff. I thought I had been relatively quiet on the course and had sat back as much as possible because in my previous job I had always been up for a fight and the governor had seen something in my actions. So we had the passing out parade and then it was homeward bound for a week off before starting at Brixton.

4. Brixton

The prison was originally built in 1820 and opened as the Surrey House of Correction; Brixton Prison was intended to house 175 prisoners. Brixton had two main roles not only did it hold remand prisoners who were on trial but it was also responsible for staffing all of the London courts as well as those as far out as St Albans. The CNA (certified normal accommodation) when I went there was 749 but Brixton was holding around 1100 prisoners. At that time they ran what was called an in and an out division which changed over every 20 weeks which meant that those in the jail would go out and man the courts and those at court came into work on the wings and other areas. That was the theory anyway, in reality, you could apply to stay in or stay out, and a lot of the staff wanted to stay out because they were getting daily subs for working out of the prison and by the end of the month this could total up to a tidy sum on top of your wages.

Brixton went onto Fresh Start about a week before I got there and so for me, that was the equivalent of a £6,000 a year pay rise from what I was earning at the Centre. Court work never really appealed to me so I was happy to stay in the prison working on visits for the first five months I was there, visits was a good way of learning your way around the prison as I did a job called a runner which meant I had to pick up the prisoners from the various wings or where ever they were and escort them to the visits hall.

We were never allowed to escort more than six prisoners at a time on our own, if they were normal prisoners or those on the "E-list" (escapers) had to be escorted on their own (if memory serves) and their movement book had to be taken wherever they went, and if you worked on Cat A visits there were always two officers escorting one prisoner, they also had a movement book that went

with them. The visits group mainly consisted of officers with ten
or more years in the job and so I had to start from the bottom and
be a runner, what we considered the more responsible jobs like
room patrol or searching were done by the experienced staff and as
the new boy I would not challenge that, it was only in the last
month or so before the changeover was due that I got the odd day
on room patrol or searching.

In my last few weeks on the visits group, I got to work in the
food room, at that time the Category A remand prisoners were
allowed to have meals brought in for them by their visitors. We
would have to search through the meals checking for drugs or
other contraband; we also kept a tally of how much tobacco or
how many cigarettes they had given in as they had a weekly
allowance. They were allowed five pieces of fruit, but we would
sit and argue with the visitors because they would try and bring in
a melon and another fruit but one melon was equal to five pieces
of fruit according to the list, the same as they couldn't have a
bunch of bananas and other fruit. They were allowed a can and a
half of beer and of course they always had Special Brew as it was
the strongest around at the time. We would pull the tabs so it went
flat in a day and they wouldn't store it and have a party at the end
of the week. Those Cat A's on Fraggle rock weren't allowed cans
or beer but they could have soft drinks but this had to be decanted
into a plastic jug, so they could end up with Vimto and Tango
orange in the same jug or any combination.

At the end of the five months I changed and became the
Orderly officer's aid, the Orderly Officer was a Principal Officer
who was responsible for the overall running of the prison daily.

It was my job to assist him by overseeing deliveries through
the main gate, dealing with contractors who came in through the
back gate and I would update the LIDS system (local inmate

database system) before lunch & tea and if I was on a late shift before final lock-up. This meant that we could run an electronic roll check of the prison and also see the location of all the prisoners.

I started as orderly officers aid and spent the day doing very little as there was no one to show me what to do, at the end of the day the orderly officer called me into the office and told me I was lazy and didn't want to work he then told me to go home as it was the end of my shift. That night I was dwelling on what he had said and to say the least I was pissed off, the following morning I went to work prepared for a row as no one had ever accused me of being lazy and I wasn't going to put up with that. I got to the centre; the area where the orderly officer's office was and the same orderly officer was there his name was Joe an old grey-haired Scottish guy who had been doing the job a long time. I was just about to have a go and he turned around and said 'I'm sorry for accusing you of being lazy I didn't realise it was your first day on the job and you didn't know what to do'.

This took the wind out of my sails a bit as I was ready for the argument to follow, and from that day on we got on well. Joe was old school and he would tell me stories of his experiences doing the job, Joe's counterpart was another principal officer named Ted another long-serving P.O I got on well with him as well, but whereas Joe would make his own decisions Ted would ask my opinion.

The general alarm bell panel was located in the centre and if someone pressed the alarm buttons located in all areas the bell in the centre would be heard by A and B wings, one day the bell in the centre wasn't working but we could still know the location of any alarms because there was also an alarm panel in the centre which lit up when a bell was pressed. Because the bell didn't ring

A and B wings didn't know there was an alarm on C wing this particular day, and so I had to run onto A and B wing like a lunatic shouting alarm, alarm there's an alarm on C wing.

Everyone thought I was a complete nutter but it was the only way to inform staff quickly of the alarm so they could attend the incident. Brixton at this time was over a hundred staff undermanned and so you weren't there long before you had to do all sorts.

With about six months in the job, I was told I was going to be I/c (officer in charge) of an escort taking six YP's (young offenders) to HMYOI Huntercoombe. I had three other members of staff with me but they were just out of their induction week so they were brand new. I had to arrange the YP's property, their valuables, arrange the gate pass which gave us permission to leave the prison and check their property cards and make sure they had current Warrants. So off we set with the YP's cuffed two together in a Pixie (mini bus) I didn't know where Huntercoombe was and the driver wasn't too sure either. I'm thinking great I'm going to end up bringing them back because we can't find the place. Eventually, we found it down a leafy lane somewhere near Henley on Thames, and as we pull up to the gates I notice not only does the place not have a fence around it but the main gates have only just been put in. I had visions that as soon as I opened the door to the van the YP's would do a runner into the middle of nowhere. But I told the other officers to stay in the van with the YP's while I went to find someone in charge.

I came across an S.O in what they described as their reception. It was an old mizzen hut as the place had been an old Internment camp in the war. So I went back to the van and we unloaded the YP's and I got the S.O to sign the body receipt book as soon as possible.

As with all escorts from Brixton, you never rushed back and so we drove down the lane to the staff mess for breakfast before heading back. I realised on the way back we would arrive at Brixton before we could claim our over five subs, (subs were a payment you received depending on the amount of time you were out of the prison.

They were to cover any costs you incurred for meals purchased while on escort or prison business) so I told the driver to take us on a sightseeing tour of London, which he was well versed at because he had done it on so many escorts before. Every new officer at Brixton went through their turn of always being the one cuffed to prisoners when on an escort, the advantage was because of all the new staff arriving because we were so undermanned it wasn't long before it was some other newbie's turn. I worked as an orderly officer's aid for three months which is shorter than it should have been, and then I found myself deployed to the security department.

I hadn't requested the move I had just been deployed there; the security department was responsible not only for the internal security of the prison, things like searching, censoring Cat A mail, drug testing but we also arranged the transport for Cat A escorts and transfers.

I started as a" Burglar" as they were known which meant I was part of three two-man teams who would wander where ever we wanted around the prison searching prisoners and their cells.

We were hated by the prisoners and as soon as we walked onto a wing the whisper would go around that the burglars were on, and the prisoners that were up to something would scurry off to hide their illicit items. Sometimes being a burglar could cause problems, prisoners were only supposed to buy batteries that were the correct size for their radios. But prisoners would often buy PP9 batteries for a small handheld radio because they lasted longer. This was an offence against prison rules, PP9 batteries made a good cosh when placed inside a sock. This particular day all three teams of burglars went onto A wing and we came off with 48 PP9 batteries we had confiscated, never mind the prisoners being upset A wing P.O banned us from the wing because of all the disruption we had caused.

One day I got told to go to the healthcare, they had a prisoner in a room with nothing in it but an electronic toilet. The prisoner so I was told was a drugs mule and he was in this room until nature took its course and he passed the drug packages.

The electronic toilet was new and we were trying it out, the idea being the prisoner uses it and his faeces drops into a plastic bag in the toilet and then it heat seals the bag. We retrieve the bag and have to squish the contents around until we find the packages; we then cut the bag open clean the packages and test them to find out what drugs they contained. Not my idea of a great job but at least the system was relatively clean up to the point of cleaning the packages.

Terry Marsh a well-known boxer and ex fireman transferred to us as he had caused numerous problems at Wormwood Scrubs where he had been previously. Marsh was in for attempted murder of boxing promoter Frank Warren, who Marsh was alleged to have shot but he was later acquitted. Although Marsh was acquitted of the attempted murder he was not the nice sports celebrity who did charity work everyone thought he was.

Marsh had been very disruptive at Wormwood Scrubs and had covered himself in baby oil several times to make it difficult for staff to restrain him; he had been moved to us and put on D wing even though he never actually made Cat A status. But this did not stop him from thinking he was something special, he was mixing with some of the country's top criminals on D wing and he acted as though he was one of them.

His mail was censored by us in security and I often read some of the crap he would write to people outside, one of his favourite things he would write was 'six screws came in again this morning and gave me a beating, but I made sure some of them got hurt' he would write this sort of crap regularly, trying to make out he was something he wasn't. When he came onto visits he would be very meek and mild, and if he tried to get above his station he would back down very quickly when challenged.

We had quite a good find rate and captured quite a lot of drugs, mainly Cannabis as at that time there wasn't so much in the way of hard drugs going around. Sometimes during the lunch break, we would take off our key chains and anything that rattled and tip toe around the landings sniffing at the doors and looking through the cracks in the old wooden doors, trying to find prisoners either smoking Cannabis or just rolling a Spliff.

One of us would be carrying a cell key and when we could smell someone smoking, or saw someone rolling a Spliff we would crash through the door and grab the evidence before they could get rid of it. They would crap themselves when we burst in and it was often funny to see the expressions on their faces as we came through the door.

We had some good finds doing this and when we retrieved the evidence we would search the cell and then go back to the office to test what we had found telling the prisoner that if we got a positive test he would be placed on report. The only problem was on occasion one of the burglars used to wear aftershave that smelled like cannabis, so you would be sniffing at the cell door and wave people over because you found one and then look at this burglar and say 'you've got that fucking aftershave on again' he would just smile and shrug his shoulders.

We used what was called a BDH test, (British Drugs House) which was the manufacturer. The test consisted of putting either a small piece of Cannabis if we had a lump or some of the contents of the cigarette if we had a Spliff on a piece of litmus paper and squirting an accelerant on it and then covering the item with another piece of litmus and squirting distilled water on it and pressing the two together. If it was Cannabis the paper would turn pink giving a positive result and if it was Cocaine or some other opiate it would turn blue. We would then tape the test paper to an index card with the details of where it was found and who had it in possession as well as the time and date and submit it as evidence at the adjudication (Governor's hearing) the following day.

I had a great time burgling every day was different although we had our regular tasks to do; we had to search at least two Cat A prisoners every day on a rota basis.

Cat A prisoners were held mainly on two wings 'A' Secure an annexe of A wing and D wing, Some of them could be difficult, one by the name of Easterbrook thought he knew the rules and would make things as difficult as possible for us. Easterbrook was due to be searched on this particular morning and as myself and the other burglar went into the cell Easterbrook was still in bed, we told him to get up and stand outside while we searched the cell but he was being awkward and slow. We finally got him outside and went to work on the cell, while we were searching he kept opening the hatch in the door to see what we were doing so we called him back in as he was complaining that he was entitled to watch the search which was true but not something we normally allowed. So we said to him if that was what he wanted we would search by the book. We told him to take one of his blankets off of his bed and put it on the floor outside the cell which he did begrudgingly, and then we made him hand every item in the cell out one piece at a time so we could search it and then we placed it on the blanket.

Eventually, he had handed everything out, the chair, table, bedding, books, personal and legal papers as well as his slop bucket, toilet roll, fags absolutely everything then we told him he had to put it all back himself, he never questioned the way we searched in future.

The search took about an hour but it sent the message and no one complained about not being present while we searched again.

On the odd occasion, we would have minor problems when searching, we had a couple of Muslim Cat A's who would often be praying when we went to search their cells. They would ignore us when they were told to get up so we could strip search them before doing the cell. We found a quick and easy way of improving their hearing, we would go to pick their Koran up and they would soon stop praying. We were considered infidels and as such we could not touch the Koran as we were considered dirty.

We would also go to visits and help out by doing their strip-searching for them; they didn't have the time or manpower to carry out strip searches. When you think that it was not unusual to have close to three hundred remand visits on a Saturday, so the search staff were too busy doing the normal rub-down searches.

One or two of us would have a walk through the visits room and pick our targets and then we would let the other burglars waiting in the search area, know who we wanted to be stripped. As soon as they came into the search area we would take control of their arms and take them to a curtained area where we conducted the strip search.

Most times it would go without a problem but on the odd occasion the prisoners would decide to fight us for whatever they were hiding, but this was not a problem because just about everyone on the burglars were always up for a fight.

On one particular day, we had pulled this prisoner in for a strip as he was acting strange, we had carried out the normal tasks of checking his mouth, ears, hair "etc" and then stripped him but found nothing. We couldn't understand what was wrong with him and so I had another look in his mouth and when I checked his ears again I noticed something very small pushed right into his ear, I told him to remove it and as soon as he had taken his hand away from his ear, I grabbed his wrist so he couldn't put it anywhere else.

The item was a tiny square of blotting type paper with a picture on it, as soon as we saw it we realised it was an LSD tab but this idiot had taken the cling film off of it so it would fit in his ear better to hide it.

Because it was not wrapped now the LSD had started to soak into his skin and he was getting his high early, and that's why he was acting strange.

Some days searching in visits turned out to be a scream, one day one of the other burglars was in the room and had let me know who he wanted to be stopped for a strip when he came off his visit.

I was told he had a big lump of Cannabis in his mouth that was too big to swallow. As he came into the search area I was waiting and grabbed his neck. Generally, prisoners would spit out whatever they were concealing in their mouths, this day though I had the prisoner around the neck and he decided to fight us, and so it ended up with me still holding onto his neck and two others trying to pin his arms, and then he was trying to chew the lump of Cannabis up so that he could swallow it. One of the search staff had a bright idea to stop this and produced a metal teaspoon and proceeded to put it in the prisoner's mouth and started scooping little balls of Cannabis from between his teeth. We were all shouting at the prisoner to stop chewing and give us the Cannabis but he was not having any of it and continued trying to swallow the chewed up lump.

It must have been some sight to see, a prisoner on the floor struggling with four screws one looking like he was trying to strangle the prisoner two trying to restrain him, one spooning little balls of Cannabis out of his mouth and one scooping the little balls of Cannabis into a pile so he could bag it up and use it for evidence. Eventually, he gave up and we retrieved the Cannabis and he was placed on report, when he went to the adjudication he never said a word about what had happened but pleaded guilty for possession of Cannabis and he received his punishment.

The searching was interspersed with other tasks such as cell removals, this is where a prisoner or prisoners are non-compliant for whatever reason and they have to be removed from their cell and taken to the Block (segregation unit). On one of these occasions, we had a prisoner on F wing which we called Fraggle rock because it was attached to the hospital wing and it was where all the prisoners who really should have been in mental institutions were kept. Most of these prisoners were raving and at that time there was a TV programme called Fraggle Rock where all these weird things run around like lunatics, hence F wing was called Fraggle rock.

This day one of them had smashed his cell up and had threatened staff with two table legs he had ripped off of his cell table, when we got there we were in PPE (personal protective equipment) this is flame retardant overalls, helmet, padded leather gloves shin and knee pads and a four-foot polycarbonate shield. We always worked in the 3 man teams, (in today's prison service you would have to say 3 officer teams) so the officer with the shield would be in front and the other two would be behind him so we formed an arrowhead formation. There was a senior officer at the door talking to the prisoner and trying to get him to give up, but he kept hitting the door with the table legs and screaming obscenities at us through the door.

Finally, the senior officer had done all he could and told us to go in and take him out, he unlocked the door for us and as he took his hand away we crashed through the door. The prisoner looked stunned and sat down on his chair and threw the table legs to one side and said "I give up" it was too late once we were committed through the door there was no surrender I hit him with the shield and knocked him arse over tit off his chair and as he was laying on his back I got rid of the shield and we went down on top of him and restrained him.

The whole thing from the door being unlocked to putting him on his back and restraining him couldn't have taken more than a couple of minutes.

We then took him in locks (wrist locks) squealing to the strip cells below, where he was placed in an unfurnished cell where the hospital screws could keep an eye on him and he couldn't smash anything else up. Incidents like these were almost a daily event on F wing, the wing held about 300 prisoners most of which should have been in mental institutions, but due to the government's policy of closing mental institutions, the Courts had no option but to place these people in prison.

Myself and another burglar walked onto Fraggle Rock one day and an officer was sitting in the doorway of a cell, the door was open and the prisoner was handcuffed to the bed. We asked what was going on and the officer said it was a constant watch as the prisoner was trying to eat himself, whatever part of his body he could get his mouth too he would take chunks out of himself, that's why he was cuffed to the bed. Strange behaviour was not uncommon on Fraggle Rock, a prisoner had been complaining of stomach pain for some time. He had been given medication but continued to complain, a prison doctor had agreed he should go to the hospital for an x-ray. When they got him there and did the x-ray they found that he had swallowed parts of a prison-issue plastic fork and spoon.

This was the sort of thing that happened on a fairly regular basis there, apart from the prisoners not being in a place able to cope with this sort of behaviour it also wasn't fair on the staff. Fraggle Rock and the healthcare had a prison doctor who was a GP, there were hospital officers (scab lifters) as they were called who were prison officers who had done a course, which was just an enhanced first aid course. Most of these prisoners really should have been in mental institutions, night shift on Fraggle Rock was an event.

You walked onto the wing and it was howling like the monkey house at London Zoo, and you also had the stench of urine and faeces that hit you like a hammer. All the cells doors had drop flaps so you didn't have to open the door to talk to the prisoner or give them things, when I started my first pegging round I would close all the open flaps because most of the lights were out and as you walked past a cell with an open flap several prisoners would put their arm out and say governor this used to scare the shit out of me because it wasn't expected. Closing the flaps was twofold, it made the prisoners quiet down, and you didn't have the shit scared out of you when walking around.

There was one officer on a landing, but you could have two or three 15 minute watches (these have to be physically observed every 15 minutes) and one constant watch (theoretically these should be observed continually through the night) and this was on top of your rounds every 30 minutes where you had to check on all prisoners on your landing, it was an impossible task and you just hoped that when you did your final count in the morning, you didn't find anyone hanging or in a pool of blood on the floor.

Checking on the F wing prisoners could be difficult, when you looked through the observation glass some would be standing at the window looking out all night, some would put their bed standing at an angle against the wall and sleep on the floor underneath it and some would sleep on the floor right by the bottom of the door so you couldn't see them.

It was a nightmare you could be going into cells all night long to check they were still alive, but we only had a cell key in a pouch for emergencies and the Orderly officer would go mad if you kept phoning because you couldn't get a response. You had to weigh up whether or not these prisoners were dead or just uncooperative.

There were lighter moments, or at least what we thought of as lighter moments. One day while sitting in the security office there was an alarm in the visits search area, we knew that one of the burglars was already there as he had asked to borrow a raincoat from another officer who normally worked in the office, censoring the Cat A mail. We ran for the alarm and even before we got to the search area there was a horrendous smell coming through the door, when we got inside the burglar who had borrowed the jacket was standing there covered in shit, it was all over the borrowed jacket and had even gotten into the microphone of the radio he was carrying.

He had decided with one of the visits lads to strip this particular prisoner, and he had tried to stuff whatever he had up his arse.

They had jumped on him and the prisoner who was so scared he shit himself and it was everywhere because they had been rolling around in it. Those of us from security that had run for the alarm thought sod this and we turned around and left them to it, needless to say, we had weeks of fun taking the piss.

One day I was asked to be part of an escort for a prisoner by the name of Nelson who was a disruptive prisoner held in the seg, he was known for committing violent crimes and in the future would be convicted of two murders one of whom was a police officer. We were taking him to HMP Leeds (also known as Armley) there was me two other officers and a P.O, we got him on the van and off we went.

Armley had a reputation for being a hard prison that didn't take any crap, when we arrived we drove around to the seg and took him in. there were three seg staff waiting and they started telling him what would happen there. Nelson was moaning about his property because he had been told he couldn't have it until reception staff had gone through it, and the fact that he had been transferred around the system so much he had a lot of property that hadn't caught up with him.

He was shown to the cell he was going into but refused because he said it was bigger than a normal cell and he thought it was a strip cell. At this point, I couldn't believe what I was seeing, these hard Armley screws allowed him to walk around the seg so he could see all the cells were the same size.

Then when he was satisfied it was a normal cell he was told he would have a strip search and he refused. Then the seg staff said to our P.O they would have to get a team of PEI's from the gym to strip him under restraint. I couldn't believe that seg staff would call PEI's to restrain someone; our P.O said if anyone is going to restrain him we would do it. While this was going on one of the officers on our escort who worked in Brixton's seg took Nelson to one side and had a word and strip-searched Nelson himself and then put him in the cell, and told the seg staff to cancel the gym staff. Nelson had complied because our seg officer had told him we would wait for the reception staff to come to the seg and sort his property out. This we did and the escort went off without a problem and we returned to Brixton.

As I have said working at Brixton you gained a lot of experience quickly, I did an escort taking a Cat A to Strangeways with another officer and an S.O. I can't remember why we took him but when we got there we took him to the seg and we got into a conversation with an officer who I shall call Duff as it seems appropriate.

He told us he had 15 years in the job and seemed proud of this as it made him a relatively senior staff member; while we were talking he looked at me and the other officer and asked who was senior out of the pair of us. The other officer said he was by about six months, and so Duff looked at me and said 'you're making the tea then' just as he said this a cleaner walked past and I pointed at him and said 'you see him he's a cleaner they make the tea not staff' Duff wasn't too impressed with the gobby London screw basically telling him to get stuffed. Not to be put off his game he carried on telling us about his exploits during his 15 years' service. A couple of years later I would see Duff again when he was on detached duty at Brixton because of the riot at Strangeways.

This day he was out at court and I was there on an escort, he was like a headless chicken he didn't have a clue what he was doing. He had spent his whole service on the landings and had never done any court work, I said to him that's the advantage of a prison-like Brixton you experience most aspects of the job in a very short space of time.

One day I was tasked with being part of an escort to Liverpool to take a Cat B prisoner called Showers to see his dying dad in the hospital, we were told his dad was the head crime boss in Liverpool and his son was second in command. The plan was we would drive up to Manchester and lodge him there overnight and then take him to Liverpool general the following day, so we travel up in a Pixie (prison van) and get to Manchester. On the way up Showers had been quite amiable and was chatting, and asked us if we were going to have a pint or two that night.

We said we probably would and he gave us the name of a club he had links with and told us to say he had sent us at the door and we would have a good night. I'm sure if we had done this we would have had a good night, but we were always dubious about things like this because when you accept these things there is generally a price to pay, so we declined and said we would just go for a quiet pint.

Our digs were in Salford and the B&B looked like something out of the Munsters, so we freshened up and went down to the bar for a couple before going into Manchester.

The bar was quite busy and there were some students in there, we got talking to them and they asked us what we did for a living (telling people you are a prison officer is not always a good thing and so it is normal to say you are an airline pilot or deep-sea diver or something outrageous) well one of the other officers said to these students you know about the IRA being shot in Gibraltar, and they looked shocked and said 'No you are in the SAS?' we just looked and said we can't say. I was about 17 stone and didn't look SAS material, people are so gullible but it gave us a chuckle. The following day Showers asked if we had a good night and assured us there wouldn't have been any comeback if we had accepted his offer. So because of the time, we would be going to see his father and the fact we would be travelling back to Brixton straight from the hospital we contacted Walton prison in Liverpool to see if we could lodge him there over lunch before heading for the hospital, Walton prison was not happy and tried to refuse apparently because Showers had been so disruptive when he had been imprisoned there years before.

Eventually, they agreed but they would only lodge him over lunch, so once we had eaten we went back to the prison to pick him up and the P.O decided it would be courtesy to inform the local police we were on their patch and what we were doing.

Well, the police had a hissy fit, saying you can't go yet as they would have to get the tactical firearms unit out and secure the hospital or his gang would take him off of us.

The P.O said so you will meet us at the prison and escort us? The police response was no we will meet you at the hospital; this now caused a problem because we didn't know how to get to Liverpool General from the prison and so we had to rely on directions from Showers (no Sat Navs back then) so off we go taking directions from Showers and then we arrive at the hospital to find police everywhere and lots were carrying machine guns. The police said it was clear and so we get out of the van with me cuffed to him dressed in my woolly jumper and the police in their bulletproof vests. We go into the hospital and are told we have to get the lift up to the floor his dad was on, as the lift doors open a nurse walks out and not noticing the cuffs tries to walk between me and Showers and gets caught on the cuffs, the police are flapping not knowing if this is some sort of ploy, and I'm saying sorry to the nurse and trying to get in the lift, we get to the room and go in and his dad is laying there not looking good.

These sorts of escorts are never good even without the armed police, I don't remember how long we were there but eventually, Showers said his goodbyes and we left for the journey back to Brixton. Showers thanked us for taking him as he said it was probably the last time he would see his dad alive, we arrived back at Brixton quite late to be told that Showers dad had died.

A week later we were on our way back to Liverpool for the funeral, the police this time said they would have the area around the church where we were going covered by armed plain-clothed officers, although they would be discreet as they expected a large number of gang members to attend and there was a chance they would try to take Showers off of us. We get to the church and again I am cuffed to him and we enter the church, family members are coming up to him giving their condolences and then a couple of what I presume were gang members come up and say 'take him off the cuffs gov' this has to be a screws worst nightmare. The police said there would be lots of armed police around but when we got off the van there weren't many people outside so where they were I have no idea, being asked to take him off the cuffs makes you feel vulnerable but to be fair to Showers he told them to back off and it was alright as he was there to pay his respects.

To say I was relieved to get back on the van and head back to London was an understatement, Showers was very good about it and again thanked us for taking him.

Day to day life at Brixton was good fun I always enjoyed going to work there. It did on occasion have its dangers though, one day we were doing our usual in visits when quite a major kick-off started in the visits hall. One of the burglars and one of the visits lads had grabbed one of the prisoner's wrists to stop him from transferring the lump of gear (drugs) he had in his hand to his mouth so he could swallow it. Because of this his visitor who had supplied it stood up and started swearing at the officers, and he was trying to come over the tables to get to them. One of the lads gave this visitor a swift right-hander and then it kicked off big time, eventually things got sorted out and I helped take the prisoner under restraint back to F wing where he had come from.

The visits room was a constant source of events, I was in visits one day with a new member of the burglars and I had pointed out a rather large black prisoner I wanted to strip search when his visit finished.

Although it wasn't allowed his girlfriend kept leaning over the centre divider of the visits table and I thought she might be passing him something, the new burglar was not too impressed with my choice as he was over six feet tall and a bodybuilder. To try and put his mind at ease I said to him if it kicks off you kick him in the bollocks and I will punch him in the face as hard as I can. I did say this with a wry smile on my face as I knew he was nervous, if it had kicked off it would have been dealt with as all kickoffs were. So this prisoner comes into the search room and I ask him to step into the strip search area, he seemed a bit subdued and avoided eye contact. Once there I started as always telling him to take his shirt off so I could search it (during a strip search prisoners can never be fully naked so we do the top half and then the bottom) I handed him back his shirt and then ask for his shoes and socks which I hand to the newbie so he can have the smelly bit.

I then ask for his trousers and he slowly hands them to me to search, at this point he is looking nervous so I put them to one side and then say right now your boxers, he pulls his boxers down a little bit and then lifts them back up. I said to him no take them completely off and hand them to me he puts his head down and does as I asked, when he gives them to me they are covered in cum.

His girlfriend had been wanking him off and that was why he was so coy during the search, I told him to squat just in case he had put something up his arse and then just handed his boxers back and told him to get dressed. Whenever I saw him after that I would smile and he would look embarrassed.

Myself and another burglar got told to go to reception late one morning as the police were bringing one in who was playing up, he came in with four policemen one of which was cuffed to him. When the copper went to take the cuffs off the one on the prisoners wrist wouldn't unlock, all of the coppers tried and we did as well with no joy. So we had to phone for a works officer to come over to try and free the prisoner, the copper took his half of the cuff off while we waited for the works officer. The works guy turns up with an angle grinder and some wet and dry paper, he puts the wet and dry between the prisoner's wrist and the cuff and proceeds to start cutting the cuff. It's not long before the prisoner is screaming the cuff is burning him, so the works guy stop so the cuff can cool down. After a couple of minutes, he starts again and in seconds the prisoner is screaming again, someone came up with the idea of the prisoner dunking his wrist into a fire bucket attached to the wall to cool thing down.

For the next five minutes, me and the other burglar are killing ourselves watching the prisoner screaming and plunging his hand in the bucket every few seconds. Eventually, the cuff is off and the prisoner is rubbing his wrist and calling us a bunch of bastards for laughing at him.

Another day in the search room a prolific drug user who we always got gear from finished his visit and came into the room, he went to walk into the strip search area when he saw me and I said hang on and I asked him if he had any gear on him and he said no. I said alright off you go; he looked at me confused and said what. I said you told me you don't have anything so you can go, he said this is a trick and I replied no I believe you so off you go, he looked at me with mistrust on his face and so I said no I'm serious off you go.

At this point he demanded a strip search, I said you can go but again he demanded a strip search so I obliged and me and the other burglar started the search (there are always two officers for a strip search to stop allegations of inappropriate touching) as soon as he took his trousers off a lump of Cannabis about the size of a golf ball fell to the floor, I retrieved it and told him he was nicked. I also told him he was an idiot because I seriously would have let him go, but he said he thought I was stitching him up.

I told him for me it was a game some days the good guys win and some the bad, it was never personal.

On another day we answered an alarm bell in the visitor waiting area, the visitors sit there waiting to go in and see husbands/boyfriends, but this day one of the young female visitors had come to see her baby father and realised there was another young woman there to see her man, it kicked off and the baby mother stabbed the other woman in the head with a Bic biro.

Luckily it hadn't gone too deep but we had to break them up and call the police and an ambulance, although it wasn't a serious head wound there was blood everywhere. One ED (evening duty) I was in the orderly office waiting for some warrants when the orderly officer got a phone call from 'A' wing saying they thought a prisoner on the two's was smoking cannabis, I went onto the wing and with another officer, we went to the cell. I peeped through the spy hole and then crashed through the door; the prisoner was a young black lad whose name was Bailey and one of his front teeth was gold (he would later be known as Gold tooth Bailey). He was in the process of cutting a bit of cannabis off his main lump to put in his fag. He grabbed the lump and put it in his mouth, I grabbed his neck to try and stop him from swallowing it but he managed it.

I told him he had won this one but I would get him another day. Everyone knew prisoners smoked cannabis overnight, but to do it before the wing was locked up for the night was taking the piss and I told him so.

The following day I was with another burglar in visits when gold tooth bailey walked in, I thought he might have the arse about me grabbing his neck but all he said was 'you're a bad man gov a bad man' (years later our paths would cross again at Belmarsh).

One of the many tasks the burglars did was to go to D wing, one of the two Cat A-wings and oversee breakfast every so often. D wing held the more able or dangerous Cat A's and it was here that I first saw Charlie Bronson, he was in his thirties then and the first time I saw him was running around the caged exercise yard on D wing. His reputation for being extremely violent and disruptive preceded him. I watched him in the exercise yard and the thing that struck me most was his stamina he just kept running, he never seemed to stop or slow down. His cell was on the ones in

D wing and you could tell it was his cell because not only did it have the usual oak door to it but it had a metal gate as an outer door. Sometimes during breakfast, the oak door was left open if Charlie had been behaving so he could talk to the other prisoners as they came to pick up their breakfast.

It was because his oak door was left open on odd occasions that I had my first encounter with Charlie. D wing was at the time also housing an IRA prisoner who every morning spoke to Charlie. This particular morning we were watching breakfast and Charlie was out to get his breakfast, all of a sudden he attacked the Irish prisoner and then, Charlie just turned around and said to me and the other lads I was with "you better lock me up now Gov" and walked back into his cell and sat on the bed. We locked the oak door and the metal gate in front of it, while other staff were seeing too the injured prisoner who had been assaulted.

This incident demonstrated how unpredictable and dangerous Charlie could be, I would speak with Charlie years later about this.

He told me the reason he attacked the Irish guy was that each morning he would give Charlie a couple of biscuits to have with his tea, and then for a couple of days the Irish guy didn't come down and Charlie was beginning to wonder if he was being set up.

Because of this, Charlie thought if I'm going to be assaulted I will get in first which is what he did. What Charlie didn't know was that the Irish guy was at court for a couple of days, and that's why Charlie hadn't seen him.

When Charlie found out he offered to let the Irish guy have a free shot at him through the cage bars but he would never take Charlie up on his offer, he was probably worried Charlie would rip his arm off through the bars and hit him with the soggy end.

As time progressed I would on occasion act up to an S.O (senior officer) on security, I always felt quite strange about this as there were officers with far more time in than me who I felt should have been acting up, but it never seemed to bother them. This job was mainly office-based and I would get involved with sorting out searching schedules for the Cat A's and arranging transport for Cat A escorts, at this time that was done through the Met police as individual prisons didn't have vans of their own. The Cat A vans the Met used were seven and a half-ton semi armoured Lorries for the purpose.

These would be used to take Cat A's to a court or transfer them to other prisons, for high-risk Cat A this would be what was called a level two escort, with two or three Met police cars with armed police escorting the Cat A van.

These cars were supplied by the S.E.G (Special Escort Group) of the Met police, their job was to ensure the convoy kept moving so they would block road junctions, traffic lights etc so we didn't have to stop.

My first experience of this was to take two IRA terrorists to Frankland in County Durham and Full Sutton in the East Riding of Yorkshire prisons, this was done in the same day and it seemed like every police force on the way up was out blocking every round-a-bout, village high street or set of traffic lights. As we travelled up we picked up another couple of police cars from some county force we were travelling through and later on we picked up three motorcycle officers as well.

When we got to the first prison we stopped there for lunch and lodged one of the prisoners there while we went to the mess, when we were done we went back to reception to pick up the prisoner who was going onto the next prison. Both prisoners had a look of surprise on their faces as they thought they would be in the same prison, one of them ended up crying because they were being separated this brought a smile to my face rough tough IRA terrorists who would happily blow people up, crying because they were being separated.

Over my time on security I would do quite a few level 2 escorts taking Cat A's to court, the S.E.G used to try and beat their previous times from Brixton to the Old Bailey, it was a bit of harmless rivalry. I think at the time the record if my memory serves me well was 11 minutes door to door.

One day the Met S.E.G took us to court but had other commitments and so the City of London Police escort group would be bringing us back, they wanted to beat the Met and so off we set. We were flying and just as me and the other officers on the escort were saying they might just do it as we were coming through Brixton high street, the van we were in clipped a traffic island with an almighty bang and the seven and a half-ton Cat A van going onto two wheels the prisoners in the cells thought we were under attack. It must have been quite a sight for the shoppers in the high street.

We got back in the prison and the driver of the van apologised and was throwing a few fucks around about the City of London escort group, he said they had gone on the wrong side of the road which is not unusual but they had not left the van driver a lot of room to manoeuvre and so he had a choice hit a car or the traffic island, but what made him madder was the City of London police had beat the Mets record.

Violent prisoners are not unusual but on this particular day, me and another burglar were told to go to A wing and move a prisoner by the name of Lieveld to the seg as he had been threatening to kill his cellmate because he wanted a single cell.

We get up to the cell and the guy is huge, over six feet and about 20 stone, we found out later he was on remand for killing his boss at a nightclub he was a bouncer at. He was relatively calm as we told him he would get a single cell but it was in the seg, he would end up there for quite some time and one day he kicked off over his meals and so he was restrained. We did hear that after a good fight he was squealing when they finally got him in locks, because of this and his size the decision was made to make him an S.O and six unlock which meant all of the security lads had to go to the seg to give him exercise, he loved the attention and would stand on the yard shouting 'My boys my boys' they are here to look after me. This was a pain in the arse because this meant it gave him kudos and we couldn't get on with what we were supposed to be doing. I would meet Lieveld again in Belmarsh when he was put on my spur on House block 4 and again sometime later in the seg when he came to give the CSC system a break.

One day I was told I was doing a funeral escort, we would be taking two brothers from the main prison to a church for the service and then on to the cemetery for the burial. We loaded the brothers in a pixie and head for the church somewhere in North London, as we were getting closer we pulled into a police station much to the brother's disgust.

They were complaining and saying if the police were going to be there we could take them back to the prison, the S.O made the excuse the driver wasn't sure where the church was and so we had to ask for directions.

Unknown to us there was a reason the police wanted to be there and so we told the brothers the police would escort us to the church and then leave. By the time we got to the church, the brothers were still complaining but we got their mother to have a word because they wanted to go back to the prison, the police made a show of leaving and eventually we got the brothers in the church. The service went off with no problems and after we came out they hugged their mum and we said we would meet the family at the cemetery.

Off we drive and as we get to the cemetery we realise there is two of them on either side of the road, we didn't know which one the burial was taking place in so we go through the gates of the one on our side of the road, and after some discussion with someone working there, it is decided we should be in the other cemetery so off we drive.

We pull into the right cemetery and drive to where we are told the grave will be, as we approach we notice lots of police trying to be inconspicuous standing behind gravestones or wherever they thought they had cover.

The brothers are now demanding to be taken back to the prison and we are trying to tell them it would devastate their family if they didn't attend. So we drive a bit closer to where it will happen and to add insult to injury there is a JCB still digging the grave. The brothers are going mental by now and so the S.O gets out and gets the mother to come and talk with her sons, eventually, they calm down and when the grave is ready we cuff them up and take them to the graveside. The rest of it goes off without a hitch and after they hugged a few family members we load up the pixie and head back. It turns out the police were looking for someone and they thought he might turn up at the funeral and that's why there were so many of them there.

Funeral escorts are never the best to be involved in; you are dealing with people's emotions at a time when they are devastated. Funerals are also places where things can go wrong very quickly, If the family approach and ask for the cuffs to come off quite often there are a lot of criminals attending making things potentially dangerous and you can't help but think how you would feel in that situation. We know they are criminals but they have just lost a family member.

With not much more than two years in the job in February 1989, I had the chance to take part in a C&R (control and restraint) instructor's course, one of the security S.O's was an instructor and asked me if I was interested.

Of course, I said yes as I enjoyed this part of the job and was reasonably good at it; it was a week-long course held in the gym at Brixton the main instructor for the course was 'A' wing P.O Tony who was a National instructor.

I counted myself lucky because although Brixton was not as bad for the time served mentality, it was rare to get the opportunity to become an instructor with two years in the job. The course consisted of learning wrist and arm locks, working as a three-man team to restrain both unarmed and armed prisoners and relocating them, ratchet and escort cuffs as well as how to apply a body belt, and how to feed someone wearing a body belt.

Dealing with fighting prisoners the role of the foreman/supervisor for incidents; stave techniques and various other situations. The course was hard physically by the end of it my arms were black and blue from being hit with staves and rolled-up newspapers, at times I thought I would pass out because of the pain I was in but this was just the way it was taught back then, you wouldn't get away with it now. I passed the course and later that year I did my initial C&R 3 course meaning I was part of Brixton's riot trained squad. In June 1991 I would become a C&R 2 instructor and in my last week as a Brixton officer in September 1991, I would be away in Lindholme becoming a C&R 3 instructor, this was the riot training instructor's course.

The training department wasn't too keen to send me on this last course because I would be starting at HMP Belmarsh when I finished it, I pointed out the course was not for the benefit of Brixton but the service as a whole.

Before I went on this course I took a prisoner to court for sentencing, the prisoner was gay and had picked up another gay man at a club. They went back to the prisoner's flat to finish off the evening, in the early hours of the morning he woke up to the man raping him. The prisoner had stabbed the rapist in self-defence as he said he was being beaten and raped, the prisoner had been charged with Manslaughter.

The judge gave a summary of the offence and said he had to decide how many stab wounds constituted self-defence as he has stabbed his attacker 27 times. The judge said because the prisoner had been woken up being assaulted and raped the shock could justify six or seven spur of the moment stab wounds, but 27 was overkill. The way the judge was talking I was expecting the sentence to be at least 18 years, and then the judge sentenced him to 9 years, I nearly fell off my chair, I couldn't believe it after this big speech the sentence was so light.

Following the HMP Strangeways riot, Brixton had taken some of those transferred out from there, on the 8th April 1990 myself and numerous staff had responded to an alarm bell on C wing and had found numerous prisoners smashing up the wing, each of the landings had what was known as Wendy houses on them and they were being smashed and filing cabinets chairs and beds from the cells were being thrown down the stairwell at staff. From my recollection a member of staff pulled his stave out and shouted charge, staff went running up the stairs toward the prisoners. A security S.O at the time had a lucky escape as he tripped on the stairs as a filing cabinet was coming down but a quick-witted officer threw a mattress on the S.O's back and the cabinet glanced off.

One officer had his wrist broken by a fire extinguisher that had been thrown down the stairwell, and there were some other lucky escapes.

The quick response of the staff pretty much stopped the riot in its tracks and the prisoners were locked in the closest cell to them, staff had managed to identify the main instigators and teams were put together to go and remove the instigators from the cells and take them to the seg. Following the incident, the C&R 3 trained staff were kitted up and we spent 3 weeks in kit working 12 hours on 12 hours off waiting for any more unrest.

I didn't go home for three days which meant I missed my daughter's birthday on the 8th, and the only notification my wife got was from Nic who I had joined the job with phoning to tell her what happened. Eventually, it calmed down and we returned to normal until one day, a short while later I was in the Orderly Office and the P.O asked if I was willing to go to the Isle of Wight as there were problems at Albany and they were calling for riot unit from around London. Of course, I said yes the P.O had said we needed to get there quick so they were going to fly us down by helicopter, I phoned my wife and told her I wouldn't be home this weekend and why she wasn't happy but she knew I wouldn't refuse.

So as is typical with the prison service they decide the problems are not so imminent and they take down by coach, I was gutted I had never flown in a helicopter. We arrived at the same time a unit from Wandsworth, we settle in and are told our accommodation will be an old staff mess. They then say they want a unit to go into Albany overnight just in case, Wandsworth volunteer or this which was fine as the weather was glorious and so the rest of the units sat around outside sunbathing. That night we went to the staff club and ad a couple of drinks, not too many in case we got called into the prison overnight. Albany told s we could have anything we wanted from the mess we just had to leave a note of what we had so they could charge the service when we got to where we were sleeping they had supplied us with piss-stained mattresses and paper sheets to sleep on to say we weren't happy is an understatement, to add insult to injury when we got back to Brixton and put our claim for subs in as we would be claiming over 12 hours for three nights, we were told we could only claim £5.00 per night residential as Albany had supplied us with food and piss-stained mattresses to sleep on.

I was at home one day when the phone went and a voice said "this is Brixton control room Tornado" this was a code word for a riot or major incident, it was July 1991 and I drove to Brixton as fast as I could.

When I got to the top of Brixton hill the place was swarming with police and they were searching parts of the road, they wouldn't let me down the road so I had to drive around the back of the prison and park up.

When I got into the prison I was told that two IRA prisoners Pearse McAuley and Nessan Quinlivan had escaped using a gun and had shot at staff. We had Special Branch crawling all over the prison for weeks afterwards.

Whilst I was continuing with my service unknown to me Steve (Shep) Shepherd a person who would become a close personal friend but a colleague who I could rely on 100% in any situation was joining the job.

Steve (Shep) Shepherd

5. Joining the Job and Training

I joined the prison service in March 1990 at 30 years of age, I joined the service because I was made redundant from my factory job and I saw an advert in a newspaper, so I thought I could do that job I'd also just met my partner and Belmarsh was being built so I hoped I would go there if I got in. I was sent to HMP Rochester for two weeks to get a basic idea of how a prison operates before going onto the training college at Wakefield.

A group of us walked around Rochester prison taking notes on how the different wings operated. Rochester was half young offenders and half adult, I remember the alarm bell going off nearly every day as the young offenders were fighting amongst themselves. We walked around the prison with the training P.O (principal officer) we were in civilian clothes with a badge saying new entrant prison officer on our jackets; we had no keys and had to rely on the training P.O and Rochester staff to let us through gates and doors throughout the prison.

When we finished our 2 weeks at Rochester we had to travel to Wakefield which is in Yorkshire for 8 weeks of training. We were the second course of the year to be trained at Wakefield and I was in G section, we slept and had our meals in the college.

On the second day, we were given our uniforms also books to read we had homework every evening whether it was report writing or reading up about the lesson for the next day, there were numerous lessons about how to deal with inmates in different circumstances, I.e. Personal space, how to calm situations down, look for signs of bullying and signs of inmates that can self-harm and commit suicide.

We also learnt about the different categories of inmates which are A, B, C, D plus E men and the types of security that goes with each category Cat A being the most high risk and Cat D being low risk.

Also, control and restraint took place in the Dojo every day you work in 3 man teams, taking control of an inmate one takes the head and one on each arm, either taking him to the floor or putting wrist locks on him standing up or handcuffing him, also we were taught how to use a small shield with 2 other officers to do the same. Then the inmate is moved off to the segregation unit, relocated in the cell and you are also shown how to strip search an inmate or just rub down and search him while he's in under restraint. Also how to carry out a rub down and strip search an inmate while he's not in locks or cuffs.

We were also shown how to use a baton if need be and also breakaway techniques if you are in trouble.

The first couple of days our control and restrain instructors were at HMP Strangeways in Manchester as the prison riots there were coming to an end, so our principal officers who were teaching us classroom work had to take us for control and restraint.

Every 2 weeks we had exams about what we had learnt the previous weeks, also we had a race relations exam. In the 4th week, we had to fill in a form about what prison we would like to work at, I was told to put any prison in London because the building of Belmarsh was not complete yet, in the 5th week I was told I got HMP Wormwood Scrubs.

At the college, we had about 200 new officers most of them from the north of England but not many of the Northern prisons needed a lot of staff, but the London and surrounding counties needed staff so a lot of them were sent there. Fifteen of us went to Wormwood Scrubs; only three of us were from London, near the end of the course the training staff from the different prisons came to the training school to speak to its new staff. The training principal officer from Wormwood Scrubs had to find accommodation for the new staff that came from up north, he also told us a little bit about the prison.

At the end of the 7th week, we had our final written exam, in the 8th week we had control and restraint exam where we were taking inmates out of the cell who were armed, we were using a shield and wearing protective clothing and relocating them in the makeshift segregation unit. At the end of the week, we had a course meal which was on the Friday at the weekend we went home; ready to start Scrubs on Monday.

6. Wormwood Scrubs

HMP Wormwood Scrubs was built in 1875 by prisoners from Millbank Gaol. It is situated Near East Acton station on the central line, Due Cane Road, west London. It is an old Victorian prison with 4 wings A, B, C, D. As you enter the main gate you will see two oval plaster reliefs on the front of the prison depicting Elizabeth Fry and John Howard both well-known figures in prison reform. As you go through the gate, in front of you is the church, visits were also near the gate, to the left was A and B wings plus segregation unit and hospital wing, to the right was C and D wings plus gym, workshops, library and reception. The officer's bar was located outside of the prison so was some of the officer's accommodation. Now the prison has changed somewhat, all 4 wings have been joined up, a lot has changed inside the prison, when I started there in June 1990 the building work was just starting.

All 15 of us from college met at the gate the training P.O took us to the gate to get our keys and key number, and then we all went over to the training room. We met the number 1 Governor who told us a bit about the prison and what he expected of us and hoped we would enjoy working at the Scrubs. We also met the chaplain and an officer from the POA (Prison Officers Association), which is a prison officers union.

We were advised to join it as it acted as a protection for staff in case any allegations were made against you and they would fight your corner or give you advice, we all joined then and there. A small amount came out of your wages every month it wasn't very much. Also, the staff that came down from up north were asked if their accommodations were ok, I don't think there were any problems, they were all living quite near the prison, for some, it was their first time in London. The next 4 days were spent touring around the whole prison, on Friday we were told what wings we would be working on. I was the only one to get D wing the lifer's wing, I was told to start on there Monday at 7:30 am.

Monday morning at 7:30 I was standing in the POs office he runs the wing and staff. P.O is a uniform grade with 2 pips on each shoulder. He was a large Welshman, he said "ok boy welcome to D wing ". He gave me my shift pattern; this would tell me every day what shift I was working for the next year.

He said, "for this week just do Main shifts which are from 7:30 - 17: 30". Then next week start your shift pattern. "Ok, I said." "A" shifts were from 7:30 - 20:30, E shifts 7:30 -12:30.

We worked 44 hours a week; he told me I would be working on the 3s, which was the 3rd landing up. I walked up the stairs in the middle of the landing to the 3s.

The end of the wing was sealed off for building work so the length of the wing had been reduced so had the number of cells and inmates. But the wings were still very long, there were over 100 lifers on the wing, some had gone to other prisons because of the building work that was taking place.

The prison role was around 1000, I went to the office in the middle of the 3s, inmates had just been unlocked they were everywhere two officers were standing by the small office, one was the i/c of the landing who had about 16 years in the other was the 2i/c who had 11 years in the other two officers had between 4 and 6 years in, me one week. I introduced myself to them the I/c said so you're with us, go and see the officer standing on the bridge, this is a bit of the landing that connects the two sides of the landing, he will show you what to do.

I introduced myself to him and he showed me how to put the shift pattern into my diary then we walked around the landing. He showed me the recess where the inmates "Slop out "there was one on each side of the landing. After unlocking we have to stand here on the bridge between the two recesses, because of the smell and in case there is trouble between some inmates we can keep an eye on it. We walked down one side of the landing; he showed me the Cat 'A' cells and the E man cell.

He explained to me that all the cells on D wing are single cells; the wing used to be the woman's wing years ago and is a little bit smaller than the other wings. All lifers are entitled to a single cell, the cells had a thick wooden door, with a bed, table, chair, water jug, a bucket to piss and shit in, cup, plate, knife, fork and spoon and a picture board to put photos on, the cell window was located high up on the rear wall with bars across it.

Over the tannoy system, inmates were called for work, they filed down the 2 sets of stairs to the bottom landing where staff were ready to rub down search the inmates before they went off to work, some staff were manning the route to the workshops and the library also the gym, for the gym orderlies and library workers.

An officer came to pick the inmates up for the officer's mess, the workshop made prison clothes it was not far from D wing. The office where the tannoy system was, was known as the bubble it was where all movement on and off the wing was recorded, inmates, officers, governors and visitors and the wing roll was adjusted.

When all the lifers that were working had gone it was pretty quiet on the wing, then visits were called, some went down to the bubble in their best prison clothing where a visits officer was waiting for them they were inspected and rub down searched, then the visits officer told the bubble officer how many he was taking off to visits. The bubble was maned by an SO (senior officer one pip on each shoulder) and an officer, when it had quietened down me and two other officers got exercise out inmates congregated by the bubble when exercise was called they were rubbed down searched before going on to the yard, it was right next to the wing once the inmates were on the yard, the other officers said in the evenings the lifers use D wing rec, it was a small building near D wing it had a full-size snooker table in it, dartboard a large TV, tables and chairs.

On Saturday mornings the lifers can go to the rec and watch a film that is shown by staff on a cinema screen and lock-up was at 8 pm every night. When we got back on the wing after exercise, the i/c of the landing showed me how LBBs (locks bolts and bars) was done.

This is where every cell on D wing and the prison should be checked every day, you check the bolt on the door to make sure it's working and has not been tampered with also check the door, check the bars on the windows to make sure they have not been tampered with, also check the walls of the cell to make sure they are all ok. We did every cell on our landing and had to sign a book in the POs office to say they were correct. Then the I/c told me about the Cat As and E man on our landing.

He showed me their books that staff had to carry with them, an officer on the landing had to sign the books every hour so you had to physically find the inmate and sign the book. If they left the landing or wing the book went with the officer escorting the Cat A or E man, the book had a photograph in it of the inmate. Also at a night the E man's kit was taken out of the cell and put in the POs office, just in case he tried to escape. The cells for A and E men had Red lights in them that were kept on all night so they could be seen and accounted for by the night staff.

The A and E men are not located on the top floor or ground floor but in the middle landings for safety, it's supposed to be harder for them to escape if they are not on the top landing or ground floor.

On the ground floor was the POs office, wing governor's office, probation office, lifer's office where all the files on the inmates on D wing were kept. Staff toilets and the tea room where the tea boy made staff tea and toast and the kit room where all spare inmate bedding and clothes were kept and the servery where the inmates collected their meals. The tea boy asked me what I would be drinking; I said "coffee please "ok gov "he said. I asked the i/c what he was in for, the I/c said, "oh he killed his wife ". I said, "what with". He said 'He poisoned her', "and we have him as a tea boy", I said. " He's alright he makes a good brew ", was the answer I got back. I was shown the cell cards on the door, it had their names, landing number, cell number, religion, lifer written on it also Cat A or E. When inmates came back in from workshops and visits, they went to their cells got their cups, plates, knives, forks and spoons and waited on the landings for feeding. Inmates came down the centre stairs went into the servery collected their meal and hot water and went back up the stairs at the end of the wing to their landings, then to their cells, where we were banging them up after lunch, another officer and me along with a cleaner, we went out around D wing, the officer had a radio and got permission from the control room to clean outside the wing the job was for the cleaner to pick up shit parcels and rubbish that the inmates had thrown out of their cell windows over lunchtime.

The cleaner was dragging behind him a black plastic bin to put everything in, which stank to high heaven when that was finished we went back onto the wing this was one of the jobs I had to do every day, once in the morning after breakfast then again after lunch.

A personal officer scheme was set up on the wing, I had to talk to one of the inmates and tell him I was his personal officer and if he had any problems to come and see me. I walked into his cell he was sitting on the bed staring at the wall most inmates have pictures and photographs on their cell wall, I introduced myself to him and asked why he didn't have any pictures of his friends and family on his wall he just looked at me. I said haven't you any pictures of your mum to put on the wall, he said no gov she's dead, I said sorry to hear that how did she die? He grinned and said I strangled her I said 'oh O K' and walked out of the cell.

After being in the Scrubs a couple of months I went on escort to Longlartin Prison in Leicestershire, we had to pick up an inmate who was a lifer and bring him back to D wing Scrubs, when we got to the reception in Longlartin he was waiting for us he was a black guy in his late 20's he had murdered his 3-year-old daughter by beating her to death with the flex of a kettle, the other lifers at Longlartin found out what he was in for said they were going to cause him harm so for some reason they thought he would be safe back at D wing Scrubs. We took him back to reception which is located at the end of D wing he was processed and searched, kit sorted out then we took him through to D wing he was located on the 3's which is my landing. The i/c on the landing gave me his cell card and told me to put him in the cell over there as I located him the cell doors were open I put the cell card on the door 2 inmates walked up to me and said, I know that cunt I was on remand with him at Brixton.

He killed his daughter, oh did he I said and walked back to the office to tell the I/c that some inmates knew him and what he was in for, the I/c said.

Just see how it works out, about half an hour later he was standing at the 3's landing office and said I think someone on here knows what I'm in for, why is that asked the I/c I went to the recess and came back have a look in my cell, when we looked in his cell his bed was covered in shit and piss someone had emptied their slop bucket over his bed, he said I think I had better go on the rule. He was taken to the PO's office and moved to the V P unit on A wing the mess was cleaned up by the cleaners for extra tobacco.

Throughout the summer months, it was very hot on the wing and also in the cells, some tempers flared between inmates, many an argument was stopped before turning into a fight, some lifers frustrations turned on the sex offenders or the weaker ones.

I spotted one inmate coming out of his cell with a cut eye, I asked him what happened. He said nothing guv I fell over, me and a couple of other officers paid a visit to some inmates we thought were bullying they were told they are being watched.

My first nicking came when an officer from the mailroom came out and said to me and another officer an inmate had written a letter to his girlfriend telling her he was hiding his cannabis in the End of his shaving brush so me and the i/c of the landing went and told him he had a cell search.

We took the inmate into his cell and asked him if he had anything in his cell he shouldn't have he said no guv he was then strip-searched he got dressed and was told to wait outside the cell, we then pushed the door to and started to search his cell we left his shaving brush till last, the i/c said to me pull the brush apart I did and it was full up with cannabis. The i/c said to me there you go you have got your first nicking, we called the inmate back into the cell and showed him what we found and where we found it he replied I guess I'm nicked we said yup. We took the evidence and the shaving brush down to the PO's office, he said well-done take it to the segregation unit and fill in the paperwork down there and take the other officers backing paper with you.

In the segregation unit I filled out the nicking sheet and gave them the other officers backing paper, the seg staff sealed the shaving brush and cannabis in an evidence bag, they said they will give the inmate his nicking sheet tonight and we will see you tomorrow at 10 am here in the seg, that evening the inmate got his nicking sheet which said he was placed on report for having any unauthorised article in his possession namely cannabis.

In the morning the inmate was unlocked taken off the wing and placed in the seg awaiting adjudication. On the adjudication he went guilty the governor gave him 28 days loss of canteen and no association for one week, which meant, he stayed behind his door of an evening when others were on.

On one of my shifts, I went along to the lifer's office, it was where all the lifer's records were kept the records explained in detail what the inmates were in for and how they committed their crimes. The officer in the office said all the files are in alphabetical order in the filing cabinet just read through some. There were some pretty horrific murders, one inmate who was on the 2s, raped his next-door neighbour buggered her then killed her and stole her money in her purse.

One inmate who was on the 2s had a partner in crime on the 4s, together they were renting a room each from this old lady who had a big house, the two of them decided to get rid of her and take over the house for themselves as she had no family. So they killed her and buried her under the new rockery they had built. The neighbours got suspicious because they had not seen the old lady; police dug the garden up and found her body. We had a couple of rent boys in for having sex with their clients, then killing them and stealing their money for drugs. A black inmate on my landing who said he was a very deeply religious man was going around London killing the ladies of the night.

Some of the lifers were in for domestic murder, where they had had an argument with the wife or found her in bed with someone else, lost the plot killed the wife and sometimes her lover too. Others were in for having fights outside the pub, either stabbing their victim or punching them to death. One lad on my landing got on a bus with his wife they went upstairs and sat down there were some young lads up there mucking about, he told them to keep the noise down one of them gave him some mouth so he stabbed him and killed the young lad.

You then had the sex offenders and child murderers the sex offenders were in for rape, a few of them had broken into old ladies houses raped them then killed them for their money and jewellery. Some child murderers raped their victims first then killed them others just lost their temper with their own children and beat them till they died. Others had murdered whilst on drugs and didn't know what they had done.

The lifer's system was that the judge gave you a tariff of say 25 years when you got to serving say 20 years of the sentence probation, parole board etc they would put you up for parole if you behaved yourself, so the next 5 years you would work on getting your release. If you got released you would be on a life license for the rest of your life.

If you did anything wrong or didn't follow your license rules you would be back in prison, hence we had some license revokes on D wing.

Just before Christmas the Birmingham 6 arrived on D wing, they were convicted of the pub bombings in Birmingham in 1975. They were going to the Appeal Court to hopefully have their sentences quashed, by this time they had nearly served 16 years. I remember standing on the landing talking to McIlkenny one of the 6, he didn't mind talking to staff, I thought he was very polite he would always pass the time of day.

The others didn't seem to care much to make conversation with staff. McIlkenny always told me that they were all innocent and that they were stitched up and spent nearly 16 years behind bars for something they didn't do and hopefully the Appeal would go their way, on the 14th March 1991 they had their convictions quashed they were free men.

Two of the Cat A's on my landing were the M25 murderers Davis and Rowe; they were convicted in March 1990 of murder and aggravated robbery. The crimes were committed around the M25, both inmates told me they were innocent and were fitted up. In July 2000, their convictions were overturned now I believe Rowe works for the BBC on Panorama.

PC Blakelock was stabbed to death in the Broadwater Farm Riots in Tottenham North London in 1985. In 1987 three people were convicted of his murder we had one still on D wing, that was Mark Braithwaite the other two had moved on by the time I had got to D wing they were Winston Silcott and Engin Raghip. Mark Braithwaite always said to me he was innocent he was nowhere near the scene; in 1991 they had their convictions quashed by the court of appeal. A few more lifers, I locked up on D wing I would meet later in Belmarsh some finished their life sentences then went on to commit more crimes.

Over the Christmas period, it can be quiet on the wing one lifer said to me "3 Christmas's down 22 to go. Staff were out and about looking for the lifer's stash of homemade hooch (alcohol) that can be made from fruit, sugar and yeast; this can be very powerful stuff. One officer told me that a few years ago two lifers ended up next door in Hammersmith hospital through drinking alcohol they had made, one went blind temporarily and they both had to have their stomachs pumped. Some of the lifers worked in the staff mess so they probably smuggled the yeast back, the fruit and sugar were bought from the canteen.

One inmate who was located on the 1s was in for killing his boyfriend he was a transvestite on the out. He used to work in the gay clubs; I would take him out cleaning around the wing with me if the other cleaner was on a visit. Mr Shepherd he would say "I can't walk around the wing in these boots; you'll have to get me a pair of high heels."

If we went upstairs he would always let me go first, I thought he was being polite but he said. "No, I just want to watch your arse wiggle as you walk up the stairs." The PO said to me "are you ok with him ". "Yeah, I said he is only mucking about." One day I took him out to clean outside the wing he said to me, "you know your safe on here don't you" what do you mean I said? He said, "I've told all the other lifers that if anyone ever touched or assaulted you, I would cut their eyes out ". I had my very own bodyguard on D wing.

After Christmas, the PO said to me if you want to go to Belmarsh go over to admin and fill in a transfer form they are trawling for staff it's going to open in April, so that's what I did.

In February I was told I would be going to Belmarsh at the end of March. So the end of March I had my leaving do and said goodbye to the lads and the Scrubs.

7. Belmarsh

September 1991 I had finished my C&R3 Instructors course on the Friday and Nic and I were starting at HMP Belmarsh on Monday, we had both transferred to be closer to home as driving around the South Circular every day had become a pain. We arrived at Belmarsh and were taken into the staff mess by the training P.O he sat us all down, me Nic and at least one other had transferred from Brixton and others had come from various prisons.

We got our security talk and shown a scale model of the prison, compared to Brixton it was huge we were told the outer wall was 1.1 miles in length, it had four house blocks holding about 220 prisoners each there was healthcare, seg, farms and gardens, astroturf football pitch for the prisoners and a gym with Olympic standard equipment.

On top of this, there was the HSU/SSU a prison within a prison with a wall built to the same specs as the main wall, this unit held a maximum of 48 high / exceptional risk prisoners ranging from armed robbers, large scale drug importers to terrorists.

The Unit

The staff that had transferred from Brixton were all deployed to the Unit because they didn't want experienced staff saying no to the prisoners on the house blocks, these were run by new officers learning the job with an experienced S.O and P.O in charge. It was obvious Belmarsh wanted to do things their way, as a general rule, the prison service used what was known as an F35 form for all general apps and other F forms for specific things.

When I got to Belmarsh I could tell you the 'F' number for whatever you wanted but someone at Belmarsh had done away with these and had their forms for everything.

Someone who was computer literate had designed all the new forms. I knew several of the prisoners on the unit because they had also been transferred from Brixton; the unit had ninety officers, four S.O's and two P.O's. There was a servery area where the meals were dispensed from but these were supplied by the main kitchen and brought over in heated trolleys before each mealtime.

The servery could at times be a volatile area, on one occasion the kitchens had decided to include poached eggs to the menu instead of just boiled or fried.

The unit's servery didn't have a poacher so those that wanted poached eggs had to wait while one of the kitchen staff boiled a saucepan of water and cracked an egg into it.

The problem with this was you never knew what shape the poached egg would be, one day an armed robber called Kendal who was always complaining about something handed his poached egg back because it was the wrong shape, and a kitchen worker took it and did him another. The staff were in an uproar this was a prisoner complaining about the shape of his egg, when he got back on his spur another armed robber who had not long transferred from Brixton ripped into him when he heard what had happened.

He said to Kendal 'you think you are hard done by, I have just come from Brixton where the meal choice is to take it or leave it' he went on to say that most of the prisoners on that spur were pussies and didn't know what prison was like. The prisoners on the unit had a daily menu with 3 options for every meal, and they would fill in a card with their choices for the following day.

Each spur had twelve prisoners on it and three officers would sit on the spur while the prisoners were on association and another officer would be in the bubble (an office with a view onto the spur, where they would monitor prisoner's phone calls and hold all the Cat 'A' movement books for the spur. Each spur had a regime whether that was exercise in the morning or afternoon, when their gym time was, first thing in the morning the officers would take applications from the prisoners.

The only prisoners who wouldn't put in applications were the IRA; they wouldn't talk to the officers unless they had to. One of them would come to the desk and ask to speak to an S.O some of us would say you can't speak to an S.O if you want something tell us, other officers would be intimidated by the IRA and would get an S.O.

It got to the stage that they would bypass the S.O because most of them told the IRA that officers could deal with their needs, and they would demand to speak with the unit governor and often the governor would speak to them much the officer's disgust.

There was however one IRA member who at that time was the ranking member on the unit and he would talk with staff, Dingus and his co-defendant were in for shooting a police special constable who died in hospital and a police officer who although shot several times survived. Dingus would talk to the officers and would have quite lengthy chats with an officer who was an ex para, Dingus told him he used to be a window cleaner on the para's barracks in Ireland.

Dingus protested several times over things he thought were wrong but he never attacked officers as he said we were just doing our jobs, he would instead smash things on the spur and throw the video player out of the window. It is strange to say that although we knew what he had done you could have a civil conversation with him, this might be because of his attitude, and he would always say he didn't agree with the indiscriminate bombings the IRA carried out like the Harrods bombing or bombings where women and children were killed and injured.

He would qualify this by saying "you choose to wear the Queens uniform so that makes you a legitimate target" and he would happily tell you that because of this if he ever got a gun and the chance of escape he would not think twice about shooting an officer who got in his way. He proved this sometime later when he and others escaped from HMP Whitemoor using guns and he shot an officer.

Most of the IRA were sullen uncommunicative demanding arseholes to be fair, but whether it was a ploy or just the way he was Dingus could have a laugh. He was known for throwing the video player out of the spur window on several occasions and smashing things, but we had a prisoner called McFadden who spent most of his association time on the phone to his girlfriend.

The phone was on the spur so you could hear him talking and one minute he would be, love you miss you and the next he was calling her a fucking bitch and he hated her and slam the phone down, two minutes later he would call her again saying I'm sorry I didn't mean it and in the next breath she was a whore and a bitch. We always laughed at his phone calls.

One day Dingus was having one of his let's throw and smash things up days and McFadden was on the phone, the next thing he was cuddling the phone box saying to Dingus "not the phone not the phone" and was doing his best to defend it. The next day Dingus was having a laugh with us about it and taking the piss about McFadden begging. One day I was acting up to S.O and Nic

who I had transferred with came to me and said he had brought
Dingus and his co-defendant off the exercise yard and as they were
coming back into the unit Dingus turned to his co-defendant and
said "I have done thirteen years for the cause in British prisons for
the cause, and this man (Nic) is the first officer to place me on
report" Nic was a bit concerned and I was smiling and said to him
" when you go home I would check your car before you drive it"
Nic didn't find this funny but I told him I was only joking and it
would be alright.

   Later that day I saw Dingus and said to him "what are you
doing telling my staff they are the first to place you on report"
Dingus smiled and told me he was only joking, but then he said,
"it was funny though wasn't it ". Before Nic went home I told him
I had spoken to Dingus and he was joking, this seemed to calm
him down.

   Along with the IRA on another spur, we had Protestant
terrorists in for plotting to kill members of the IRA, one of them
was called Doherty and he was quite an amiable person who
would laugh and joke with the staff. Doherty's big thing was when
he had visits he would tell his wife the staff were rough and treated
them badly and never fed them properly.

   We were not supposed to interfere with their visits or talk to
them whilst on a visit, but one day I decided to put Doherty's wife
straight about his treatment. Every mealtime they had a menu with
three choices of main course and sweet, they could also order a
video to watch on the spur on association. So this particular day
while Doherty was on a visit with his wife, I put a tea towel over
my arm like a waiter and took the menu into his visiting room. I
asked him what he would like to choose for dinner that night and
what video he would like to order, his face was a picture and his
wife just sat there bemused.

Eventually, his wife asked what I was doing and I put the menu on the table and explained they get three choices at every meal and that they could order video's, his wife read the menu and then slapped him on the arm and called him a lying toe rag, Doherty looked at me and called me a bastard and then said his wife had been bringing extra things in for him because she thought he was not being looked after.

After that, he never slagged the staff off to his wife again and whenever I saw her she would ask how I was and if Doherty had been behaving.

Sometime later Doherty would get involved in a problem on his spur where he had to back up the rest of the prisoners on that spur in refusing to go behind their doors at bang-up. He was not the bravest of people and so when he and the rest of the spur refused to bang up, the plan was for loads of staff to wander onto the spur and as soon as there were enough just grab the first prisoner you came to and put them behind their doors.

Well this not very well thought out plan turned into a fight scene from the movies, bodies and chairs were going everywhere, Doherty lost his bottle and ran into his cell and when a member of staff went to lock the door he found Doherty taking his trousers off because he had shit himself.

The unit had its own segregation unit but it was never used for adjudications as no one knew how to equip it or run it until the unit P.O decided I was the man for the job, and so I had to contact the main seg and find out where to order the rubber stamps for the different charges and sort out all the paperwork needed. Eventually, it was up and running and another officer and me were the main people to run adjudications when they happened.

Now it was up and running we started to have prisoners down there on punishment, we got quite busy and one day we had an armed robber by the name of Bolden down there on C.C (cellular confinement) and next to him was McFadden who absolutely hated it because he was not allowed phone calls whilst located there.

I got on alright with Bolden but one day he called me to the cell door to talk with me because McFadden was driving him mad shouting at the night man all night, Bolden said to me if I didn't move him he was going to shit up because he couldn't take anymore. I told Bolden to leave it with me and a decision was made to move McFadden to the Box (special accommodation cell) because of his disruptive behaviour. Our office could be seen from McFadden's cell and he was again shouting and swearing at us, but then an officer turned up to be one of the team to take McFadden out and move him.

He was about six foot six and twenty stone, when McFadden saw him getting his kit on he suddenly went quiet and asked to speak to the S.O McFadden said he would shut up and just finish his time in the seg quietly which he did.

As I have said we also dealt with armed robbers and big crime families, we had a group of armed robbers in the unit on Spur 1. Field, Forder, Parker and Russell were all on that spur.

One day I was working on unit visits and Parker was there having a social visit, when he finished me and an officer escorted him back to the main building so we could strip-search him in the search room before returning him to his spur. All Cat A's had to be strip-searched before returning to the spur, at this time we were having problems with several of them not taking their underwear off so it could be searched.

The standard for a strip search was that they removed the clothing from their top half item by item and handed these to staff to search, they then replaced this and took off their shoes and socks for searching, and then their trousers and underpants. They then had to lift their upper clothing so we had a clear view of their genitals and they turned full circle before putting the bottom half of their clothing back on, they were never allowed to be fully naked during a search.

Anyway, Parker complied with the first part of the search but instead of removing his underwear he just ran his thumbs around the waistband of his boxers and refused to take them off.

I wasn't happy with this and so I said to the officer with me stay with him while I go and see the P.O, I went and saw the P.O and told him what had happened. He asked me what I wanted to do and so I said I wanted to take Parker to the seg and strip him under restraint.

The P.O said well go and do it then so I returned to the search room with another officer and the P.O following on behind, I told Parker I was taking him to the seg and so we all walked there and I put Parker into a cell where the search would take place.

I told Parker I intended to strip him under restraint if he did not comply, and I asked him what he intended to do? Parker moved to the back of the cell and took up a boxers pose, I gave him a last chance to comply and he told me to fuck off, so I moved forward and took hold of his head and pulled it down, the two other officers took control of his arms and we took him to the floor under restraint. This hard armed robber was crying like a baby and squealing so loud another prisoner heard him from the exercise yard.

The three of us had him controlled but we could not remove his trousers or underwear because we had him in locks and so the P.O had to take these off, this time he was fully naked and we left him to get dressed once his clothes had been searched.

Unknown to us at the time was that the prisoner called Kendal on the exercise yard had shouted to those on spur 1 and told them we were killing Parker because of all the screams he was making. The result of this was that Field, Forder and some others smashed the spur up and were throwing pool balls at the three members of staff who were retreating from the spur. When the other two officers and me along with the P.O returned to the main unit all hell was breaking loose, it was decided by the governor not to get lots of staff kitted up to take the spur back, but to talk to the prisoners and find out why they had done it.

As I have said it came to light that Kendal had heard all the screams and told them we were beating Parker up, I went to the seg to speak to Kendal who was located there at the time and Russell the other member of the gang was located in the cell next to where Parker was now. Russell asked me what we did to Parker and I just told him we had restrained him like we do anybody else but he started squealing like a girl.

Russell had heard me talking to Kendal and blaming him for the spur being smashed up and asked me to let him out on the yard to explain to Field and Forder that Parker was alright and had just been restrained for refusing a search.

Russell went onto the yard and called across to Field and told him what had happened, Field went mad because they had smashed up the spur for nothing and would all now be nicked for doing it and they didn't have to.

After that Parker had to stay in the seg for a couple of weeks because Field and Forder wanted to kill him so he was there for his own protection until their trial started. When the trial started for these hard men I was on the escort and went to the seg to get Parker who then pleaded with the P.O not to be cuffed to me because I had hurt him big tough armed robbers that's a laugh.

We did have lighter moments in the unit; we had another well-known criminal by the name of Johnson who had two young sons that visited him with his wife. The eldest was Alfie who was about nine at the time and Charlie, who was about seven; they were a real pain on visits and would run around the visits room causing mayhem. To get the visitors to the unit they had to ride in an electric bus from the visitor's entrance to the rear of the unit.

The bus was a bit like a milk float, and when the bus got to vehicle gates the officer driving it had to get out and open the massive gates by hand and then get back in and drive-through and stop, get out and shut them.

Over some time Alfie had clocked this and noticed when the officer got out no one was in charge of the bus, so one day when the officer got out to open the gates, Alfie jumped into the driver's seat and made off with the bus full of passengers wondering what was going on and the officer running after the bus like something out of the keystone cops. When the officer finally got control of the bus back he told Johnson what his pain in the arse son had done, but instead of telling Alfie off Johnson just laughed.

Eventually, Alfie's mum had a go at him and said he would never do anything like it again although she did have a smile on her face. It turns out Alfie and Charlie had nicked a milk float the day before so they would know how to drive the bus. A few weeks later I was acting S.O in the visits room and Johnson had a visit, again Alfie and Charlie were running riot and I informed Johnson he had to keep control of his kids or they would end up hurting themselves or someone else.

He said he would and carried on with the visit, I had my radio standing on my desk in front of me so I could hear any messages.

Alfie crept up and took the radio, when I saw him I shouted at him and Johnson heard me and looked out of the room he was in.

I told him again about Alfie and he said to me just do what you have to, to control him and so I got hold of Alfie and handcuffed one of his hands to a chair that was fixed to the floor in front of my desk. Alfie was shouting about it and again Johnson looked out of his room and saw Alfie cuffed to the chair with Alfie moaning, he just laughed at Alfie and said it was his own fault and gave me a thumbs up. Strangely after that, if I was on visits when Alfie came his behaviour was a lot better.

We had three members of another well-known London crime family called the Arif's as well as their brother-in-law, they were into all sorts they could be problematic on the spurs but in general, weren't too bad. They were there for some time and one day we received notice that their father had died because they were Muslim most Muslim funerals happen within 24 hours, with this in mind a very rushed escort was arranged so they could see their father in a chapel of rest before his burial to pay their respects. The body was being held at Rotherhithe chapel of rest just down the road from Rotherhithe police station.

It was agreed we would take the Arif's to Rotherhithe police station and then take them one by one to the chapel of rest for them to say their goodbyes.

So off we go in a Cat A van with a police escort because they are a very powerful crime family and as we are approaching the police station both sides of the road are manned by police and armed police, we pull into the police station and place the prisoners in the cells. They sort out an order of who is going to the chapel of rest first to see their father, once this is done we load the first one on the van and I have been chosen to be cuffed to him. We get to the chapel and before we get out of the van I am cuffed to the prisoner and then we are shown to where his father's body was laying.

As I was about to find out Muslims are very tactile when viewing their deceased relatives, so in we go and the first thing he does is say a few words then he lays his head on his dead father's chest and puts his arms around his shoulders basically pulling me virtually on top of the body. He is talking to his father in words I don't understand and I'm looking at the S.O thinking get me out of here, eventually, the S.O says it's time to go as the other family members have to come to see their father.

We get back on the van and off we go, unfortunately, I had to do this three more times to the amusement of the S.O, each time being pulled over the body, That was one escort I was glad to see the back of.

I have mentioned working with the IRA in the Unit and although they were pretty much all the same demanding, uncommunicative it was noticeable that the public view of them was changing when they were going on trial. Dessie Ellis had been extradited to England to stand trial for conspiracy to cause explosions, as his fingerprints had been found on explosives that had been found in a cache of bomb-making equipment near Pangbourne Berkshire.

If memory serves me correctly he had been charged with conspiracy to cause explosions in England, but his defence was that he had truly believed the bombs he made were for use in Northern Ireland and not the mainland. The trial was not too long after the Birmingham six had been released for being wrongly imprisoned and I think this cast doubt over several IRA trials. As I say if memory serves Ellis was found not guilty because doubt was cast on the charge because it mentioned England, had he been charged with conspiracy to cause explosions in the United Kingdom the result might have been different as Ellis always maintained the bombs were for use in Northern Ireland.

This change in attitude to the IRA carried on with the case of a young IRA member O'Donnell who was stopped by police in this country for running a red traffic light, his car was searched and weapons and ammunition were found.

Again a jury found him not guilty and he was released, I think the Birmingham six case had caused doubt amongst juries sitting on IRA cases. Sometime later O'Donnell was killed by the British Army while taking part in an attack on a Royal Ulster Constabulary police station in Northern Ireland.

I did about sixteen months in the unit and worked with some really good officers male and female, when it became time to move to another area of the prison I was told I was going to work on house block 2 a residential unit. I had found out that had I gone there I would have been one over the staffing levels for the house block, and so I approached the P.O and asked if I could go to the visits group as in my eyes the unit was residential albeit on a smaller scale.

8. Belmarsh

Monday, March 25th 1991, I sat in the officer's mess which is located outside of the prison with about 20 other officers; we had come from different prisons from all over the country. There was a lot of staff from up north; apparently, most of the courses from the 2 training colleges had sent most of their officers to Belmarsh. A lot of them were stacked up at London prisons then went on to Belmarsh when it opened and others like me transferred, some others came on promotion.

We filled a few forms in; one of them was about where we wanted to work within the prison. I put down for the segregation unit and in a couple of days found out that I had got it. We went over to the prison and collected our keys and were given a key number and tally, then we were given a tour of the prison with the training P.O, it's very strange walking around a prison with no inmates about.

We were told it was built on the former site of the Woolwich Arsenal and the prison cost around £150,000,000 to build with cameras everywhere linked to a control room above the gate. Belmarsh had 4 house blocks (wings), each with 3 Spurs, 70 inmates on a spur, 210 inmates on a house block.

A secure corridor upstairs that linked the house blocks, chaplaincy, education area, security office, duty governor's office, Watson office (intelligence), orderly office, main stores, visits, reception, healthcare, segregation unit, and workshops. There was a corridor downstairs that linked all these areas as well but was not secure enough for inmates to walk along unescorted, these areas were mainly patrolled by dog handlers.

Past the workshops, you had a building for the dog section. Then across the field from that, you had the Cat A unit, a prison within a prison. It had a wall around it and inside the wall was a fence just like the main prison, the unit had cameras on all 4 of its spurs, and each spur held 12 inmates a roll of 48 inmates. It had cameras everywhere, it had a visits area, and exercise yards and one yard had a roof on and a small segregation unit that could hold about 4 inmates.

Between HB4 and HB2 there is a newly equipped gym and an education area with a library. On the other side of the prison was the farms and gardens area for inmates to work, Astroturf football pitch, running track, admin offices and the visits area.

When you walked through the main gate you were in a sterile area, reception to the left, the whole area was fenced in with gates to let you through into different areas of the prison, this was where the cell vans waited, to collect and deliver inmates to and from the reception area that were going or coming back from court or escort.

Seg 1st Tour

After a couple of days of finding our way around the new prison, we went to our places of work, I went to the segregation unit with some other staff to introduce ourselves to the S.O.s and get our shift patterns. The seg unit is on 2 floors, with 2 holding cells, 10 normal cells, 2 special cells, 1 recess, storeroom, staff office, and an Adjudication room. Downstairs, 2 holding rooms, 10cells, entrance to exercise yard, recess, servery, storeroom and another staff office. Because the exercise yard was located between the Healthcare centre and seg, it was a small yard and the walls of the

2 buildings were about 60ft high. The yard looked like it was in the bottom of a well. We had 1 P.O. 4 S.O's and about 12 staff, 2 S.O's and 6 staff on each weekend. Everything had to be ready for when the prison started to accept inmates which would be on 2nd April.

We had to learn all the prison rules and learn how to write nicking sheets out, and we practised mock adjudications, and how to escort inmates in and out of them. Adjudications are when an inmate is put on a charge for breaking a prison rule, he goes in front of the governor, with the reporting officer and the seg S.O and escorting staff from the seg.

The governor then listens to the charge read out by the reporting officer then decides with all the evidence in front of him if he is guilty or not. After the 2nd April, the prison started to get inmates, mostly from other London Prisons (mostly their trouble makers), the rest came from courts around London. Belmarsh has a crown court outside the prison, with a tunnel leading from the secure corridor right into the cells area of the court. Gradually the prison began to fill up; it didn't take long until we ended up with some customers.

One of the first we had in the seg was an inmate called Owen, he was brought down from reception under restraint, and he was probably in his thirties and about eight stone wet, and about five foot six tall. He would try and punch anyone around him, we had him as a 3 man unlock, every time you opened his cell door and tried to talk to him he would take a swing at you, sometimes he made contact.

He would get restrained put in the special cell stripped and left in there for a while to calm down, then he would be placed on report for assault, taken in front of the governor in handcuffs so he didn't punch anyone.

The next day we open him up, he would try and punch staff again. In the end, we just used to push him back into his cell and shut the door. We had a female officer working with us in the seg he never tried to assault her.

He was visited by a doctor who managed to get him to take some medication he recommended for him, after a couple of weeks things started to improve, he didn't try and assault staff, we managed to shower him and put him on the exercise yard without incident, he even started to except visits from his mother. Later on, we moved him to a house block where he finished off his sentence, he wasn't in for long (criminal damage I think).

About a month later an officer from the house block that Owen went to said to me, 'remember Owen you sent us from the seg',' yeah 'I said, "apparently he hung himself last week at home'. That I found quite sad, I think his mum got in contact with the prison and thanked the staff for trying to help him while he was in prison.

We had a few inmates that spent time with us in the seg, and then went back to their house blocks, finished their sentence went out on the street and within a month or so they had been shot or stabbed and killed.

Another inmate we had in the seg, had refused to bang up on one of the house blocks, he was escorted down to the seg by staff, we strip-searched him and located him in a cell.

The next day he was on adjudication for refusing to bang up on the house block, he went in front of the governor and got punished, he ended up staying with us for a few days, the next day he asked if he could shave, he was given a razor and told we would be back for it in about 5 minutes. When we went back for the razor, blood was running out under his cell door. I looked through the inspection hatch, he was sitting on the bed, he had cut both wrists, and the cell floor was covered in blood. I opened the door the other officer pressed the alarm bell. We both entered his cell, me and the other officer grabbed some of the inmates clothing, that was on the floor and tried to wrap it around his wrists, then we both pushed our thumbs into his cephalic vein, which runs down the inside of the arm in the elbow joint, I had one arm the other officer had the other. By this time the cavalry had arrived to answer the alarm bell, a nurse or hospital officer always attends an alarm bell. Luckily we had both as the health care was only next door.

They took over from us, and got him into the health care next door, then on to the hospital. Officers were slipping and sliding on the blood inside and outside of the cell. The razor was broken up and the two blood-stained blades lay on the cell table that is bolted to the wall.

When things calmed down, the cell was taped off and had to be specially cleaned, the other officer and myself had to get a new pair of shoes from the stores, as ours were covered in blood. We had a meeting in the office and any inmates who want to shave after that had to do it in the recess under the watchful eyes of staff.

My first cell takeout was when we had a black inmate in the seg, he had been playing up on one of the house blocks and was escorted down to us he had a big attitude problem.

His face was scarred all down one side; he was blind in one eye where someone had thrown acid in his face years earlier. He had covered his observation hatch in the cell door and refused to move it, so he got nicked for that then we saw water coming out from under the cell door he had to flooded his cell, which was another nicking. The cells have sinks and toilets in them made of metal so the inmates can't smash them up he was trying to kick the sink off the wall.

The S.O. Said to me and another officer "get kitted up were taking him out and putting him in the Box ". (Special cell) which is a concrete box smaller than a cell with no windows, just a blanket and mat to lay on nothing else one observation window in the roof and one in the door.

We get kitted up the S.O had the shield and me and the other officer on either side of the shield, the other staff were standing by the cell door of the box. The other S.O opens the cell door in we go water all over the floor, the S.O hits the inmate with the shield and pins him up against the rear wall of the cell, and me and the other officer run around and grab an arm each. The S.O Throws the shield to the floor and grabs the inmates head; the other S.O takes the shield out of the cell.

The inmate starts to struggle so we take him to the floor and start to put wrist locks on. When we have locks on we stand him up, we are all soaking wet then we move him to the box in locks. In the box, he is strip-searched under restraint and his clothes taken out of the box, all this is done while he is in locks. Another officer takes his legs and puts a figure of 4 on them he also takes his wrists, we leave the cell one at a time when the last man is out the door is shut. Then the inmate is observed every 15 minutes we got changed and had a cup of coffee.

There were many more cell removals to come, we would have some inmates that came to us in the seg that liked to self-harm, and they would swallow anything they could for attention or just to be a pain in the arse.

Small size batteries and razor blades seemed to be their favourite, one even had a razor blade pushed down his foreskin and threatened to cut his penis off. Another inmate would put chicken bones from his meal into an open wound on his side, we tried to get these inmates off to the Health Care Unit but they wouldn't have any of it, so we were stuck with them.

One inmate we did have from the Health care was Lenny McLean, the unlicensed boxer known as the Governor. He was located on the HCC upper floor, he apparently was abusive either to a member of staff or another inmate, so he got placed on report he was found guilty of the charge and the adjudicating governor decided that he would be better off in the seg away from other inmates because of who he was. He wasn't the type of person to take fools gladly, not just that but someone on one of the house blocks might have wanted to have a go at him so they could say, "yeah inside I had a pop at Lenny McLean." More fool them.

When the adjudication was over he was placed in a holding cell, opposite the adjudication room. My S.O said, "come on we will have to strip search him because he is staying with us ". I looked through the observation slit and opened up the cell door and walked into the cell thinking the S.O. Was with me, when I looked back he was standing at the door.

This mountain of a man stood in front of me, he must have been 6ft 3 INS tall and about the same in width and about 20 stone. I said, "Hello mate, you're staying here with us in the seg, before we can locate you, you will have to give us a strip search."

He looked at me took his reading glasses off and put them on the small table in the cell that was bolted to the wall, he took a

newspaper out of his trouser pocket and put that next to his glasses
he said in a deep voice," Listen, son, I don't really want any
trouble ". I said, "Do you really think I want to roll around the
floor with you." He started to laugh, he sounded just like Frank
Bruno. Then he started to get undressed, that's when my S.O
decided to enter the cell and assist me. We finished the search
checked his newspaper gave him his glasses, off we went
downstairs located him in a cell told him when his kit came down
from the HCC; we would search it and give him what he was
entitled to. He seemed happy enough over the next week we took
him out on the exercise yard, he would walk around for a bit then
come and talk to us.

He would tell us all about the fights he had in and out of the
ring, he was very interesting to listen to.

One day we were getting kitted up to take a black inmate out
of his cell he was banging and crashing and trying to smash his
cell up. Lenny McLean's cell bell went on, I answered it looked
through the observation slit and said through the door" what's up
Len "you boys alright out there "he replied. I said "yes Len why
", he said, "if you are going to take that noisy twat out down the
end and want a hand, come and unlock me and I'll come in there
with you." I said" Thanks for the offer Len, but we will be
alright." Five minutes later one noisy twat was in the box.
Sometimes me and another officer would sit in his cell and listen
to him telling us about his case, and he would show us his legal
papers he was concerned that he was charged with murder, he
thought the police were stitching him up he went to court later that
week and the charge was reduced to manslaughter, he seemed a bit
happier.

We said to him don't worry, it'll all get sorted out at court, a
couple of weeks later he went to court again and never came back

to Belmarsh, I think he went on to Wandsworth. I never saw him again until a few years later when I was working in the Cat A unit If you showed him respect you got it back (Old School).

This is what happened: Lenny McLean was working as the head doorman at The Hippodrome in Leicester Square when he ejected a man named Gary Humphries who suffered from serious mental health problems and was reportedly on drugs.

 He was streaking through the night club urinating on the floor and harassing women. McLean admitted to giving him a backhander, Humphries died later that night and was found to have a broken jaw and severe neck injuries. McLean was arrested for the murder of Humphries, McLean's charge was reduced to manslaughter and he was cleared of this at the Old Bailey when it emerged that Humphries had been in a scuffle with police after being ejected from the nightclub.

Reportedly the police had forcefully restrained him with a stranglehold; the stranglehold applied by the police probably caused the neck injuries which led to Humphries death. However it was determined that McLean was responsible for Humphries broken jaw, McLean was charged and found guilty of grievous bodily harm and was sentenced to 18 months. The seg was a very busy place, what with dealing with adjudications and inmates; little did I know I would return to the seg 12 years later.

9. Visits

I would spend about 2 ½ years on visits with the last six months as acting S.O, Our job on visits was varied we had two desks in the visits room, the visitor control desk where the visitors came and booked in and handed over their V/O's (visiting orders) and they were identified. The V/O's were then sent to the other desk, the inmate control desk where they were sorted into different house blocks and runners would take the V/O's and collect the prisoners from the individual house blocks and bring them to the visits hall. Once in visits, the prisoners went through the search room where they received a rubdown search and anything they had with them was put into pigeon holes as they were not allowed to take anything onto a visit. The prisoners then put on a coloured bib to identify them as remand or convicted before entering the visits hall, they then went to the inmate control desk to be told what table their visitors were at. Remand prisoners were allowed a 15-minute visit daily up to 1 ½ hours per week, but if they behaved and we weren't busy we would give them ½ an hour a day. Convicted were allowed two V/O's a month each visit being ½ an hour, they could also get privilege V/O's depending on their behaviour which would give them four visits a month.

I was detailed various jobs daily, I could be room patrol which meant patrolling the visits hall looking for anything untoward. The Search room is where all prisoners were searched before and after visits, and sometimes during the visit if it was suspected they had concealed something. I could be on either desk controlling visitors or prisoners. The visits staff were very proactive at finding drugs being passed to the prisoners and fights were a regular occurrence when the prisoner did not want to give the drugs up.

The room patrols would look for anything that didn't seem right, prisoners were not allowed to touch their trousers on a visit, so if they put their hand down their trousers we would go up and pull their hand out and take them for a strip search. Plugging as it is known was a favourite way for prisoners to hide drugs, it involves them pushing a package of drugs up their anus so that we couldn't get it when they were searched and they would retrieve it later when they got back to their cell.

We would also look out for prisoners kissing their mums, nans, and dads full on the mouth which is when the visitors passed drugs from their mouths to the prisoners. If we saw this we would take them off to the search room for a strip search.

It was while I was working one day in the search room that a prisoner was brought in for a strip search, and I was convinced he still had the package in his mouth. I grabbed him around the neck and squeezed while I was telling him to spit it out. He was struggling a bit, it was just then when the S.O walked in and said "put him down Mr Richards you're not at Brixton now" this was a favourite technique used at Brixton to make prisoners spit the packages out.

The S.O turned around when I had let go and walked out of the search room, the prisoner took this time to swallow the package and I told him he had won today but I would get him next time.

We were proactive and this lead to a lot of fights in the visits room, if we thought a prisoner had a package in his hand because it had just been passed we would walk up and grab his wrist and pin it to the table, then we asked him to hand it over. It was then up to him what he wanted to do, he could hand it over and have his visit terminated and get nicked or he could fight us for it and get restrained and then taken to the seg and nicked.

A lot of them wanted to fight us for it, which was fine as all of the staff on visits at that time were quite happy to oblige.

If an alarm bell was pressed on visits at that time staff would come from everywhere because it was not unusual for half of the visits room to be fighting, if you restrained a prisoner in the room not only would his visitors be irate but other prisoners would join in. We carried on having a good success rate and if we had seen the visitor pass something and we managed to retrieve it we would arrest the visitor and call the police to have them charged. This mainly became my job as the caution you had to give visitors was long-winded and most of the staff couldn't remember it, and so because I was used to hearing it from family members and friends in the police it was me that made the arrests.

This was fine until one day I arrested a young woman for supplying a controlled substance (what most people don't realise is that prison officers have the same powers as a constable whilst working) because I had been told we had retrieved the package when the prisoner was searched. Unfortunately, this was not the case and I had been misinformed, we had moved her to a quiet room just outside visits for her to be searched by a female officer and then the police were going to be called. Just as we were about to call the police I was told we didn't have the package and therefore no evidence.

I had no idea at the time if it was possible to de-arrest someone but I made it sound as if it was possible and informed the woman how lucky she was that the prisoner had managed to conceal the package where we couldn't get it, so I told her she would be on closed visits (behind glass) next time and sent her off with a bollocking for what she had done.

I worked with a lot of good people while on the visits group, and it was here that I started working with Steve Shepherd who had started his career at Wormwood Scrubs; he would become one of my closest friends and someone I could completely rely on, I would trust Shep as he would become known with my life.

I was working in the search room one day with another ex-Brixton officer when again someone was brought in for a strip search; yet again I was convinced he had some drugs in his mouth as he appeared to be rolling something around in his mouth. I grabbed him around the neck as always in these situations and told him to spit it out, he managed to say he didn't have anything and so I told him again to spit it out and squeezed a little tighter. You could see the fear in his eyes and Shep had walked in and stood with his open hand under this prisoners mouth waiting to catch the package, just then the prisoner spat and all that came out was a plate with false teeth on.

It landed squarely in Shep's palm, I was so surprised that I let him go and just looked at Shep in amazement. The prisoner grabbed the plate back; I told him to bugger off back to his house block and said he was lucky not to be nicked for wasting our time. When he left the room me and Shep just looked at each other and pissed ourselves laughing.

The thing with all of these incidents was that to me it was a game if they managed to get their drugs in one day they won, but I would get them another day. I never took it personally; it was a game of cat and mouse, this was the day to day life on visits and this made it fun.

Again one day I was in the search room when another prisoner was brought in for a strip search. The search room was just a small square room with rubber mats on the floor for the prisoners to stand on while being strip-searched, around the wall there was bench seating suspended from the wall in case the prisoners had to sit down. On this bench was a plastic bin which we kept the bibs the prisoners wore when on their visit, this day the prisoner was brought in and he was a smallish young black lad who came in sucking his teeth because he was being searched.

Amongst the black prison population sucking your teeth is done as a sign of derision toward the staff or whoever winds them up, so he's sucking his teeth at me and saying "this is because I'm black" this made me see red and I bent at the knees and pushed both my palms into his chest as I stood up. He just took off his feet came off the floor and he went into the wall behind him and slid down ending up sitting in the bib bin with me leaning over him telling him there's no black and white with me because prisoners are all scum. We got him out of the bin and completed the search and he went off with his tail between his legs.

I don't know why but I always seemed to have problems in the search room, another day I was sitting at the desk taking names and the other officer was doing the searching when a prisoner by the name of Coakley came in and he just wouldn't stop winging about being searched. In the end, I took my glasses off as I didn't want them broken if it kicked off and came around the desk, the other officer thought it was going to kick off but I stood there and gave Coakley such a bollocking by the end of it he was calling everyone sir and couldn't comply with our instructions quick enough.

Every time he saw me after that he would call me sir and ask if I was alright, he was always in and out of Belmarsh but whenever he was in he was always polite to me, years later I saw him in a local town when I was shopping with my wife and he was still the same when he spoke to me, it's nice to know I can have an effect on people.

One day I was walking through reception and I saw a blast from the past, Gold tooth Bailey was coming in. He saw me and remembered me and shouted across reception 'Mr Richards do you remember when you had me around the neck at Brixton' I walked towards him saying 'you can't shout out stuff like that in front of everyone. We had a chat for a while and I carried on with what I was doing, little did I know he would cause problems further down the road.

Nearing the end of my time on visits we had a change of P.O and we got a woman, she was a no-nonsense P.O and nearly everyone in the group was scared of her. Around the same time one of the S.O's went off long term sick and she was looking for a temporary replacement for him, she decided the choice was between me and another officer. So she said she would observe both of us for a week and then make her decision, eventually she made her decision and called me to the office and asked if I would act up to S.O for at least six months.

I said yes and as was her style she walked down to the visits hall where another temporary S.O was working on the visitor's desk. She walked up to him and told him to hand over his S.O's epaulettes or she would take them off of him. He handed them over and she told him he didn't work on visits anymore and came back upstairs and handed the epaulettes to me.

She asked if I had a problem with what she had done and I told her I didn't as this TSO was a complete Pratt and was in trouble for things he had allegedly done in reception. She was very strong-minded and I'm sure she only picked me because she preferred my way of working as opposed to the other officer. He was a lot quieter in what he did but very good all the same.

We had some real characters on visits and she wanted them managed, she would give everyone 100% backup but she wouldn't take any crap. Things didn't change much for me apart from getting paid a bit more and doing more desk work. If there was trouble on visits I was still there, one day I was on visitor control and one of the other S.O's went to deal with an incident at one of the tables.

The prisoner had been captured with drugs in his hand and decided to fight for it, the staff were rolling around the floor with him and his visitors were getting irate.

The S.O went over to sort it out but just stood there watching, the prisoner was shouting we were killing him and the visitors were calling us all the names under the sun. I couldn't leave the desk I was on because I controlled the visitors in and out and this was the only place a prisoner could possibly escape during a disturbance.

I was shouting at the S.O to cuff the prisoner and move him into the search room, the visits governor was shouting at the S.O from the balcony above telling the staff to let the prisoner go. Someone pressed the alarm bell just as the whole room kicked off, we had about 60 prisoners in the room and over a hundred visitors.

I told the officer on the desk not to let anyone out and I went for the fight, the tables were arranged in a snake around the room and prisoners and visitors were coming over the tables to have a go at staff. I got to the main incident and told the staff to get the prisoner into the search room, there were staff attending from everywhere as an all available staff call had been put out on the radio. It was like a pub fight tables and chairs were flying everywhere, there wasn't enough staff to C&R everyone so it was a mass brawl.

One S.O arrived and was trying to calm a visitor down when she tried to hit him over the head with a chair, I stopped her doing that and as I did her friend hit me across the back with a chair. As staff were arriving I was standing in the middle of this chaos sending staff to different fights like I was directing traffic, it was surreal. A prisoner called Mullis came running at me and I just pointed at him and shouted at him to stop and sit down, and to my amazement he did.

Eventually, things calmed down when the dogs came into the room. It took ages to sort out who was who and make sure no one was released from the room that shouldn't be. Things like this were fairly commonplace but we did have our lighter moments. On this particular day, we were short of staff and so the P.O came down into the room to run the inmate control desk, things were fine until I decided to wind her up. I decided to write out a fake visiting order, I put the surname as Boeing and the prison number as BA0747 and the name and address of the visitor as Mr A Plane, No1 the Runway, Heathrow. I sent this to her desk expecting her to send it back, but instead, she sent a runner off to the house block to pick the prisoner up.

When the runner returned and said there was no such prisoner on that house block she phoned outside to the officer responsible for booking in. The officer on the front desk with an alpha list (list of all prisoners in Belmarsh alphabetically) was a very meek and mild person who was very intimidated by our new P.O she told her that there was no such person in Belmarsh.

She wouldn't have it and shouted at her to find him before she contacted ECR (emergency control room) and had static posts (a place where staff are deployed to watch areas of the outer wall if an escape is suspected) deployed because we had lost a prisoner. She even sent a member of staff to the table number I had put on the V/O to tell the visitor to put his proper address on the V/O. It was at this point she looked up at me across the room and saw me laughing; she gave me a real glare and shouted across a packed visits hall at the top of her voice "Richards you fucking wanker" the whole room went quiet and I was sitting at my desk in hysterics, I couldn't stop laughing I just couldn't believe she had fallen for it. Luckily she did, in the end, see the funny side of things, but the poor officer at the front desk was a nervous wreck.

Things quietened down for a while and we went on to dealing with the day to day issues, then one afternoon a couple of men came to visit a prisoner by the name of Kenny.

Kenny was a real toe rag and so were his visitors; they were drunk and should never have been allowed in because they had been drinking. But they managed to come in and one of them tried to pass Kenny a piece of cannabis the size of a tennis ball this was seen as they weren't really trying to hide it and one of the officers went up and challenged them.

One of the visitors punched the officer and it all kicked off, I got hold of the one that had punched him and took him to the floor where myself and two others restrained him; the other didn't want to know when he saw how many staff had arrived. The P.O turned up, on hearing the alarm bell and told me to stand my one up, when we did his face was covered in blood and it looked like his nose was broken as we had gone down on the floor hard.

He was complaining to the P.O but she just told him to shut up and leave the premises, the police should have been called but they weren't; I think this is because from the state of them they were the worse for wear. Things started to change and the visits governor wasn't happy that we were having so much success capturing drugs as this reflected badly on Belmarsh and meant Belmarsh had a problem with drugs and this showed in the statistics for the amount of drug nicking's we were doing.

So he never said it directly but he would try and encourage us not to pin prisoners' hands to the table and start a fight for what they had. As far as the staff were concerned we didn't start the fights, we pinned their hand and told them to hand over whatever they had, it was prisoners who chose to fight for it. Because of the pressure, things did slow down but we would still have the odd kick-off involving most of the room.

On one occasion me and Shep were on the visitor control desk and it kicked off in the search room, as the only S.O on duty in the room I went to see what was happening and just as I got to the search room door it kicked off on the convicted tables at the top of the room. I turned to look at the visitor control desk to see Shep jumping over the desk to go to the convicted tables, I shouted at him to stop as he needed to stay at the desk in case anyone tried to get out. I went into the search room and a prisoner was under restraint but he was so close to the rear door no one was protecting his head.

Staff from other areas responding to the alarm were trying to get through this door and kept smashing the door into the prisoners head. They couldn't understand why they couldn't get through, as they didn't know a prisoner was on the other side. I had to shout at the staff to go another way before the prisoner was knocked senseless.

Eventually, enough staff arrived and both incidents were dealt with, Shep was moaning because I wouldn't let him get involved but he understood why.

I was responsible with the other S.O's for detailing 52 officers and 18 auxiliaries (members of staff employed to assist officers in various tasks but without direct prisoner contact) visits at the time was one of the biggest groups in the jail, we didn't just run social visits we also ran legal visits and I have to say some solicitors are nearly as bad as their clients. They know the rules of what can and can't be handed over on a visit, but some would try their best to give their clients cigarettes, tobacco and other things they were not allowed.

I would have to say most of our problems on visits were caused by visitors who generally looked at us like we were something they had stepped in. Where you might think it would be the male visitors who would cause the most problems, it was actually the women. One woman on this particular day had brought Methadone into the person she was visiting in a bottle she had concealed in her vagina, she had gone to the tea bar in the room and got a polystyrene cup then gone into the toilet emptied the Methadone into the cup and came back to her seat.

An officer on room patrol had walked past her and noticed this almost fluorescent liquid in the cup and knew it was nothing that could have been purchased at the tea bar. The visit was terminated and she was arrested and the Methadone was taken as evidence. These women were always how dare we lock up their poor little boy he hasn't done anything, (no just mugged or raped some old lady or got their visitor to bring drugs in).

On one afternoon a new officer who would become a good friend had a woman visitor spit in his face, this woman was in her late 30's or early 40's an age where you would think they would realise we had a job to do.

When the officer told me what had happened I was furious, I took the woman off the visit and in front of the whole visits room (shouldn't have done that) gave her such a bollocking for spitting at my staff. By the time I had finished with her she was balling her eyes out and apologising profusely, I ended her visit and banned her from visits for three months. It's not right but you learn to expect things like this from prisoners but we are not paid enough for the public to think they can do it without some form of comeback. I ended my time on visits soon after, the S.O who had been long term sick returned to work, and from there I was deployed to the segregation unit.

10. Visits

Visits was a place where inmates would try and get articles into the prison such as drugs and also money. You would have family members, friends, ex-inmates bring drugs into visits to try and pass them over to the inmate, either by kissing passing the drugs from mouth to mouth, or putting the drugs into a drink the visitors could buy in the visits room and the inmate would swallow the drugs with the drink.

The other way was to pass the drugs to the inmate he would try and hide them in his clothing or literary try and bottle them (push them up his backside so we couldn't get them) on his visit. Another trick the visitors used was to put the drugs in the babies nappy, when the inmate picked the baby up he could remove the drugs.

The visitors were searched coming into the prison, but there are places on your body to hide them. The visitors are checked against the visiting order if convicted and remand, you just made sure the inmate had one visit per day. Some convicted inmates would save up their V.O.s and have a couple of visits in a day, one morning, and one afternoon.

Some inmates came on accumulated visits, which meant if the inmate was in a prison up north and his family were in London, he might get to be located in a London prison for a few weeks for visits, once his V.O.s were used up, back to the other prison he would go. When the visitors got through to the visits room they were stamped on the hand and had to sign in, then they were given a table to sit at and wait for the inmate. When the visit was finished the visitors would sign out and the signature would be checked and the hand that was stamped would be put under a lamp so the officer could see the stamp, just to make sure the right person is leaving the prison, and not the inmate.

Officers called visits runners collect inmates from all around the prison, except the Cat A unit, to take inmates on visits. They are taken into the search room rubbed down and searched, anything in their pockets is taken off them and put in a bag, they are given an orange bib to wear when they get out of the search room they go to the desk where an officer tells them what table their visitors are on. Also, there is staff patrolling the room walking up and down seeing if anything is being passed. If they have a suspicion that an inmate has been passed something he can be taken off his visit and taken to the search room and strip-searched.

If nothing is found then the inmate can go back onto his visit. If drugs or anything else is found he will be nicked and sent back to his house block and the visit terminated or the inmate could go down the seg in locks if he plays up. Visitors can be nicked by the police for bringing unauthorised articles into a prison.

Also, any inmate in the visits room who officers thought might be acting suspiciously was strip-searched when they came off a visit, and the search room staff would strip search 1 inmate in 10. If an inmate was found guilty of being in possession of drugs on a visit by a governor on adjudication, he would go on closed visits for as many as the governor thought fit.

Closed visits was a room with about 6 tables in it, all the tables were partitioned off with glass, so all you could do was talk through the glass to your visitors. Nothing could be passed and no touching. This is how all visits should take place, but there you go. In the visiting room next to the desk where staff supervised the coming off and on of inmates was the VP visits tables, then the remand tables, at the far end was the convicted tables. The tables were laid out so the officers could walk between them it snaked so the inmates were sitting on the inside of the rows of tables, they would have to climb over them to try and escape.

Upstairs was legal visits where solicitors, barristers, police, and probation came to see inmates. There were about 20 rooms with tables and chairs in them. The inmates again were brought down to the legal visits by the visits running officers, they were rubbed down and searched everything was taken off them that didn't have anything to do with the legal visit, it was put in a bag and the inmate locked in one of the rooms.

The legal visitors were searched at the visits entrance, they then came upstairs, we checked their paperwork, they signed in and were shown to a room where the inmate was waiting, and when the visit was over they signed out.

Staff patrolled around the rooms. I remember being on legal visits one day when 2 black blokes turned up at the door, I could see them through the glass in the door. I said to the other officer I was working with. "I bet they want social visits." I went over and opened the door, one of them had dreadlocks halfway down his back, a brown leather jacket, gold chains around his neck, sovereign rings on nearly every finger, the other one had short hair and a long black coat on. I said." Social visits are downstairs fellas." I thought these looked like a pair of drug dealers.

The one with the dreadlocks said." I think we are in the right place." And handed me some paperwork, then he said." Sorry mate." And they both showed me their ID cards, they were both Detective sergeants. When I looked at the paperwork it said can my two sergeants' visit one of your inmates, signed by a Detective

Inspector from Plaistow Police Station. The one with the dreadlocks said, "We have come to visit one of your little scrotumbags.

They signed in and went off to a room. As they went my S.O came in I said to him" Did you see those two." He laughed and said," They have been here before; they go undercover a lot." Respect to those two; they didn't look like what they were.

The visits search room is where I met my mate Bob, we went through different departments together after we worked on visits, he became someone I would trust with my life and I knew he would always back me up, and I would do the same for him. We always looked out for each other, I walked into the search room Bob was in there with another officer, and they had both come from Brixton.

I used to call them the Brixton thugs Bob who was searching this inmate suddenly grabbed him around the neck and said to the inmate "Spit it out" the inmate started to choke. "Spit it out," Bob said again, I put my hand up to the inmate's mouth. Then I said to the inmate, "Spit it out into my hand" As Bob's grip got tighter the inmate choked and swallowed. The next thing I knew I had a plate with false teeth on it sitting in my hand. Bob let go of the inmate's neck and said, "I know you swallowed it, you got away with it this time".

The inmate said," I didn't have nothing" I was standing there looking at this plate with teeth on it; Bob and the other officer were in stitches, I gave the plate back to the inmate and said" You swallowed a package "when the inmate had gone out the back with the other inmates, Bob and the other officer were still laughing. Still to this day Bob reminds me of that incident (Brixton thugs).

It got quite a regular thing; you would walk into the search room and find the searching officers rolling around the floor with an inmate saying "Spit it out "or trying to stop an inmate from trying to hide drugs up his backside. Once when I was in the search room with the searching officer an inmate came in acting really nervous, we decided to strip search him, he stood on the raised platform and when he was stripped we found a hypodermic syringe and needle in his underwear.

I remember saying to him" what the hell are you going to do with that" He said," It's not for me, I've got it in for someone else". He was either in debt to someone or was paid for doing it. He was placed on report the hypodermic and needle went as evidence on the Adjudication, the inmate wouldn't say who it was for so he got closed visits for a long time plus other punishments. The hypodermic and needle then went to the security department for them to find out who had the drugs problem. If you were a visits runner you would carry a radio with you, as you would be all over the prison except the Cat A unit picking inmates up, often the alarm would go off it would be the visits room or search room.

Officers would be rolling around the floor with inmates in the search room or inmates and sometimes visitors in the visits room (ex-cons) to stop them from getting drugs into the prison.

Another officer and me saw a visitor pass drugs to an inmate, the visitor was held until the police arrived, the inmate was taken off his visit and searched, we found the drugs, and both got nicked. The inmate got closed visits and the visitor had to go to court, so did me and the other officer. When we got to court we were not needed, he went guilty, he probably only got a slap on the wrist, anyway it was a day out.

We had a couple of tables near the desk where staff sat that organised the inmate visits and the timing of the visits, on those small tables sat the E men they wore a blue bib and brace with a big yellow stripe down one side so they can be easily seen.

This E man had his wife and mate visiting him, he had his hands on the table, I noticed he hand something under one of them, I walked over to him with another officer who was suspicious of him as well, and I put my hand on top of his and said." What you got there mate." Then I moved his hand, it looked like a Mars bar without its wrapper on.

It was a lump of cannabis. I said to him." You had better finish your visit off now." He said goodbye to his wife and mate and followed me and the other officer into the search room.

We strip-searched him in case he had anything else on him but nothing else was found. He said." Look Gov, my mate gave it to me not my wife, I didn't know what to do with it, and it was too big to hide." I told him he was nicked, the drugs went to the security department for testing, to make sure it was cannabis before he went on adjudication, if the inmate had still said it wasn't drugs on the Adjudication the governor would have sent it off to be tested.

Then if it had come back positive he would have got a bigger punishment for time-wasting. Anyway, he went guilty and got closed visits and other punishments. After the Adjudication, I said to him lucky we didn't catch your mate passing it to you otherwise he would have a cell next to you.

I picked a black inmate up from the seg unit for a visit dropped him off at the search room and went through to the visits room, the inmate came through and because he was in the seg unit he sat near the desk where staff could watch him.

His mother was sitting there when he walked over to her, she stood up but not to kiss or cuddle him, she smacked him right round the face in front of a packed visits room." Why are you in the segregation unit, what have you been up to." I thought nice one lady.

Staff went over to them and calmed things down and they got on with the visit. When his visit was over he was strip-searched and I took him back to the seg, he was really embarrassed. I told the seg staff what happened, they thought it was hilarious.

I remember patrolling around the visits room one shift and spotting Charlie George the ex-footballer who played for Arsenal, he was sitting there with his wife, they were visiting an inmate on remand, he gave a couple of officers who were Arsenal fans his autograph, he seemed a nice bloke he visited a few times he would always talk to staff when he came in.

Whatever department you work on you will always get a couple of sets of nights in your shift pattern. Ours was done in the health Care Centre, upper floor, where most of the nutters were, it was like the film One Flew over the Cuckoo's Nest up there. You work 7 nights from 7 pm till 7 am and get a week off after it. We had one inmate that would literally howl at the moon when he could see it out of his cell window.

Most of the inmates up in Healthcare would be awake all night, either walking around their cell talking to themselves or just staring out of the cell window. One inmate was on his cell bell nearly every hour asking for a light, he never had any cigarettes or tobacco; he was probably going to set fire to his cell, when nights had finished I was glad to get back to normality.

The officers on visits would confront anyone with drugs on them if they were trying to get them past us on visits.

One shift it kicked off in the visits room the alarm bell was pressed and staff were rolling around the floor with inmates and visitors (ex-cons). I came into the room and was going to join in when my mate Bob who was in charge of the visits room shouted to me." Stay there" What he wanted me to do was guard the door so no one could get out.

The room soon was flooded with staff, gradually things came under control with inmates being taken off visits and visitors (ex-cons) being removed. Another time it kicked off again with staff rolling around the visits room with inmates a woman visitor fainted, if I remember right I think an ambulance was called for her I don't think she went in it. The Governor got to hear about it and said he didn't want staff to roll around the floor with inmates or visitors in the visits room. Wait until you got in the search room for it to kick off. The staff were willing to fight to try and keep drugs out of the prison.

There were still a few rolls around the floor, with stroppy inmates refusing to come off their visit or give their drugs up. In the visits room, we saw some good arguments between visitors and inmates on visits.

An inmates wife threw a drink over him when she found out another woman had visited him during the week. One inmate I picked up from one of the House Blocks said to me. 'Gov after ten minutes can you finish my visit off, the wife's coming to visit me and she does my fucking head in.

Can you say the wing governor wants to see me, I'll come straight off' I dropped him off in the search room he came out and went over to his visit. After about 15 minutes he started to look around the room for me, I smiled walked over to him and said." Then wing governor wants to see you after your visit." He said."

No, it's alright gov I'll come now it's probably important." He said goodbye to his wife and followed me into the search room, he was strip-searched because he came off his visit early. He said to me when I took him back to his house block. "Thanks, Gov I owe you one." Another inmate refused to go on a visit to see his wife, because he sent out a letter to his wife, and put the wrong name on the visiting order he put his girlfriend's name on it, and he was shitting himself.

As my time on visits was coming to an end the P.O. Of the Cat 'A' unit asked if I wanted to go and work over there. Cat 'A' unit here I come, I said goodbye to my mate Bob, and we would meet up and work together again later.

11. Seg Unit (first tour)

I started in the seg unit around Feb – March 1993, I was told by an officer who was already working there that I was deployed there even before the official deployments were announced, but this was nothing unusual at Belmarsh for everyone to know things before you. The seg at Belmarsh at that time could hold a maximum of 14 prisoners in normal cells; we had two boxes (special accommodation) two holding rooms for those coming down on adjudication and two dirty protest cells. The seg was over two landings, with the main office and adjudication room on the top floor. The staffing levels were an S.O and five officers in the morning and an S.O and four for the afternoon, and two on the evening duty and one on nights. The seg was an all or nothing type of place, you were either full up and busy, or there was little to do.

We were detailed daily duties by the S.O, these tasks included Doc's officer responsible for the completion of all adjudication paperwork as well as the daily logs and GOOD paperwork (good order or discipline) cleaning officer responsible for the collection of meals, supervising the cleaners, collection of newspapers and magazines.

Adjudication escort responsible for searching prisoners before the adjudications and escorting them into and from the adjudication room, finally landing officer ensuring that the prisoners in the seg got what they had applied for that morning, showers, exercise, razor, mirror etc.

One morning I came into the seg about 7 a.m. and was speaking to one of the officers and said 'I have a bad feeling about today' she told me not to jinx things. Well about two hours later my prediction would become reality, it started with a prisoner we had in the box going on dirty protest. Then one of the prisoners downstairs started flooding his cell, this started a chain of events by mid-afternoon we had one in the box on dirty protest, three downstairs flooding their cells and ripping up their floor covering (a thick industrial kind of Lino) and another one upstairs setting fire to his bedding.

The problem was we were quite full and so we didn't have enough cells to move them all, so for those flooding and damaging the flooring we just turned their water off and left them where they were.

The one on the dirty protest was left where he was; the only one moved was the one who had set fire to his bedding we went in and got him, put the fire out and took his lighter away with a warning that any more trouble and he would be going into the other box.

Along with this we still had to run applications for the other prisoners, showers, exercise, phone calls etc. The only good thing was they cancelled adjudications, so a governor had to come down and open and remand them to keep the nicking s active. I eventually got out of there about half nine that night which wasn't bad as I should have finished at five.

I worked with many members of staff over my time in the seg, and we dealt with many incidents generally involving a small hard-core of prisoners. We tended to have the same prisoners come back to us again and again. One of them by the name of Hutchinson was always a pain in the arse, we had him for quite a long time and he was always pushing the boundaries. On one particular day, this would result in an officer being quite badly bitten on the arm by him.

It was lunchtime and Hutchinson had been playing up for the past couple of days always complaining and trying to intimidate staff.

So the acting S.O at the time who I had worked with at Brixton plated his meal up, (beef stew) and got a cup of hot water for him and walked down the landing, it was the policy at this time that all prisoners had to stand on the door threshold of their cells at feeding times but were not allowed over it. Anyway, the S.O comes down the landing with this plate of stew in the palm of his hand, as he gets to the door.

Hutchinson kicks off well all hell broke loose we were trying to restrain Hutchinson who of course had tried to punch the S.O, but we were sliding all over the place on the stew that was now all over the floor along with the cup of hot water. It was chaos no one could get a proper hold of Hutchinson because he was covered in the stew, someone hit the alarm and we carried on fighting. Another seg officer had just walked into the main gate as he was a late shift, he heard the alarm and came running.

As he came into the seg he ran down the landing toward us but just kept going as he trod on a potato and slid past us rolling around on the floor. It was funny to see the expression on his face as he went past. Eventually, more staff arrived and we got Hutchinson under control and the decision was made to move him to the box (special accommodation) upstairs. It was then that we found out that the S.O had been bitten on the upper arm and Hutchinson had drawn blood, the bite mark was very distinctive.

We took Hutchinson to the box but instead of him being moved in one go we took him to the floor four or five times on the way because he wouldn't stop struggling. Hutchinson spent several hours in the box before being relocated and placed on report.

Hutchinson would have several run-ins with seg staff during my time in the seg, on another occasion when he was in the seg he had to be produced at a police station for them to make further enquiries over something he was involved in. The police picked him up at the back of the seg instead of reception and three coppers threw him in the back of a van and took him away. They brought him back later that afternoon face down on the floor of the van as he had been playing up all day, they offered to bring him into his cell but I told them we would do it.

He came off the van cuffed in rigid police cuffs behind his back, we don't use these cuffs but they work the same as ratchet cuffs but the piece between the ratchets is solid. The effect this solid bit has is that if you twist it the cuff twists against the wrist and it is very painful. Well these cuffs were black and the cell I put him in was not well lit, and so I had trouble seeing the keyholes.

I was twisting the cuffs and he was squealing like a girl because it was hurting, I kept telling him not to struggle as this made it worse. Eventually, I got the cuffs off and left him in the cell, I gave the cuffs back to the police who were laughing because they had heard him squealing.

When we went back to move him to his proper cell he was threatening to assault me and anyone that opened the door. I tried to reason with him to no avail and so I decided we would kit up in PPE and take him out. We went and got ready and then we came downstairs and were standing outside his cell in kit. He could see us there through a small gap in the side of the door, he then started saying he was only joking and wasn't going to assault anyone.

I told him it was too late and to help himself he should face the back of the cell on his knees while we came in or we would crash through the door and this would be more painful for him. Unfortunately, he complied and so we went in and controlled his arms and relocated him to his proper cell upstairs.

I would see Hutchinson again and again over my time in Belmarsh, he never came in for anything much, but because he had pissed the local police off they would nick him for whatever they could. When I see him now I just laugh and tell him we are both getting too old for this shit.

Working in the seg was a good experience and a place to learn a lot; it was also an area where at weekends you could chill out a bit. After adjudications on a Saturday morning, things slowed down and there was a different atmosphere.

Even the prisoners were generally more laid back at the weekends, Sunday mornings were breakfast mornings. We would take it in turns to supply and cook the breakfast; sausage, egg, bacon, beans and toast were the norm.

This started to get out of hand though as everyone tried to outdo the other, we ended up having all that was already mentioned and then someone added burgers, then someone else added pork chops then one Sunday we ended up with all that and a tray of chips from the kitchen that would feed about twenty of us. At this point we called a halt to the one-upmanship and went back to full English, the duty governors would also come down for breakfast. If there was anything left over which there generally was the cleaners could have it.

We took advantage of the quiet times because they were few and far between, another regular to the seg when he was in was a prisoner called Renford. He was a lump only about 5 ft.10 but very stocky and powerful; I am not exaggerating when I say on occasion it has taken eight of us to get him to the floor.

Renford came to the seg one day under restraint we put him in the box because he was resisting all of the way from the house block to the seg, we went into the box and the cuffs were taken off.

He was face down and I made the decision we would cut his clothes off as he was so powerful it was dangerous to strip him under restraint. He was wearing a grey sweatshirt that I thought was a prison-issue one, and so I asked someone to get the cut-down scissors. When I was handed the scissors I cut his top all the way through the back of it, and then up each arm to make it easy to pull off. Like I said I thought it was a prison shirt but it turned out to be a designer top and Renford was not happy I had cut it to shreds. He kept threatening me saying he would remember me and see me later, I told him to comply with the strip and then we would get out of the cell as soon as possible. An officer had Renford in a figure of four leg lock, and Renford's arms were up his back and we prepared to come out of the cell, every time we started to leave Renford would start to push the officer off and we would have to go back in and restrain Renford again.

We tried this about four times, each with the same result. Eventually, I just went up to Renford and said if he didn't let us out of the cell I would put him in a body belt.

The body belt was used for violent prisoners and was a steel-reinforced leather belt with handcuffs on both sides and a D ring at the back to secure it.

Prisoners tend not to like this as their hands are cuffed to their sides and this greatly restricts their movement. And so Renford agreed to let us come out of the cell, even so before the cell door was shut Renford was on his feet and coming for the door. Renford didn't stay in the box for too long and was then located in a normal cell, the next day Renford was playing up again and had used his body to barricade the cell door.

The cell design wasn't the best, Renford had placed his shoulder against the cell door and his feet were wedged against the cell table which is made of steel and bolted to the cell wall, he clung onto the sink and this prevented us from opening the cell door without causing injury to Renford. Luckily all modern cell doors have what is called an anti-barricade kit which means by undoing a few bolts the door can be opened outwards allowing staff to gain entry. When we went to open the door there were six or seven staff around, but only the three officer team were in PPE.

The door was covered by the shield man of the three officer team while the bolts were removed from the door, as soon as the door started to open outwards Renford rushed the door and got out of the cell onto the landing.

The team grabbed him and he started struggling, in the end, it took about seven of us to get him to the floor and as soon as this happened he put his arms under his body so we couldn't get hold of them. The struggle continued and even one of the seg staff who was a bodybuilder who was in PPE couldn't get Renford's arm from underneath him.

This officer is a big lad very strong and always up for a fight, but he was struggling until I told him to kneel on Renford's tricep with the edge of his shin guard. As soon as he did this Renford grunted and his arm shot out from under him, and the officer got an arm lock on him. Eventually, we got him to the box and re-located him, again by the time the last man was out of the cell

Renford was on his feet and we only just got the door closed in time.

From mid-May of 1995 until mid-September I was off work with a knee injury, It was getting close to six months off sick and after that, I would go down to half pay and so I decided that I would go back to work and have a word with the S.O's about doing mainly desk work until my knee had settled down. I was on strong anti-inflammatory tablets and the pain was bearable. Whilst I was off sick I had missed the yearly C&R instructor's refresher and so after I returned I found out there was a course taking place in Lindholme the next week.

I went to see the governor in charge of the seg at the time who said that as I had just returned from sick I wasn't fit and there were another five members of staff applying to be instructors. I wasn't happy with this and asked him if he was prepared to lose six years' experience of instructing on the chance these new guys might pass the course, he told me 'that's tough and I wasn't going'. I was fuming when I came out of the office and I wasn't going to give up something I enjoyed so much without a fight, I went to see the number one governor and explained how I was signed back fully fit even though I wasn't and that he would lose six years' experience on the chance the others would pass.

He told me he knew nothing about this but would give me an answer the following day, the next day he called me and said I could go and so I had to make a quick call and arrange my digs and on the following Monday I went to Lindholme. The seg governor was not a man to be crossed and he had the right hump because I had gone to the number one, he would demonstrate this at a later date when he blocked me from getting a (TSO) Temporary Senior Officers post in the seg.

Things carried on and one day we had a prisoner by the name of Amah who was a zoomer we had got him from healthcare because according to them he was bad and not mad. Anyway he was in the box and kept putting the call buzzer on an officer went to answer it and I went to see what his problem was, we both looked through observation windows and the officer asked him what was up. He said we couldn't judge him as he spoke to god and we would all pay the price, the officer said to him if he spoke to god then he should demonstrate this and ask God to turn the light on in the box. Amah asked god to turn the light on and the officer flicked the switch and it came on. The officer told him that was great but to be sure he should ask God to turn it off, and so Amah did so and the light went off. We did this several times just to make sure and by the time we had finished Amah was convinced he has spoken to god and he had answered him. This would confuse Amah in the end because when we had finished he couldn't understand why God was not listening anymore.

Over time we would have Amah in the seg several times and we had great fun with him, on another occasion he was on dirty protest downstairs in the dirty protest cell, this was a basic cell with just a mattress on the floor and a grill in the floor outside so that any piss or liquefied shit could be washed down the drain. Amah was on dirty protest as I have said and we had to open the cell to place his meals in there, we were all dressed up in paper boiler suits and masks when we went in.

This particular day an officer drew a face on a football we had in the cupboard and placed it in the hood of his paper suit and we opened the door to put Amah's food in, Amah was looking at the face on this ball and was asking questions.

The officer was answering but Amah couldn't understand why the officer's mouth was not moving when he was speaking, he had no idea he was talking to a football. Later that week Amah decided he wanted to come off dirty protest but we told him he couldn't because he hadn't been on it long enough and we were getting £10 a shift extra for this.

He thought he would be clever and the next day he was pissing on the piles of shit to liquefy it so he could push it under the door, what he didn't know was that we were on the other side of the door with a broom sized squeegee pushing it back under. Over time dealing with Amah would result in an officer snapping his cruciate ligament. Amah was in a day cell used when prisoners were on CC (cellular confinement) it just had a metal table and stool attached. The idea of this was to stop those on punishment from lying in bed all day.

Amah was in this cell and wouldn't stop singing; he was at it all morning. The S.O that day just looked up at me and said he couldn't take it anymore it was driving him mad. He asked me and two other officers to come with him, he opened the cell door and three of us walked in, the S.O told him to stop singing but he carried on. Amah was sitting on the stool with his legs under the table and so the S.O took hold of one of his arms to pull him up and I leaned across the table to take his other arm and pulled him. He resisted a bit and the other officer came around behind us to take control of Amah's head, but as he did this he slipped on a piece of paper on the floor and fell over twisting his knee.

He was shouting in pain and holding his knee; we took Amah to the floor and put him in wrist locks.

All the time the officer was wincing in pain and I was so annoyed with Amah and what made it worse was that although I had a good lock on he was showing any signs of pain. The S.O went out of the cell to press the alarm bell not because we couldn't handle Amah but because he knew that a nurse would attend the seg with the other staff and so they could look after the injured officer.

A governor turned up and started taking the piss out of the officer who was rolling around in agony, this annoyed me even more and when we moved Amah to the box this governor told us to leave him in there standing. I told him this was not the way and he had to be placed face down and a figure of four applied but he said no. I then got into a row with the governor about how to relocate a prisoner and told him the only way Amah was going to remain standing was if I put him in a body belt, the governor said that would not happen and ordered me to leave him standing as we came out of the cell.

I did as I was ordered but carried on arguing with the governor, and told him not to interfere in things he knows nothing about. Eventually, the incident was over and the injured officer was taken to hospital where it was discovered he had snapped his cruciate ligament.

In March of 96, I took a TSO (temporary senior officer) board but didn't get it, the governor doing the board was the seg governor at the time he was an arrogant man who wrote with a fountain pen containing green ink, he thought he was something special and had to be different. We never really got on and when I questioned him about his reasons for not giving me the TSO post he said it was because my knowledge of escorts wasn't good enough, I told him this was rubbish as he had not touched on that subject during the board. I also told him I was responsible for arranging escorts when I was at Brixton as well as booking the transport and all aspects of Cat 'A' escorts.

I told him I was not happy with his answer but he just said he wouldn't be either but that was tough I didn't get it. That minor run in setting the stage for our relationship, he gave the TSO post to someone I had worked with within several departments, who I would find out later was a complete snake in the grass.

This officer was always sucking up to the seg governor and in the not too distant future, I would have run-ins with both of them. The S.O on my weekend was ex-forces; me and this S.O got on well and were C&R instructors together.

The S.O on my weekend moved on and I started a long period of acting up and because of this I went onto the S.O's shift pattern, not long after this, we were told we were getting Charlie Bronson.

I knew Charlie from my days at Brixton, we were told we were getting him on a lay down to give other prisons a rest, he came to us as an S.O + 4 unlock and we were to try and work with him to break the cycle of hostage situations and damage to prison property. Almost as soon as Charlie saw me he said 'I know you from Brixton' this was nearly six years on and he must have seen hundreds of screws but he recognised me. I didn't know if this would be a good or a bad thing, he seemed to take to me and things settled down. Charlie would go on the exercise yard every day and do hundreds of sit-ups and press-ups; an officer in the seg I have mentioned before was a bodybuilder and well into his training and he was the ideal candidate to go on the yard with Charlie.

Whilst Charlie was there a governor of ours who I had worked for in the unit decided to make a project out of Charlie and stop the cycle of hostage-taking and smash-ups. This governor suggested we help Charlie to become more compliant and therefore easier to deal with.

We started the process by giving Charlie what he wanted, he said he wanted to learn to use a computer and so we arranged this but we were concerned he would break the keyboard because he would press the keys so hard. To overcome this we got hold of a plank of wood a bit bigger than a keyboard and drew keys on it that were larger than normal, a bit like the phones for people that can't see very well.

Charlie would bang away at this practising typing. Eventually, he got bored with this and so we convinced him to play card games on the computer so he would only have to use the mouse. Charlie loved this but would get annoyed at times because he couldn't cheat.

The governor then suggested we have him as the seg cleaner to keep him occupied; Charlie agreed but said he would clean but he wouldn't make tea for the staff, and so we drew up a compact that we all signed. We would unlock Charlie first thing in the morning after we had given everyone breakfast and he would come around with us collecting the plates and cups. This on occasions would get a bit iffy; we had Hutchinson in the seg overnight for adjudication the following day, through the night he had been shouting out of the window to Charlie.

Hutchinson didn't realise it was Charlie he was shouting abuse at, and he had been shouting out for a light most of the night. When we opened Hutchinson's door for him to pass his plate out Charlie was standing there and he said "You want a light? I'll give you a fucking light" Hutchinson went white which is no mean feat considering he is black, Charlie stepped forward and we had to shut the door quickly before he could get at Hutchinson.

All we could hear then was Hutchinson shouting through the door that he was sorry and he didn't realise it was Charlie he had been shouting at. I had never seen Hutchinson look so scared, and he was glad he didn't get CC when he went on adjudication because he would have had to face Charlie every day. Charlie was still a multi unlock which caused a bit of a problem because he had to have three staff with him whenever he was out cleaning, but we would wander around with him and sometimes when he was washing up he would pick up a large soup ladle and say "imagine if I hit you over the head with this" and I'd just go yeah it would do a bit of damage and then he would laugh and carry on washing up.

We had an industrial waste disposal in the kitchen and one day Charlie said to me "just think if I stuffed your arm in there and turned it on" he would have a smile on his face and I'd just reply yep that would make a mess.

Charlie had stated he would never make tea for staff, but one day I was sitting in the office when he came past and he knocked on the door and asked me if I wanted a cup of tea. This was an opportunity I couldn't pass up even though in the back of my mind I was thinking I wonder what he will put in it. So I was the first staff member ever to have a cup of tea made for him by Charlie Bronson to the best of my knowledge.

It was around this time that Charlie was walking past the office daily, and one day he said to me 'you are always sitting in that fucking chair' I explained that I had to do the Spar forms (these detailed the officer's shifts and times for the seg). A day or so later he gave me a cartoon he had drawn of me stuck in the chair, and so the chair man as he called me was born. A couple of years later this would resurface when I was on House Block 4.

Part of his compact was for him to learn to use industrial cleaning equipment and so we got onto the workshops which ran an industrial cleaning course and arranged for one of the tutors to come to the seg to teach Charlie. The first time the tutor turned up you could tell he was quite nervous as he had heard about Charlie's reputation; it didn't help when I told him Charlie was a pussy cat really.

We made sure there was staff about as Charlie would have to use chemicals and a scrubbing machine and none of us was really sure how Charlie would take to criticism if he did something wrong. Charlie took to it like a duck to water, his only problem was that because he had spent so many years behind his door he couldn't focus more than eight feet in front of him and because his eyesight is so bad he wears dark glasses. Charlie passed the course and carried on as our cleaner, over time he had more and more leeway and the staffing level dropped when he was out and about.

This would cause a problem when the governor who was behind giving Charlie a job and another governor decided to take him for a walk around the inside grounds of Belmarsh. Their first mistake was doing it then they compounded it by not informing the ECR (emergency control room) and not informing the dog section who patrol the grounds. On their walk a dog handler spotted them and nearly had a heart attack, he thought Charlie had taken them hostage and called the ECR. The governor spotted the dog handler and told him all was fine, but it did cause a stir.

One evening I was the ED (evening duty) officer in the seg and the governor had come down to see Charlie, he was sitting in Charlie's cell with the door open talking to him.

That evening we had a prisoner by the name of Doyley who was being disruptive and making a lot of noise because he wanted to see a doctor. I told Doyley the doctor was busy in reception and if he carried on I would put him in the box. As I walked away from Doyley's cell I passed Charlie's cell as he was talking to the governor. Charlie called to me and said "I'll put him in the box for you Bob if you want", I declined Charlie's offer but told the governor I was contacting the orderly office to get a team together to put Doyley in the box (when intervening in the cell of a difficult prisoner a three officer team is used in kit).

I went to my office and made the call, Doyley was on his cell bell again and so I went to the cell to ask what was wrong now, Doyley again said he wanted to see a doctor.

On the spur of the moment I said to Doyley come with me the doctor was waiting, so I opened the cell door and told him to come out and see the doctor. We went past the cell with Charlie and the governor in and then I turned left and took Doyley into one of the boxes. I told him to wait here and get undressed, he took his clothes off and I threw them outside the box.

As I was going toward the door Doyley said this is not a waiting room and I said: "And I'm not a fucking doctor tough shit" I closed the door to the box and as I did it Doyley shouted this is the fucking box and started kicking the door. I just looked at him through the observation hatch and laughed. When I came back onto the landing the governor was standing In Charlie's doorway and asked me what I had done and when I told him he and Charlie pissed themselves laughing, this had taken all of five minutes and so I phoned the orderly office and told them not to bother with the team and I would get the governor to sign the paperwork for putting Doyley in the box.

You would never get away with things like that today, everyone is scared of their own shadow and the governors would never back the staff up like that. Charlie also carried on with his training and with the officer who had now become the person I would always put on the yard with Charlie; Charlie had the bright idea of setting a world record for the highest number of consecutive sit-ups using a medicine ball in an hour.

It was arranged and there was an independent adjudicator present. Charlie was set and our bodybuilding officer would be throwing the medicine ball to Charlie.

The idea was that Charlie would sit on the ground and our bodybuilding officer would throw the medicine ball at Charlie who would catch it raise his arms straight above his head at the same time laying down, he would then sit up arms still straight and throw the ball to the officer and the process would start again. Charlie and the officer did this for an hour continuously resulting in Charlie gaining a record. The work with Charlie would result in myself and the seg staff getting nominated for a Butler Trust Award.

The house blocks were busy with lots of incidents and restraints; this meant the seg was busy. One day we had a prisoner brought down under restraint and when we put him in the reception cell he was still fighting and so the order was given to strip him under restraint.

He was taken to the floor and the strip began all was going well until his trousers and pants were removed and one of the officers said he could just see the end of a piece of cannabis poking about an inch out of his arse.

We are not allowed to do internal searches and so we would have to let him have it and hope he would hand it over, the next thing we know the officer has put a latex glove on and is pulling this piece of cannabis out of the prisoners arse and the prisoners is screaming, our view was with an inch or so of the cannabis protruding from his arse it was not an internal search.

When the officer was finished he had a piece of cannabis about the size and shape of a finger of Kit-Kat in his hand and so he handed it over to be tested and bagged as evidence for adjudication. Later on, the prisoner would put a complaint in accusing the officer of stave fucking him, he told the governor dealing with the complaint that the officer had stuffed his stave up his arse.

Of course, nothing came of the complaint and the adjudication went ahead. It was not unusual to strip someone under restraint when they came to the seg, and we would help with the process as it can seem quite complicated if you are not used to doing it. We had one come down who again was not cooperating and it was decided to strip him under restraint.

On this occasion, a different officer did the figure of four leg lock, as always when they are face down naked and you are the one on the legs the last thing you want is the prisoners arse in your face and so we would place a towel over their arse.

On this particular occasion, the prisoner kept struggling and so we were convinced he had something up his arse, we got him naked and placed a towel over him. When the officer who was on the figure of four all of a sudden he said "the dirty bastard has farted" and then there was a waft of shit coming up.

Someone said I think he's shit himself and then one of the officers pulled the towel away from his arse and there it was a big dollop of what looked like crunchy peanut butter. The officer's face was about 12 inches from it and he started retching, we all thought he was going to be sick and the rest of us started laughing at his face. I have never seen a team of officers come out of a cell so fast, the leg man was the last out and he was still retching and between his retching, he was calling us all wankers.

I carried on as ASO in the seg and dealt with whatever the days threw at us, the governor overseeing Charlie's progress decided that Charlie had progressed enough to be tried out on normal location and so he was moved to House block 4 spur 2.

This was a smaller spur than the others as it had an area at the end which was used as a segregation unit and so the part of the spur he was in was quite small.

He was employed as a cleaner to keep him busy and this would affect the other prisoners if anyone dropped fag butts on the floor after he had cleaned he would have a go at them and they would shit themselves. This would lead to some hairy moments for the staff that had to stand in between Charlie and whoever he was having a go at.

On House block 4 at the time were several Iraqis who had taken over a plane and forced it to fly to Stansted airport and they would become Charlie's victims. He was becoming more frustrated as he couldn't deal with all the prisoners around him; he became more confrontational and eventually took two of the Iraqis hostage along with another prisoner by the name of Greasley.

In true Charlie style he demanded a helicopter, blow-up doll and some ice cream, during the hostage incident he stepped out onto the landing with Greasley under his arm, looked around and then dropped Greasley on the floor and went back into the cell.

In total the incident was just short of two days and when eventually Charlie released the hostages it was decided to take him to HMP Wakefield whose segregation unit had an area called the cage where violent and disruptive prisoners were put, as it was almost self-contained and there was little interaction between staff and prisoners.

The escort to Wakefield was arranged and coincidentally I was due to go to Wakefield around the same time to do a C&R element on a POD course (principal officer's development) and so me and two P.O's and another instructor did the escort.

On the way up to Wakefield Charlie kept me amused, he was talking to me about the hostage incident and he said "Bob they took me hostage and those Iraqis kept tickling my feet, they wouldn't let me go. I told them to bash me over the head with a metal tray but they wouldn't I think they were scared of what I might do, so I took the tray and smashed myself over the head until I had bent it". Charlie went on to tell me that he was getting bored but because of the way he is he couldn't surrender to end it.

He told me he knew there would be teams in full kit outside ready to go into the cell and take him out, and so he stepped out on the landing with Greasley under his arm knowing that as soon as he did this he would be jumped on and after a struggle, it would be over. He said I stepped out and looked around but the teams weren't there.

Because he hadn't been jumped on he dropped Greasley and walked back into the cell not knowing what to do. Eventually, he let the Iraqis go and negotiated his surrender.

When we arrived at Wakefield we drove around to the segregation unit where the cage is located, there must have been about twenty prison officers waiting for Charlie to be unloaded as well as five or six dog handlers.

Charlie told us he wouldn't get off the van because they were waiting to give him a beating, and so after some negotiation, he agreed to come off if we took him to the seg and put him in the cage.

We did this and walked him in and did the strip search and put him in the clothes they had waiting, we went through his possessions he could have I/P (in possession) and gave them to him, he then turned to all of us on the escort and shook our hands and thanked us for dealing with him decently.

Before we left Charlie said to me he was writing a book called Legends, it was about people he had met and had either done right by him or had him over. He told me he was going to include me because of how I had always treated him; we left the prison and went to Wakefield Prison College where we were going to do the course, and so three days of fun began.

The other instructor and myself were there to do C&R training for the P.O's but that was not until the last day of the course and so me the other instructor and a P.O were free to do what we wanted for the first two days, most of that time was spent wandering around Wakefield town centre going from pub to pub. In the evening we would have our meal at the college and then go to the pub with the rest of those on the course.

On the last day, we did our C&R bit and then we were asked to help out with the command training which involved the P.O's being in a mock ECR (emergency control room) where they had to deal with Major incidents like fires, floods, escapes etc. To do this the other two and me were in a different room and we would choose different videos to play on the monitors to simulate someone climbing over the prison wall or fires and so on. I was also told to play the part of a police liaison officer and keep going into the ECR asking for updates for the police who would surround the wall in a real major incident.

We put all sorts of tapes on and I kept going in asking questions, the P.O who was in control was getting stressed and I kept going in and asking questions and making a nuisance of myself, eventually, he lost it and told me if I didn't leave he was going to punch me in the face.

I stayed in character and told him that was not helpful, just as he was about to come around the desk another P.O came over and ushered me to another desk and started to explain what was happening. I couldn't help but laugh and when I went back to where the other two were they were killing themselves with laughter as they had been watching and listening.

We returned to Belmarsh and I carried on acting up in the seg, during this time we would have Gold tooth Bailey turn up for some reason, he was with us for a few days and then he decided he had the arse over something so he covered his cell walls in E45 cream, set fire to paper on his bed and flooded the cell. He then sat on the floor and worked his way under the metal cell table which was bolted to the wall. His legs were under the bottom shelf and he put his arms were through the middle shelf. Because of the fire, it was discovered and we saw what he had done, we open the cell and put the fire out and shut the door, we then got a team together in PPE to go in and take him out. The visits P.O turned up as Oscar one and the duty governor attended as well.

The team went in and tried to put wrist locks on him but because he had his back against the stool attached to the table they couldn't get control of his arms without pulling them against the legs of the cell table.

This caused problems but I went in to see what was what, I then had an idea and told the duty governor to go and get me two pairs of escort cuffs. When he returned with them I went back in and attached one-half of the cuffs to each of his wrists so the team could use them as leverage, Bailey was smiling at me and said 'you should be an S.O because these wankers wouldn't have thought of that'.

The team managed to get control of Bailey and he was moved to the box, he was strip-searched and left in there with just a rip-proof gown to wear. He was only in there about ten minutes and someone went to have a look through the hatch to see if he was alright and they noticed he had removed the cell call button from the wall. How he had done this with just his fingertips I have no idea, and so he had to be moved again.

This time he was put in a holding cell normally used for prisoners attending for adjudication, he was in there a few minutes and he shit up. It was decided to leave him where he was so we didn't have another cell out of action.

Eventually, I went home that day and was glad when my shift ended, I came in the next day to find Bailey out on the landing ironing his clothes, I asked him what the fuck was he doing and he just grinned and told me he was being released.

I said to him 'you knew this yesterday when you did all that shit' he just smiled again and said 'good though wasn't it'. Just before he was taken to reception he shook my hand and said it was good to see me again, prisoners like Bailey were a pain in the arse but you couldn't help but like him.

It wasn't long before the problems with a certain TSO and Governor became more and more frequent. These problems were to culminate in a meeting between the Governor, TSO and myself, which ended with me calling the Governor a Muppet and me leaving the meeting. The following day I was redeployed from the seg to House block 4 as my permanent place of work.

Shep

12. The Unit

The Cat 'A' unit is a prison within a prison, it is basically in a middle of a field within the main prison. It has a wall around it and a fence inside the wall with Geophones on it, which means if you shake the fence lights start to come on in the ECR (control room).

This was one of my first jobs when I joined the unit to walk around the inside of the fence and kick certain sections of it to see if the panels lit up in the control room. When you entered the unit you got searched just the same as you did coming into the main prison. Walk under a portal, turn pockets out, bag and contents of pockets X rayed.

The unit had 4 Spurs, 12 inmates on each spur and I think 4 cells in the seg unit. Everywhere in the unit was on camera. I think 1 exercise yard at the time had a roof on it, later on, all that changed. The visits room was out the back near the exercise yards.

It housed a room where visitors and the contents they brought with them was searched and X rayed, legal visits and social visits were held in the same rooms, unlike the main prison. The search room was located back in the main unit; this again all changed a couple of years later when the unit shut down for refurbishment.

On social visits, you sat inside the room with the inmate and his visitors, on legal visits you sat outside the room but looking in through the glass in the door.

The inmate's meals were brought over from the kitchen on a trolley and plugged in to keep them hot, they were located outside the 2 Spurs downstairs, the inmates came off the Spurs collected

128

their meals and went back to their Spurs and got hot water from an urn, then got banged up.

We fed one spur at a time, the S.O.s office and gym downstairs, upstairs was the P.O's and Governor's office, staff restroom; the spare room was used for staff meetings and a room that acted as a church on Sunday if any inmate was interested, also Spurs 3 and 4.

On the Spurs you had 12 single cells, recess with toilets shower and bath, furniture for inmates to sit on, TV, staff table where we sat, a bubble with Perspex around it so the officer could see the spur and us, also he had access to a phone and alarm bell.

His job was to monitor the inmate's phone calls, make sure they were not ringing any unauthorised numbers, their numbers had to be authorised by the police.

Three of us were on the spur one officer with a radio, we all had personal alarms, a phone on the desk, and an inmate phone on the wall next to bubble. When I started on the unit I was working everywhere, on the Spurs, visits, seg unit if anyone was down there and sometimes out on escort.

You do get nights in your shift pattern but they were easy to get rid of, somebody would do them for you to get the week off afterwards.

Escorts was a day out of the prison, usually, you took your own inmates from the unit along with other officers from the main prison, we would go to court or sometimes you were out at a hospital, being High-Risk Cat A's they rarely went anywhere else. Normally an S.O would be in charge of the escort with one more officer than inmates.

When we took the IRA and some other prisoners to a court whether it was magistrate's court or crown court for trial, as soon as we drove out of the prison gates we had a police escort and a helicopter flying above us, same for the way back. In court when the Judge walks in we all rise (stand up) they just sat there saying, we don't recognise your rules or system, also they didn't listen to what was going on they didn't care, they knew they were going to get about 25 years, and they did for conspiracy to cause explosions. One actually got released from the Old Bailey at the beginning of the trial because they found out that he was not a member of the IRA, he just hired some Labourers for a job and hired IRA men looking for a cover, even the IRA said he wasn't anything to do with them. He had spent about a year and a half in the unit on remand protesting his innocence.

We took a few London criminals to court for drugs and firearms, also a few yardie (Jamaican) criminals, one of them had shot a police officer, and luckily he didn't kill him. We took him to the Old Bailey for sentencing, he got about 25 years, and he was a horrible fucker.

Two other inmates who were nasty pieces of work were going back and forth to the Old Bailey on trial for kidnap and robbery.

One of them was allowed to sit in the back of the Cat 'A' van because he was supposed to suffer from Asthma, so he was cuffed to staff, the other was locked in a cell on the van. What happened one day on the way to court this inmate cuffed to staff dislocates his thumbs gets out of the cuffs and produces a blade, threatens staff with it, he then pulls a switch and releases the safety hatch in the roof they then climb out of the van, the driver and his mate suspect something is wrong and call the police. (So I was told) .No police escort because they are not dangerous enough. One gets caught later on spends a few days in police custody then back to us in the unit.

The other is on his toes for a good few months till he is caught, then sent back to Belmarsh to the main seg to carry on with their court case that was suspended because one of them was on the run, there was a massive inquiry.

I felt sorry for the officers on the day this happened, it was rather embarrassing because the other inmates kept asking where the other two were, knowing what had happened one inmate asked me the next day with a stupid grin on his face why two cells on his spur were empty, I told him to " fuck off ". Inmates must be searched properly, and use your sticks when necessary. I don't think he should have been sitting in the back with staff even if he had Asthma; he pulled a fast one and got away with it.

On one of the Spurs, I was working on we had an inmate who was black about 6ft 4 INS and about 20 stone not fat all muscle. He said he was on the books of the San Francisco 49ers, he was huge. He had killed someone back in the USA and done a runner over here, he was found in London somewhere and arrested; he was waiting to be extradited to the US.

He said 'At least they haven't got the death penalty where I come from'. In the gym in the unit he would bench press with nearly all the weights on the bar, also on the exercise yard we would play volleyball with the inmates as me and a few other officers were sports and games trained, everyone tried to get on his side, I haven't seen anyone hit a ball over the net as hard as he could. Sports and Games was a good course that was 2 weeks out of the unit and in the gym learning and playing different games.

He used to eat two meals to everyone else's one because he was so big. Me and another officer had to take him over to the

Health Care to see a doctor; we put the cuffs on him they were on the last notch as his wrists were that big. I was cuffed to him I said 'If you are going to do a runner remember I'm cuffed to you' he said, 'don't worry I'll just pick you up put you under my arm and run with you '. Then he started to chuckle like Frank Bruno, and patted me on the head, he could have got the whole of my head in his hand they were huge.

We had another American inmate he was a white bloke always winging and moaning, he got a life sentence for murder in the U K and was being deported back to the USA, three police officers from the USA arrived to pick him up, after he was strip-searched they cuffed him, he started to moan about the cuffs being too tight. The police officer in charge said, 'There's an easy way and a hard way to do this, you ain't going to like the hard way. He soon shut up, another time on one of the Spurs an inmate was getting annoyed with the officer in the bubble because he wouldn't let him phone a number, the officer said the number hasn't been cleared the inmate said it was. The inmate picks a chair up and I walk towards him, he says' Duck Gov this ain't meant for you. He throws it at the Perspex window in the bubble.

The officer in the bubble pressed the alarm bell, the inmate runs back into his cell; other officers arrived for the alarm we got everyone banged up. The P.O and Governor came on and had a chat with the inmate and left him on the spur. I said put him down the seg, the P.O said if we put him down the seg we will have to man it as it is empty at the moment.

We had three inmates in for armed robbery for two of them it wasn't their first time the other one I think it was.

The one who's first time it was, walked with a stick when he went off the spur to exercise etc, at this time they were on remand before their trial came around the one with the bad leg was going over to the health care to see the doctor about his leg or so we thought.

When they went to court for trial the other two got about 17 years the one with the bad leg got a couple of years, apparently, he was not seeing the doctor but secretly talking to police, he had to be kept away from the other two after the trial. Sitting on the Spur one day I said to the other officer I was working with." Nice and quiet today ain't it. Next thing two inmates start arguing about who is next on the phone, then it turns into handbags at fifty paces the officer in the bubble presses the alarm, in come the staff everyone gets banged away. The two inmates are taken to the P.O's office and bollocked, both stayed on the spur. The other officer I was working with said.' Shut up in future'.

We had this inmate come to us who was supposed to have been high up in the Mafia; he was in his fifties, short and bald. He was waiting to be deported back to Italy to finish his sentence off; he said he had a few years left to do.

We searched his kit and gave him what he was entitled to, he asked for this magazine you get out of the Sunday paper, on the front of it, was a house that looked like a castle. Red sports car and a very pretty young woman, he said to me, my house, my car my wife; l gave him the magazine and said.' you wished'.

The next day I walked onto his spur he said. 'Governor follow me', I followed him to his cell and he showed me some photos on his wall. He said. 'Look my wife, my car, my house and my boat.

His boat as he called it was like a battleship. The photos were exactly the same as those in the Sunday magazine. Later I asked him how long he would serve when he went back to Italy, he said.'

If my friend is in charge it will be a couple of weeks, if he is not in charge a couple of months.

They say crime doesn't pay, speaking to a couple of Columbian drug dealers we had, I asked them why they sold drugs? The one that spoke English said, 'you don't know what it is like to be poor and have nothing, then someone comes along to you and says work for me selling drugs. Suddenly you have money to buy things you could only dream of, it's worth the risk'.

Working with the IRA, was an eye-opener, they really didn't like anyone in a British Uniform or anybody who represents the Monarchy or the British Government. Some of the officers I worked with had served in Northern Ireland in the Army, so there was a bit of tension there sometimes. We had some IRA scattered about on different spurs, one of them that we had on Remand was waiting to be sent to America to face charges for trying to buy surface to air missiles, to take helicopters out. Another one was not Irish but Scottish; he just hated everyone and moaned about everything. One Irish inmate was released from prison the police dropped all charges on him, he got the sack from his building job, got drunk nicked a JCB and with a 45-gallon drum of fuel in the digger bit and drove towards the police station. Just what the IRA does but with a bomb in the digger, he got stopped and arrested and put in the Cat A unit until the police were happy he wasn't IRA.

I was feeding at lunchtime on the spur I was on when the inmates left the spur to get their lunch came back on and queued up at the urn for hot water, I moved back out the way and suddenly felt something sharp in my back. I turned around and one of the IRA was standing there with his plastic knife in his hand he said with a grin on his face 'Sorry about that '. I looked at him and said 'you would like to 'he just smiled and walked off.

On Friday 9th September 1994, 5 IRA and 1 London Armed Robber, escaped over the wall at HMP Whitemoor they shot a dog handler while escaping luckily he didn't die. The police were alerted and the escapees were caught hiding in a ditch outside the prison. Inmates were moved around in our unit and we were told the escapees would be coming to us and all 6 would be put on a spur on their own, they were all convicted inmates. The spur was searched and everything was removed apart from a desk and 3 chairs for officers. They were not allowed off the spur, their meals were brought onto the spur, and if they come out of their cells they would have to wear E man clothes, blue jacket and trousers with a big yellow stripe down one side. One of them wore the E man's clothes just to give the meals out, but they just sat in their cells all day with just shorts and a T-shirt on, they wouldn't wear the E man clothing.

If you want to go on exercise you will have to put the E man clothing on, they all refused. We went into their cells to conduct locks, bolts and bars, these have to be done every day and fill in their Cat A Books every hour, they just sat there. It seemed strange not having inmates wandering around, or having them in your face moaning.

In the mornings they had letters they wanted to post out and make applications for different things, we would not accept anything unless they put the E man kit on, and come out their cells, eventually, they did all except the London armed robber, and he just stayed in his cell all day banged up.

The 5 IRA started to take exercise walking around the yard for an hour, they even started to keep the E man kit on in their cells. After a couple of weeks, the S.O came on the spur and said to them.' If you want to watch TV you can we will put one on the spur with some chairs as well'. They said 'no thanks '. I said to the

S.O 'fuck em then'. Then one of them came out of his cell and said 'I'll watch the TV the horse racing's on'. Then he said 'Take no notice of that lot, I'll watch it and so can the officers'. I thought this one does what he wants to do he is a bit of a loner, he never really mixes with the others.

So a TV gets put on the spur, one happy IRA man and some staff that like horse racing, the others aren't interested they just sit in their cells reading. When mail started to arrive for them it was addressed to POW (prisoner of war) then the name, it made me feel like I was working in Colditz.

The only time I saw the others watch the TV (not the London Armed Robber he was still banged up) was when the news was on about the football match between Ireland and England, it was abandoned after England went 1-0 down and the England supporters starting fighting with the Irish supporters.

You could hear on the news the England supporters singing, 'Death to the IRA'. One of them said to me 'You seem to have a problem in England with football violence.' I said 'Yep' he said I think it is a big problem'. I replied, 'and you don't have any problems in Ireland with violence." He just looked at me and walked off to his cell.

One of them you could have a conversation with he would talk to staff no problem. He said he joined The IRA in the late 60s, he said being a catholic I could not get a job, being a catholic I couldn't get credit. So I decided to fight for my rights. He said to me' you know I would shoot you to get out of here don't you 'I said 'I know that'. He said, 'I think you're alright I wouldn't kill you but I'd shoot you in the leg, and good luck with the compensation money you would get'.

I knew he meant what he said; he was the one who shot the dog handler when they were escaping from HMP Whitemoor.

I got a day out of the prison an S.O and another officer and me were asked to do an escort, we had to take this other IRA inmate who had just got convicted (25years) for being caught with explosives in the boot of his car, to HMP Frankland way up north in County Durham. Early start home late, this IRA inmate would not wear prison clothing so we took him in a Cat A van all the way to Durham with just a blanket around him, it was winter and no heating in the van he must have been freezing.

After some time the IRA was wanting to have visits, they were saying there shouldn't be a problem as all their visitors were approved, the prison authorities seemed to drag their heels they wanted to put them on closed visits, because of the escape from Whitemoor prison and the shooting of the dog handler. So they did what they do best and 'Shit Up 'dirty Protest, they covered the cell walls with shit, but they didn't cover themselves. The London Gangster decided to join in.

We all got dressed up in white suits with hoods, masks gloves and plastic bags on our feet, we still had to take applications from them and we gave them their meals at the door, all they did was hand over their mail that we put in a sterile bag, I'm sure the auxiliary officers that deal with the mail were aware of the situation.

When we got to the cell of the IRA member the one who wants to watch TV, we opened his door up and he was laying on his bed, "' thought you were shitting up we asked him'. ' I have ', he said pointing to a foot square patch shit on his wall. Me and the other officer started laughing, he said.' I'm told old for this game, don't tell the others'. His secret was safe with us; the place was starting to stink now as soon as you walked on the spur you could smell it. We even taped the gap up around the door frame to try and stop the smell from coming out. After about a week they were told they could have visits from their families and it would be a normal Cat 'A' visit, and not behind glass. So they came off the dirty protest. We moved them into the clean cells next door to their dirty ones Chucked them in the shower, got some inmates over from the main prison that were doing an industrial cleaning course, got the shitty cells jet washed out and cleaned.

I think they got nicked for going on dirty protest, if I remember rightly they refused to attend the adjudication and basically just got banged up for a few days on the spur. Which didn't make any difference really because only one of them came out of his cell.

When their punishment was over back to so-called normal, the one who wanted the TV said he only got about 2 visits a year because his family couldn't afford to keep coming over from Ireland to visit him, I said to him wouldn't the IRA pay for them to visit you, he said 'Your joking aren't you'. I said 'no it's the least they could do if you have put your life on the line for the cause'. He just shrugged his shoulders and went back to watching the TV.

We had a few inmates in and out of the seg unit for different things, one had assaulted an officer, he was a bit of a punchy fucker, he would assault a member of staff then stand there when staff arrived and put his hands up and say 'I'm not fighting' he just got escorted to the seg not bent up. One got put in the seg for punching our P.O we had an inmate who was an Australian who escaped from a prison in Australia, came to England murdered someone spent his remand time on the unit got found guilty moved somewhere up north, comes back to us, to the Cat 'A' seg because he was playing up in the other prison.

It's said in his record, he must be kept away from the IRA apparently in the other prison he punched a member of the IRA in the face and knocked him out for laughing when a bomb went off in England somewhere. The IRA member who got knocked out was one of those who had escaped from Whitemoor.

Another inmate in the seg was there for his own protection, he was grassing a lot of people up, even some of his own family.

Sometimes we would have to help out on the unit visits, if they were busy, even if it was just picking inmates up or taking them back and strip-searching them, then putting them back on their Spurs. One morning I took an inmate over to visits after me and another officer had strip-searched him, delivered him to the visits S.O when someone picked me up off the floor from behind, the voice boomed. 'Hello Boy,' when he put me down, I turned around. It was Lenny McLean, who we had in the seg in the main prison a few years ago. I said." Alright, Len how are you." He said. "Yeah Fine Boy." he was with Roger Daltrey the singer out of The Who.

A couple of female staff were getting Roger Daltrey's autograph and Lenny McLean was kissing the female staff on the cheek. They had come to visit a London Gangster. The control room phoned up to see if we were ok, they were watching everything on the cameras.

The S.O. then told me I had to stay there with them on visits; I ended up sitting on the visit with Lenny McLean, Roger Daltrey and the London Gangster they came to see. When the visit was over Lenny McLean shook my hand and said." See you boy." That was the last time I saw him before he died.

On spur 2 in the unit, it was mostly all London Gangsters (or they thought they were) all on remand waiting for trial. The other

Spurs had at least one inmate that would keep the spur clean and tidy, not spur 2; they just left their mess on the floor. We refused to open them up unless they tidied the place up. They refused a couple of them that were the mouthpieces for the spur got quite vocal about it, even telling the others not to clean up. So they all stayed banged up, we got some inmates over from the main prison who were doing an industrial cleaning course, they cleaned the spur up the 2 mouthpieces were removed to the unit seg. One stayed in the seg for a while the other was transferred to I believe HMP Liverpool to spend time in their seg, he came back weeks later when his trial started.

Whilst in the unit I went on 3 courses 1 was a sports and games course, 2nd was the C and R 3 course which is riot training.

You get petrol bombs thrown at you, and you practice taking, landings, wings, and the prison back from inmates. The 3rd was a Cat 'A' course all officers that were working in a Cat 'A' unit with High-Risk Cat 'A's were supposed to attend the course at one of the training colleges.

It was a course that was supposed to bring staff closer together and to stop the conditioning of staff. This course happened after the escape at HMP Whitemoor, when I came off this Cat 'A' course me and the other unit officers were told that the unit was shutting down for refurbishment and house block 4 had been upgraded for us to move into. So the inmates were moved over to HB4 in cell vans and the unit closed.

We used spur 2 and some of spur 3. The IRA and the non-clothes wearing London Gangster were put on Spur2 near the makeshift seg. The governor said you will need some cleaners to keep the Spurs tidy, get the convicted inmates to work you can't legally make remand inmates work. The only convicted inmates were the IRA and the London Gangster who escaped from Whitemoor plus one inmate who came to us from another prison because his sentence had nearly finished and he lived locally, (Still a High-Risk Cat 'A').

Some of the IRA said that they were in the middle of completing education courses when they escaped from Whitemoor, they had all their course work with them now, as all their kit had been sent from Whitemoor, and they wanted to continue with their courses as they had paid for them. Education is classed as work.

One IRA member was doing nothing nor was the London Gangster, or the other Cat 'A' waiting to be released. They all said," Fuck that" when asked to clean. The next step if they refused was a nicking as they were convicted and expected to work. They were asked again, the same answer. They got nicked and a small punishment, when that was over, they were asked again "Fuck Off ". Was the answer this time, so they spent some time in the makeshift seg on punishment.

In the meantime, a couple of inmates who were on remand volunteered to clean when they heard they would be paid for it. I was told by the unit P.O that my time on the unit was up and had to move somewhere else.

The S.O on HB3 said come on here we want staff with some experience, so I collected my shift pattern for HB3 and started on there a week later. For the last week on HB4 come the unit I worked on the makeshift visits we had that was turned from a servery into a Cat 'A' visits area.

I heard that one of the IRA that refused to work, who was in the makeshift seg was thinking of going on dirty protest good luck with that lads, me and the IRA would meet again a few years later.

13. House Block 4

When I went to House block 4 I had approx 10 years in the job, the staff on there at the time had on average 3 or 4 years. Because of this the S.O's said I should be I/C of whichever spur I worked on, I told them I needed time to settle into the regime on the House block and the staff they already had were doing the job without problems. The first few weeks I was there I worked on various spurs and landings, at the time all the spurs had regular staff which was one of the reasons it ran well.

The House block also had high-risk Cat A's as the unit was being refurbished, eventually, I became a regular on spur 1 and whenever I worked on the spur I would usually be I/C. On one of my first evening duties on spur one, I was sitting with the I/C and another officer and it was getting close to bang up time but the prisoners were watching "The Bill" on TV. Roll check was supposed to be 20.30hrs which means all the prisoners have to be behind their door so they can be counted.

I mentioned this to the I/C and he said the staff normally let them watch TV until the adverts about 20.45hrs and then they fill their flasks with water and go behind their doors, I said I wasn't happy with this as roll check is 20.30hrs but he said it wasn't worth the aggravation to do it earlier.

I said next time I am on ED (evening duty) this would change and he said it won't happen, sure enough, the next ED I was I/C and at 20.20hrs I went up to the TV and turned it off and took the Ariel. This didn't go down too well and soon I had several prisoners around me, I told them roll check was 20.30hrs and that meant they had to be behind their doors for this to happen. They weren't happy but I said the more they complained and hung around the earlier I would turn the TV off in future. They reluctantly got their water and went away, after a couple of weeks of moaning they got used to it and got their water straight away when I shouted for them to get it. I soon found that the easiest way to run the spur was to be consistent and although I would shout at them for things if they came to me for a genuine reason I would do what I could to sort their problems out. They soon came to realise I wouldn't be messed about but if they were entitled to it I would do my best to get it for them.

We had two Nigerian prisoners on spur 1 by the names of Shotonwa and Olaku; they were on remand for murder unusually as most Nigerians are in prison for fraud.

These two were ok but very full of self-importance and this showed itself on association one night, everyone was on the ground floor for association and all of the chairs were taken when Shotonwa and Olaku came down and went up to another Nigerian and told him to stand up so one of them could have his chair.

I saw this and asked them what they were doing? They replied that the other prisoner was of a lower caste than they were and so he had to give up his seat, I told the other prisoner to stay where he was which he reluctantly did, but he looked very nervous. I told Shotonwa and Olaku that I was the highest caste on the spur and only I can tell someone to give up their seat. They weren't happy about this and tried to argue, I told them if they kept on they would find life very difficult being unlocked last all the time or the first to be locked up. They went away calling me god knows what in Nigerian but there was no way I would put up with bullying on my spur.

Day to day life on house block four carried on we had a good crew of staff and me and the rest of the lads had a laugh whenever possible. In July of 97, it was the tenth anniversary of my joining the job and so the staff thought they would get me something to celebrate this and got one of the prisoners to draw a picture for me. This was presented in front of most of the staff on the house block, and even the house block governor was in on it.

I was congratulated for doing nothing for ten years and told to see if I could do the same for the next ten. On the 11th of October 97, I took a very large prisoner by the name of Farquharson to the S.O's office for a warning about his behaviour toward a female officer, she was tiny but very fiery and wouldn't take any shit. During the warning, Farquharson kicked off and we were getting thrown around in a very small office bouncing off filing cabinets. What struck me as funny was that this petite officer had jumped up and grabbed him around the neck and Farquharson stood upright and she was left dangling like a necklace around his neck.

She was swinging around but wouldn't let go, unfortunately, he swung her against a filing cabinet and she got hurt. We eventually got him on the ground and someone pressed the alarm bell, we managed to get him under restraint just before the cavalry arrived.

I was supervising what was happening and talking to Farquharson when a new S.O tried to take over, but an S.O who was there told the new S.O to fuck off because I knew what I was doing. Unfortunately for him, he didn't know I was also a C&R instructor, he was quite taken aback by her tirade and stood there with a stupid look on his face.

We got him to his feet but he was still trying to fight us and we had to drop him to the floor several times on the way to the seg.

One Sunday we had a new officer, he was detailed the top landing of spur one and I was the officer for the middle landing and another experienced officer was I/C the spur. Sundays are pretty boring and when it was time for association the new officer was on the top landing I was talking with the I/C on the ground. He shouted for the newbie to unlock all the 42 cells on the spur, he told him it would be good practice. Being new did as he was told and unlocked all the cells down to the ground floor.

I told the I/C he was a bastard with a big grin on my face, the policy then was that prisoners had fifteen minutes to get whatever they needed (shower stuff, phone card etc.) before the doors were locked again. Sure enough, fifteen minutes later the newbie was told to lock all the doors again, and so off he trotted and locked 42 doors. On Sundays, we did toiletry apps where they could ask for soap, shampoo and the like, we also exchanged their bedsheets.

Just as the newbie locked the last door the cleaning officer came onto the spur and shouted sheet exchange, the I/C looked up at the newbie and said unlock for sheet exchange, his face was a picture he looked so pissed off and the I/C and me were sitting downstairs pissing ourselves.

Luckily the newbie eventually saw the funny side of it, but if you did that to a new officer now you would be reported for bullying, in total he had locked and unlocked 126 doors in something like 25 minutes. I would end up as his mentor officer and his shifts shadowed mine so he could learn from me and I could keep an eye on him.

This would lead to his first restraint, on the 1st of April 98 a prisoner called Staggs had a bad visit and when he came back to the spur he asked if he could have a phone call.

I allowed him to make the call which didn't go well and when he finished he asked if he could get a cup of hot water, I told him no and that he had already had a touch by having a phone call on bang-up. He was agitated and went upstairs where another officer on with me who was my bodybuilding friend from the seg was waiting, Staggs told him I had said he could get a cup of water and so he got his cup and came back out of the cell.

He started down the stairs and the other officer shouted to me asking if I had permitted him to get water, I told him no and so he started to follow Staggs down the stairs. I was standing by the water urn and as Staggs approached I told him he wasn't getting water, he ignored me and went to walk past me, I stood in his way and he put the cup under the tap to the hot water urn.

Because he couldn't get it under the tap properly the water splashed and some hot water went on my arm, I grabbed Staggs and put him on the floor, the other officer was level with us then and also grabbed him.

He shouted for staff and just then the newbie walked on the spur and saw us fighting on the floor, he jumped in and took an arm and so we restrained Staggs.

We stood him up and as we were taking him out of the door Stagg's co-defendant a prisoner called Curry who was a cleaner started shouting for us to let Staggs go and that we were out of order.

We took Staggs to the seg and I nicked him for refusing a direct order. When I returned to the spur I went straight to see

Curry, he was on the escape list for running away from a coach he and his co-defendants were being transferred in. I had made him a cleaner against the odds as E-List prisoners did not normally get employed as cleaners. I was mad and went into his cell ready to rip him a new arse, I told him I had done him a favour getting him employed and I didn't expect him to take the side of a shit like Staggs.

He said to me before I go off on one that he had no option as Staggs was his co-de and he had to be seen to support him, I was just about to have another go and Curry said "that was great I have never seen Staggs squeal so much "he apologised for what he said but said he didn't have a choice.

I had calmed down by then and, I understood what he meant about being seen to be supporting his co-de, as he was already under pressure because I had got him the job as an E-List prisoner. It was Curry who had drawn the picture for my ten years in the job. He made me laugh because his main offence was armed robbery, which he committed with a cucumber concealed in a plastic bag which he pretended was a sawn-off shotgun.

One afternoon I was sitting on spur 1 enjoying the quiet time because most of the prisoners had gone to work.

I was having a cup of tea and laughing with the cleaners and staff when we heard a shout for staff from spur 3. I went running over to spur 3 and when I got on there I saw a prisoner by the name of Ola who had sat on the railings and tied a noose to the suicide netting above and jumped off the railings. He was hanging from the anti-suicide netting on the middle landing (ironic I know). Two officers were on the netting trying to support Ola's weight and stop the ligature tightening, I ran to the middle landing and another Officer had been to get the cut-down scissors from the bubble and he was in the process of cutting the ligature. We pulled Ola over the railings and laid him on the landing, the ligature was so tight at first I couldn't get the cut-down scissors under it to cut it free from his neck.

Eventually, I managed to get two fingers under it which gave me the space to cut the ligature and when I did this Ola took a massive breath. A medical emergency had already been called and we were waiting for healthcare staff to arrive. The S.O at the time arrived in answer to the alarm bell and then as the nurse arrived and asked what had happened.

He told the nurse that 'Ola had just been hanging around', (this seems harsh and uncaring, but this type of humour is how prison officers and those that work in the emergency services deal with potentially life-threatening situations) she didn't see the funny side of this and she would later put in a complaint about him. Ola was taken to the healthcare and I took the ligature to the office to write my incident form and bag and tag the ligature.

This has to be done because if he had died the police would have investigated the death, and they can tell from the way the knot on the ligature is tied whether it was tied by the dead person (suicide) or by someone else (murder) Another S.O from the staff care and welfare team arrived on the house block and was asking everyone if they were alright. Eventually, she walked into the office I was in, she looked at me and said 'I'm not even going to ask if you are ok because you just don't give a shit' and then she walked out.

I was quite hurt by this, as it happens she was right but this could have been the one incident that pushed me over the edge and affected me. The irony to this story is that Ola was Nigerian and he had tried to take his life because he didn't want to be deported back to Nigeria. But because we saved him he was deported and basically, the Nigerian authorities took him around the back of the airport terminal when he got there and shot him.

I was on the spur one day with the new officer who had locked all the doors and we were banging up, so we were walking around the ground floor. At the time we had a new female governor on the house block and unknown to me she had walked onto the middle landing without me seeing, so me and the other officer were chasing the prisoners to bang up and I was telling them to get behind their fucking doors. Just then I looked up and saw the governor and she had obviously heard me swearing at them, I just looked at the new officer and said 'that is an example of how not to speak to prisoners' I looked at the governor again and she had a wry smile on her face.

There were always minor things going on, it was on house block four that I met up with my old friend Shep. We were sitting on spur 1 one day supervising association when a black prisoner came up to us at the desk and said he wanted to change cells.

I asked him why and he said he didn't want to share a cell with a white man, I told him to go away and he got quite angry and again said he wanted to change cells. I said tuff it's not happening and so he started shouting at me and Shep, which attracted some attention from the other prisoners.

He was ranting and raving and shouted that he wanted to be taken to the seg, I looked at him and said 'the only way he would be going to the seg was bent up and for this to happen he would have to assault me'.

Bearing in mind this is in the middle of 70 prisoners associating, and I'm sitting down at my desk which is not the best position to be in if it kicks off. He said 'what did you say? I repeated myself and said 'you will have to assault me and I dare you! He looked around for support and said 'you can't say that in front of all these, so I said I just did 'so either do it or fuck off. He looked around again and at this point, everyone was looking in a different direction and getting on with what they were doing. Because he had no support he just walked off to his cell all despondent, and me and Shep looked at each other and laughed.

Another day Shep and I were on spur 1 again at the desk talking when a Russian prisoner with a bad attitude came up to the desk and asked for something while I was speaking to Shep.

I told him to wait a minute as I was talking, I turned back to Shep and this Russian again said something so I told him I was talking and he would have to wait.

He said 'you can't talk to me like that I am ex Spetsnaz (Russian special forces) and I have fought in two wars' I just looked at him and said yes and you lost both of them! He looked at me and Shep and said ' I don't talk to people with tattoo's ' so in unison we both said best you fuck off then, he looked completely dumbfounded and walked back into his cell. Life carried on as normal on house block four and I acted up to Senior Officer on many occasions, if I wasn't doing this I would normally work on spur 1.

One day I did an escort with Shep to Thames magistrate's court, we took a Cat A that was represented by an obnoxious solicitor who always represented terrorists, and was well known for making complaints against staff.

Thames mag has no legal rooms to interview clients so me and Shep had to stand in the corridor which was only about six foot wide while this solicitor interviewed her client at the cell door.

In a cell directly behind us was a Rastafarian who started abusing Shep, by saying "you eat pussy" the significance of this is that a lot of black people think oral sex is dirty.

Shep retaliated by saying shut up you thick fuck, the solicitor was only a couple of feet away and I had visions of her turning around to have a go and make a complaint.

I decided to try and divert the conversation, so I said to him 'Rastafarians hate Africans right 'and your Rastafarian right?' he replied 'yes so what', I said 'you worship Haile Selassie who is Ethiopian yes?' again he replied yes so I said 'if you hate Africans so much how can you worship an Ethiopian? Ethiopia is in Africa, and so you worship an African you fucking idiot' He had a puzzled look on his face as he had never considered this before, so I said to him 'basically you use Rastafarianism as an excuse to smoke Ganga (cannabis) and say it's part of your religion.' He didn't know what to say so he went and sat at the back of his cell, just then the solicitor turned around and said she was finished, so we let her leave and phoned for the van to take us back.

On the 13th November 99 The S.O I had worked within the seg who had transferred to HMP Chelmsford and was also a C&R instructor picked me up with another instructor from Chelmsford to take me to Gatwick airport because we were doing a C&R demonstration for the immigration service.

We did the demo because the Immigration Service had no idea what to do with refractory prisoners they were holding for deportation.

If they had a kick-off in one of their centres they just let it go on until they burnt themselves out and then went in and moved the prisoners.

We demonstrated how we do cell removals and how we dealt with spontaneous incidents, at the end of it the head of the Immigration service came up and thanked us and mentioned they also have problems restraining deportees. When they try to get them on a plane they have problems and also keeping them still while in flight. He asked my od S.O and me if we would be interested in devising a system to get refractory prisoners on and off planes and how to keep them compliant while in flight. We said we would have to get permission from the National C&R centre but we were more than willing to do this. Unfortunately, this never happened and we later found out the National instructors were teaching Immigration staff clearly, they didn't want us stealing their thunder. I did C&R training as often as I could get off the house block, when there were problems on the house block the S.O's would normally ask me to supervise it as they didn't have a clue.

We had probably one of the best cell smash-ups and one of the funniest on the 12th of August 2000. We had another Russian prisoner who had been placed on basic regime, he was not happy about this and so he smashed his cell up. He smashed the porcelain sink to pieces, he flooded the cell.

From the outside of the cell, there is a door that can be opened to gain access to the water stopcock and the power supply so we can turn their water or electricity off when needed. Once this door is opened there is an observation window above the toilet, this not to look at them on the toilet but if when you look through the observation hatch in the cell door and you can't see them, they could be on the toilet.

This small observation window above the toilet allows you to see the top of their head and so you know they are using the toilet. Because he had flooded we would normally open the door outside the cell and turn the water off, but he had done such a good job he had smashed the small observation window, reached through and pulled some of the piping out. This meant if we opened the door to turn off the water he could reach through and injure staff turning the water off.

As I have said this was one of the best smash-ups I have seen. Because of the danger, we had to get a three officer team together in full PPE. I arranged the team and a couple of extra staff in case anyone was injured during the removal.

The funny part came when our house block governor turned up to interfere, this governor was a cross hierarchal governor he had worked in the health service before changing to the prison service.

He went up to the cell door and knocked on it, he got no response so he knocked again and said 'Mr Maernurn, Mr Maernurn people in silly uniforms are going to come into your cell and arrest you' all the staff were standing around pissing themselves with laughter. He was such a plumb, eventually, the S.O got the governor out of the way so I could look through the observation hatch in the door.

Maernurn was standing in the centre of his cell with a piece of copper piping in his hand, shouting and swearing at me. I told him to face the back of the cell and put the pipe down but he refused and so I committed the team and they entered the cell.

They didn't fuck about they splatted him good and proper, to be fair to him he put up a fight all the way to the seg.

The cell was a right mess broken porcelain all over the floor and lumps of copper tubing, the floor was also about an inch deep in water which made it difficult for the team. They were all soaking wet rolling around in this, on the way to the seg with Maernurn in cuffs but still bent over under restraint because he was still struggling.

I tried to talk to him to calm him down but he just ignored me and so we located him and stripped him under restraint because he was holding a weapon when the team went in and we couldn't take the chance that he might be concealing a weapon. When we got back to the house block everyone was taking the piss out of the governor for what he did.

I would have more cause to doubt this governor's abilities a couple of weeks later. We had a prisoner on spur 3 who was a real big lump, the governor said to me he wanted to go and talk with him. I took him up to the prisoner's cell and the Governor said ok I'm fine, I told him I would sit in the cell with him if that was where he wanted to interview him because we never sit in a cell alone with a prisoner. So we went in and the governor asked all sorts of questions and this prisoner was stating he was being bullied by someone on the spur and he was afraid. The interview finished and we came out of the cell and went downstairs, the governor turned to me and said "I think this prisoner is being bullied and we will have to move him because he is scared for his life" I looked at the governor with a look of disbelief on my face, I said 'I have never heard such a load of bollocks in my life. This prisoner is 6ft 5ins about 20 stone and is covered in bullet wounds and stab wounds' I told the governor this prisoner is an enforcer for some gang and he is trying to manipulate the system.

The governor said 'do you really think so? I was dumbstruck this governor is off his trolley he hasn't got a fucking clue, I just said to the governor do what you want and walked off in disgust.

We had a prisoner called Tomlinson come in as a Cat A, he worked for MI6 and had got the sack so he was somewhat disgruntled and decided to write a book about MI6 and expose them. He came into us because the authorities were trying to do him for breaking the official secrets act by writing about MI6. Belmarsh was a shock for him, but he was quite up himself, after he had been with us some time myself and another officer were approached by one of our S.O's and asked if we would try to find out as much as we could about him and produce a regular report. We would talk to him quite a lot and play dumb asking what it was like to work for MI6. He liked to brag about what he did in MI6 and the places he has been like Bosnia, and he would tell stories of his exploits. In a lot of ways, he was very naïve and at times it was difficult to believe he worked for MI6.

Eventually, he was convicted but basically because of the time he had spent in prison on remand he was all but time served. To add a twist to this tale about a year later the other officer had moved prisons and was now up North.

He phoned me one day and said that he had received an anonymous e-mail from Russia and the e-mail contained a draft copy of Tomlinson's book.

To this day we still don't know how whoever sent it got hold of his e-mail address. Tomlinson throughout his description of the events at Belmarsh and his way of describing me were very odd. If you read his book he seems to think of me as some jovial Dickens character, and when he describes the prison as dark and dank like some Dickensian prison.

Eventually, the staff were moved around I ended up working on spur 2 as my main spur along with Shep and several other good staff. We had a prisoner by the name of Knowles who came to us with a bad reputation for smash-ups assaults and all sorts. The P.O on the house block at the time used to call me and Shep up to his office and say to us that we were getting a shit bag on our spur and we had to deal with them, the P.O said I don't care how you do it but I don't want to hear about it. So Knowles came onto the spur and me and Shep just said to him we don't care what he's done in the past, we will treat him depending on how he is here on the spur.

He progressed and we ended up making him laundry boy, one day I was on the spur with two other officers, I was walking around on the middle landing when I saw a prisoner called Fossett who was a right little weasel, hanging around in one of the cell doorways on the ground floor.

He had something in his hand, the two other staff on the spur were sitting at the desk, Knowles walked across the spur in front of the desk and this prisoner Fossett walked up behind him and hit him across the back of the head with a weighted sock.

Knowles turned around and grabbed Fossett, I ran from the middle landing and down the stairs and managed to grab Fossett's arm before the other two staff had even reacted. When they did react we restrained Fossett, and I have to say I was hurting him a bit because I don't like people who use weapons and haven't got the balls to do things face to face. We took him to the seg and when we got back a couple of prisoners who had seen it, said to me you were on the middles how did you get down the stairs and grab Fossett before the other staff who were only at the desk.

I said I know I'm a fat fuck but don't judge a book by its cover, the prisoners on the spur already knew I wouldn't put up with any shit, but this did my street cred on the spur the power of good. Knowles came and thanked me, and also commented on how fast I had got down the stairs.

Unfortunately in the confusion, the weapon disappeared, but it was almost certainly a tin of tuna or two in the sock. Knowles didn't sustain any lasting damage just a bump on his head, and he carried on as laundry boy.

Again one day me and Shep were called to the P.O's office and those famous words were again said 'you've got a real shit bag coming on your spur called Day' this one was supposed to be super paranoid with a history of assaults, shit ups, smash-ups, you name it he was supposed to have done it. That afternoon he came onto the spur in E-List kit and we took him to his cell and told him it would be association tonight. He said he wouldn't come out on association so we just said we would unlock him and shoot the bolt (this means unlocking the door and releasing the bolt that keeps it closed so that until we put a key in the lock the door can't be closed) this way if he wanted to come out he could if he didn't he could stay behind his door. We went back downstairs and had a cuppa and then we looked at each other and both said shall we see what he is really like, we went back up to his cell and walked in.

We told him he had a strip search as he was E-List, when you strip-search a prisoner they should never be fully naked, but we got him to take all of his clothes off and then turned around and left the cell locking the door.

He shouted through the door what are you doing? We shouted back we were only joking, he started kicking the door shouting you pair of bastards no one has ever done that to me, you are a pair of wankers.

We just laughed and went downstairs, that evening we unlocked him and said come out if you want but it's up to you.

Later on, we were sitting at the desk and he came down dressed in his E-List bib and brace, he looked around and then looked at us and started to take his bib and brace off. I said to him what are you doing? he replied 'I'm going to shit on your floor', me and Shep sat there with a grin on our faces and he said again 'I'm going to shit on your floor' I looked at him and said 'all I will do is say cleaner clean that up' he looked at us in disbelief and said 'I'm not going to win with you pair of fuckers am I' me and Shep just laughed and said no, he did his bib and brace up and went back to his cell.

Day was paranoid and we worked with him to see how he would respond, in the end, he ended up like all these other so-called shit bags.

We made him a cleaner, like a lot of them he responded to being treated with a bit of respect and being given some responsibility. Day (Popeye as he liked to be called) was a wide boy and you had to keep a check on him, but when we were around he was a bloody good cleaner.

However when we were off duty he was a handful, he would refuse to get out of bed and do his job and other staff members wouldn't know how to handle him so they let him get away with it.

When we were on he would occasionally try to do the same but me and Shep would go into his cell and throw a cold soggy flannel in his face and shout get up you lazy bastard. Sometimes we would tip him out of bed and throw his stuff on top of him. Because the staff on the other weekend couldn't handle him they were jealous and put complaints in against me and Shep saying Popeye was conditioning us, when in fact it was the other way around and they were conditioned to be afraid of him.

Popeye was a barber by trade and in all my time in the job he is the only prisoner I have trusted enough to let him cut my hair, and I have to say he didn't make a bad job of it. He was also something of an artist and ended up giving me a picture he had drawn to say thanks for giving him a chance.

Popeye was always up to something, one Sunday we had several Muslim terrorist prisoners on the spur, one of which for some reason hated me. We had unlocked for breakfast and this prisoner was on the top landing, he looked over the railings and shouted at me that I was a racist and then he started hitting himself on the head with a metal flask which they were issued with.

He would often hit himself on the head when he was angry for whatever reason.

Popeye heard him shout out that I was a racist, and promptly shouted back from the ground floor that I couldn't be a racist as I fucking hated everyone. The spur just fell about laughing, a little while later I saw Popeye coming down from the top landing with another cleaner with stupid grins on their faces. I called Popeye over and asked what he had done and he denied doing anything, I didn't believe him and so I went to the top landing to have a look around.

As I walked to the end of the spur I looked into the cell that the terrorist was in and saw loads of rashers of bacon on his bed. I went in and this bacon was everywhere, on his bed in his bed in his pillow. I collected as much as I could but there were bacon fat stains all over his sheets and pillowcase, I couldn't be caught with the bacon in my hand because no one would believe I hadn't put it in his bed.

I came out of his cell and went off the spur from the top landing so no one would see me with all this bacon. There were about 20 rashers, I left the landing and dumped the bacon in a bin and then walked back onto the spur from the ground floor.

Popeye was standing there pissing himself, along with the other cleaners. I waited for the terrorist to go back to his cell, I was expecting him to come out and start accusing me.

His cell stank of bacon and the sheets were covered in grease, why he never complained I don't know, but even though I couldn't prove Popeye had done it I gave him hell for weeks after that.

Whenever a prisoner is restrained around the prison Oscar1 or 2 normally turn up and take over the supervision of that restraint, and see it through to the prisoner's relocation in the seg. This on occasion caused problems, because the P.O'S and S.O's that worked as Oscar's 1 and 2 didn't always fully understand the process of supervising a restraint and they would all do things differently. To try and stop this it was decided by some governor that we would have a duty C&R instructor every day that would carry a pager and when there was an incident involving C&R they would attend and supervise the relocation, for the sake of continuity.

So this particular day I am duty instructor and my pager goes off and I trot off to House Block 3, I get there and Oscar 1 is in attendance and he asks me to supervise the move to the seg. Off we go with the prisoner under restraint; he is resisting us all the way making it difficult for the team.

We get to the seg and the female S.O in charge of the seg points toward a cell, I said to her get the box open he is going in there and we walk with the prisoner still struggling to where the box is.

We are now standing outside the box with the prisoner still non-compliant arguing with the S.O because she says only a governor can authorise the use of the box (technically true) but I told her she can get the governors permission afterwards.

She is not having this and the prisoner is still under restraint, just then Oscar 1 turns up to see what's going on and she starts telling him about the argument and that the prisoner is not going in the box unless he says so or a governor. Oscar 1 just looked at her and said 'who do you think teaches me who should or shouldn't be put in the box? He does he's an instructor' so with her tail between her legs she opens the door to the box and we relocate the prisoner. Whilst we are doing this Oscar 1 phones the duty governor to tell him he needs to come to the seg to sign the paperwork authorising the use of the box.

Unfortunately, sometimes people with rank think that means they know better than others, but this is not always the case.

1st of September 2000 and we got a call to HMP Wandsworth as they had 40 plus prisoners staging a sit-down protest on the exercise yard. We got a Tornado team together (14 riot trained officers) and jumped in a van to go to Wandsworth to help remove them from the yard.

We were all stuffed in the back of a works crew bus, and so our equipment had to be put in a Cat 'A' van as there wasn't room in ours. We started to make our way but the traffic was horrendous, it took us ages just to get the Forrest hill. We pulled over and the S.O in charge decided that as the Cat A van had lights and sirens the driver should use these to lead the way and hopefully get through the traffic easier. We are not supposed to use lights and sirens unless there is a cat A in the van and it's an emergency. The S.O said he would take responsibility, so off we set siren wailing, the trouble was the traffic moved to let the van through because they thought it was the police. But we were in a yellow works van behind and so we were hanging out of the windows shouting get out the way, it must have looked like something from the Keystone cops. Eventually, we went past vans from other prisons and so they joined on the end and we had a convoy.

We arrived at Wandsworth and went in and then as always came the waiting. We were located in their reception area and they put food on for us; there was sausage and egg or pretty much whatever you wanted. This is done to break the boredom; you never go straight in and fight, there is always ages of negotiation. Eventually, we were told to form up in our units and move forward to the gate that leads to the yard.

We had psyched ourselves up and were ready to go and batter some prisoners when we were told to stand down. The prisoners had caught sight of us and bottled it, they agreed to come in and return to their cells. This happens a lot on these call-outs but it is frustrating when you have got the adrenaline pumping and then you have to stand down without using it. Callouts didn't happen often and one of the problems, when they did, was getting the payments for them. If you were a rest day or ran over your shift time you would be paid a set amount per hour, for any time over and above your shift. The trouble was you are expected to respond as quickly as possible and put your safety at risk but it could take months to get the payments owed.

Our argument has always been we volunteer to become trained in riot control and we put our safety on the line when we are called out. But we only get paid if we are off duty when called or we go over our shift times.

I have over the years wasted a lot of time on callouts, I have been in a riot and I have spent many days and hours training to do this part of the job. The powers that be respond by saying you volunteered to do it, not of course we will pay you as soon as possible. Over the years I was part of this, I had spent weeks training and putting myself in harm's way as part of that training.

On one refresher I got injured and was off work for ten weeks because of it, I came away with injuries of some description from every refresher I did.

Yes, it was my fault because I volunteered and I enjoyed every moment of the training, but that doesn't detract from the fact that all of those that volunteered saved the service millions of pounds potentially over the years. The powers that be then quibble about paying these officers what is usually less than a hundred pounds each, and make us wait months for it. Eventually, in 2001 I had enough and stopped doing the riot part of C&R and later that year I would even give up instructing, bitch over let's get back to lovely house block four.

November 2000 and the infamous Dome raiders struck, this was a daring raid to steal a diamond that was on display at the Millennium Dome. The diamond was estimated to be worth £200 million, they intended to get away by a speed boat they had on the river Thames.

We knew they were coming to us as they were made Cat A and so we sorted out the cells they were to be put in. We put pictures of a JCB in each of their cells to welcome them to house block 4.

They turned up but didn't seem to see the funny side of the pictures in their cells, we all thought it was funny and didn't stop making jokes about it for ages.

Some of the gang were gipsies from Kent; one was from the Adams family a well-known crime family in South London. Once they had settled in and got over the shock of the police beating the crap out of them whilst they were trying to smash the case surrounding the diamond. What made it worse was that they found out later it was a fake made just for the display, they gradually became more confident and demanding. After being told in no uncertain terms to wind their necks in we came to an understanding, if they were entitled to it they got it if they were trying it on they got told to piss off. Amongst the gang were a father and son the Wenham's, one night while the spur was on association Shep was I/C the spur and I was listening to the prisoner's phone calls because they were high-risk Cat A's and their calls had to be monitored.

I was sitting behind Shep with the headphones on and Papa Wenham as we called the older one was giving Shep a load of grief about something and wouldn't stop.

I took listening to his drivel for as long as I could and in the end, I turned around and shouted at him 'what part of fuck off don't you understand' the whole spur stopped what they were doing and stared. Papa Wenham said 'you can't talk to me like that' so I told him to piss off, at which point Knowles the laundry boy who I have mentioned before pulled him away to have a word with him.

Papa Wenham came up to me a few minutes later and apologised, I told him I don't hold grudges and shook his hand. I also told him that if he didn't do what he was told in future I would make his life hell but for the moment we would start afresh. I later found out Knowles had spoken to him when he pulled him away and told him to apologise as I could be his worst nightmare or his best friend. It worked and I had no more problems with Papa

Wenham, his son would take a bit more guidance but he ended up being a cleaner. Things on the spur settled down again and the day to day boredom resumed, with just the normal round of applications, feeding and exercise.

Each spur had an Anti-Bullying officer on it and for spur 2 it was me, I never liked it when prisoners picked on weaker ones and so I would make it my business to intervene, there was a sign on the wall telling the prisoners who their Anti Bullying officer was and some bright spark (probably one of the cleaners) had crossed out the word 'anti' so the sign read your bullying officer for this spur is officer Richards. I don't believe I ever bullied prisoners but I wouldn't take any shit.

Around the end of 2000, I would attend a C&R advanced refresher that would have an effect for years to come. The refresher was at Kidlington in Oxfordshire, Belmarsh sent the best part of a unit up there and this meant a fun time for me. As a C&R instructor we never really got to do an advanced refresher, it was assumed we knew what we were doing and so on these refreshers, local instructors like me would be given Orange overalls (Tango man) to wear so we could be identified when things got lively, and we played the part of prisoners during the exercises.

The upside of this is you get to throw lumps of wood at your mates; the downside is at some point they will capture you and get payback.

I put a long piece of 2x4 on top of a barricade and when the Belmarsh boys approached I was ready for them, we always told the lads not to poke their heads out from behind the shields.

Boys being boys they never listen partly because over time the shields become so scuffed it's difficult to see through them. So I have my lump of 2x4 ready and the Belmarsh lads come toward the barricade and sure enough, the S.O who is the unit commander pokes his head around his shield, bang I hit him on the visor of his helmet, not hard but enough to wake him up and tell him not to do it. He does it again bang I hit him again and tell him to stop giving me a target, he does it again bang I hit him again.

Now he has the right raving hump, draws his PR24 riot baton and is ready to come out from behind the protection of the shields and try to come over the barricade to get me.

I stopped what was going on at the barricade and told all of the unit why they shouldn't do this because if I was a real prisoner the S.O would probably be on his way to the hospital now because I wouldn't have been tapping his helmet I would have been trying to put my lump of 2x4 through it, teaching point acknowledged.

Later on in the day after a break, the National instructors gave us tango men our instructions, and in this scenario when whatever unit finally breaks through the barricade I am to run down to the bottom of the hanger, sit on the floor and when the three officer team gets to me surrender. This I promptly do and so I'm sitting on the floor as a team from Swansea approach and I tell them I am surrendering, (I don't know why but it always seemed to be teams from Cardiff) I can see the red mist has taken over because of the shit they have taken getting through the barricade, they shout at me to stand up and I slowly start to get up. This was clearly not quick enough for the shield man and he hits me with the shield, I said to him I was getting up and he tells me not quick enough and hits me with the shield again.

This time I have the hump and sweep the shield man's legs from under him and he goes down, now I'm rolling around the floor with this three officer team who are trying to get control of me. They are suffering from the red mist even more and are trying to bend my arms in ways they are not designed to bend, at this point, they are not listening to me and it's pretty much a free for all. Luckily a National instructor turns up and pulls the team off of me saying they will break my arms if they are not careful, the Nationals bollocking over I am stood up and cuffed behind my back and taken to a secure area.

While I'm standing there waiting for the exercise to end I'm talking to Shep who is on the course and these Cardiff lads come over and one of them is shoving me in the shoulder saying 'you think you're hard in your Orange suit' bearing in mind I'm still cuffed behind my back, I'm saying to Shep get the keys and get these cuffs off me and I'll show them how hard I am. The exercise is ended and they return to their unit and once the cuffs are off Shep is taking the piss and I calm down.

The red mist should play no part in this training but unfortunately, some teams/units are like that, as I have said it always seemed to be Cardiff. You knew they were Pratts as they always turned up to these refreshers with specially printed tee shirts like they were something from a US Swat squad.

The following day we are back in the hanger to practice one more landing clearance before we leave for our establishments. The way of clearing landings had recently changed from using long shields to having two short shields covering the landing with numerous officers behind. The idea is that if a prisoner attacked the shields they would fold inward and the prisoner would be drawn into the waiting officers who would secure him in the first empty cell and deal with him later.

So my brief was to attack the shields and see how it worked, for this part of it the Tango men had boxers head guards on, I attacked the shields with my head down as I knew when they pulled me through I would get some punches thrown at me. In I go and it worked as it should, I don't know how far down the landing I was when I realised I was in a cell but something wasn't right! I was off the floor upside down, how I don't know because I was about seventeen and a half stone then and the next thing I know is I'm dropped on my head.

It's a good job I had the boxer's helmet on and I end up in a crumpled heap, at the end of the exercise I come out of the cell still wondering what happened. We returned to our establishments and I didn't think any more of it, about a week later I woke up one morning and as I tried to get out of bed the whole room was spinning like I was pissed.

I would be off work for nearly ten weeks because the GP didn't know what was wrong and I had to wait to see a specialist at the hospital, the specialist asked me if I had been in any car crashes as these symptoms happened a lot in people who injured their heads in crashes.

I told him I hadn't but that I had taken quite a beating on a riot training course recently, he told me that was probably the reason and said he wanted to try an Elpy manoeuvre on me because I had the crystals from my inner ear dislodged and this move should put them back.

Eventually, I returned to work as I was feeling better, I never put it in the accident book because the effects hadn't happened until a week after the injury and I didn't know the long term effect it would have, I did however stop being part of Belmarsh's Tornado response. I still have occasional episodes of vertigo now years later and these episodes would contribute to my eventual medical retirement, even though it was listed as a serious underlying medical condition and shouldn't have counted towards my periods of sick.

16th March 2001 I was called in because there were three prisoners barricaded in a single cell and they were refusing to come out. I shouldn't have been called out because I was no longer part of the riot unit, but all officers are trained up to cell removal standards.

I think the instructor in charge of this incident also wanted to entice me back onto the team, and he thought I might change my mind.

When I arrived there were several other instructors there and the teams had been decided, with three prisoners you need three teams of three staff.

It was decided that because they had a lot of potential weapons in the cell, the three shield men would go in first followed by the rest of the teams. We set up a distraction in the cell next door by banging on the wall to make them think we were coming through the wall. We were in reality undoing the anti-barricade lock on their cell door, we got the anti-barricade plate off and with the three teams outside ready to go, the door was opened outward. The shield men went in closely followed by the rest of us; they didn't know what hit them, it took 90 seconds for all of us to get in the cell and subdue all three of them.

I went to control the head of the one my team were dealing with but I couldn't because another instructor had his foot on the prisoner's face. Eventually, we got them up and cuffed and took them to the seg, where they were all stripped and located. Daniels who was the one my team were dealing with still had the dirty sole print on his face from the instructor.

A couple of weeks later and Daniels was back on the spur and starting to get a bit gobby, so me and Shep just looked at him and so everyone could hear we said 'just remember it only took 90 seconds to get you and your hard men out of that cell'. He would go quiet and walk off and whenever he got gobby again we reminded him.

After this, we got on alright and when he was out of his cell me and Shep would go and look around his cell to see what we could find. We would make him paranoid by looking over the railings outside his cell when he was coming back with his food or whatever and say to him 'you better find it before the DST (dedicated search team) turn up' he would run-up to his cell and look around like mad, thinking we had planted something.

I was working on the spur one day when a cleaner approached me and he had a copy of Charlie's book Legends in his hand, he showed me and said 'you're Bob the chair aren't you' and so it went all around the house block and it was a nickname that stuck with me until I medically retired. It wasn't helped by the fact that whatever spur I worked I was normally I/C and so stuck at the desk controlling the spur and staff.

Several of us were sitting in the Bubble on house block 4 when another officer who had been checking the landing over the tea break period, came in and told me a prisoner was trying to hang himself on spur 2. I went with two other officers to the cell which was occupied by the Thompson's a father and son who were always a pain in the arse.

When we entered the cell the younger Thompson had a ligature around his neck and this was tied to the heating pipe. The elder one appeared to be still trying to tie the ligature around his son's neck, but he denied this and said he was trying to untie it.

One officer took the father out of the cell and I removed the ligature from the son's neck with a pair of cut down scissors I had taken from the bubble. I called a medical emergency over the radio and told a different officer had turned up to place the ligature into an evidence bag. I didn't believe Thompson was trying to hang himself I just think the pair of them were up to something. The young Thompson was lying on the floor pretending he was trying to get his breath; I gave him a couple of gentle taps in the stomach with the tip of my boot just to help him, he was no more trying to kill himself than I am the pope. I don't think I've ever known anyone hanging themselves from a heating pipe 6 inches above the floor.

The healthcare officer arrived and checked him over and said there was nothing wrong, and so the elder Thompson was put back into the cell and they were both told to stop pissing around, nothing more was said and we went on with our break. The boring routine carried on as normal, with various little wind-ups to pass the time.

On the 17th of September house block 1, they had called their prisoners off the exercise yard but several of them had refused to come in. They were contained on the yard while the governors were making their minds up what to do. It was decided that they would negotiate a peaceful end to the problem so they had staff talking to them to find out what their problem was. I can't remember the cause but I was a late shift and so we fed our house block their tea meal and then we went to get kitted up to act as receivers for a controlled surrender on house block 1, we were briefed by a governor as to what they wanted to happen, and as usual, the plan was crap.

This was the same governor that had prompted me to quit C&R instructing, he refused to take advice from the C&R

instructor on scene and he wanted the prisoners cuffed in front when they came in, he was told that nowhere in the C&R manual does it mention cuffing in front because you can't restrain them further if needed.

They are cuffed behind their back so if this is not enough control, wrist locks can be applied against the cuffs. It also makes it more difficult for prisoners to reach into their trousers if they are concealing weapons.

Sure enough, a prisoner comes off the yard and on the way to the seg he kicks off and the staff don't know how to deal with this because he is cuffed in front and that is not what staff are trained in. they are now in a position where they have to take the prisoner to the ground and remove one cuff so they can put his hands behind his back and re-cuff him. Eventually, the rest of the prisoners came off the yard without any major problems, my shift should have finished at 9.00 pm but I didn't get off duty till 02.00 in the morning.

The next few months were the normal round of being I/C a spur and messing around with the other staff and going on escorts for an extra payment. I worked with a lot of good staff on house block 4, but it had its share of idiots as well. We had a young female Asian officer who really was a fish out of water; she had a horrendous sick record. One of the S.O's decided he would take her to task about this and she was called into his office to sort it out, as he was dealing with her he received a phone call saying to leave her alone and her sick record would be wiped clean.

She came into the bubble after the meeting with a smile on her face, we asked what had happened and she told us her sick record had been cleared.

She went on to say 'I'm female and Asian what are they going to do to me' this really pissed people off.

The service was changing and afraid of being called racist and discriminatory, and so she thought she was invincible. At one point she had to place two prisoners on report for fighting, she went to the seg for the adjudication and gave her evidence, the governor asked her 'were they really fighting or was it handbags at twenty paces' her response was 'oh no there were no handbags there' this was the level of recruit the service was taking on.

On another occasion, she had booked a holiday in Canada for two weeks, and while there decided to stay for an extra week even though she didn't have enough annual leave. She sent a postcard to the central resourcing department saying 'I have decided to stay in Canada for an extra week, I know I don't have enough leave but I'm sure you can cope, see you when I get back' she received no comeback for this because she was female and Asian. On another occasion, her mum phoned the house block and said she wouldn't be in for duty at the weekend because she had recently married and she had to stay home and cook for her husband.

Another officer who worked on house block 4 would also test me to my instructing limits, myself and another C&R instructor were taking a refresher course and the officer concerned was on it.

He told people on the house block he used to be in the R.U.C (Royal Ulster Constabulary) we were teaching knife defences this day and I was demonstrating how to defend against someone slashing from side to side with a knife. The technique involved allowing the slash to go past you and then attacking the weapon arm on the return swing. I showed the class how to slash at someone in one fluid movement and then return the other way.

This officer had the dummy knife and as he slashed toward his partner he would keep stopping and then move again. I told him no not like that and demonstrated again, he had another go and did the same again. Four or five times I did this and to my regret, I was losing my temper, this had the effect of me telling the other instructor to come at me with the dummy knife for real so I could show the class the technique in real-time.

By doing this both of us instructors would hurt each other because one was attacking hard and fast and I was defending hard. How this idiot ever got in the R.U.C if indeed he did I will never know, he was probably a storeman for them.

A lot of the day to day work could be quite boring so we would do what we could to brighten things up, this could be with the help of staff or our cleaners.

One day we were messing around with a couple of our cleaners, we had forgotten that some of the cameras were still in operation from when house block 4 had been used for high-risk cat A's. Me and Shep were trying to push one of the cleaners back into his cell and he was hanging onto the door jamb, so I got a broom and was using that to push him in, the phone went on the spur and it was the emergency control room who were watching on the cameras. I was glad they had phoned instead of putting out a general alarm thinking there was an incident on the spur, I apologised profusely and told them we were just messing about.

One E/D we had a young black cleaner called Jelly, don't ask me why he was called that but during the day me and Shep had put about 200 used phone cards in his cell under the closed door, we told him we would contact security because he was trading in phone cards. I told him he could not come out on association that E/D because of all the cards he had, at the last minute I was asked to man the bubble for the E/D and so I was sitting there watching spur two when Jelly appeared at the doorway of his cell as if he was going to come out.

I came out of the bubble and shouted down to the spur ' Jelly get behind your door I told you not to come out' he was looking all around saying to those on the spur 'how the fuck does he know I'm coming out' he didn't know the cameras still worked. The next day he asked how I knew and I told him I know everything, he didn't know what to say.

Nothing much happened until we had a new P.O take over the house block, he came to speak with me and Shep on spur 2, as soon as he had finished he went up to our S.O and told him to stop the "Spanish practices " me and Shep were doing. By this he meant running the spur our way, the S.O told us what he had said and the three of us decided we would carry on the same as normal but keep the P.O out of it. These Spanish practices were things like giving the prisoners the option to get nicked if they had done something wrong, or take our punishment. This might be stopping them from going to the gym if that was their thing, we would also unlock someone last all the time and bang them up first if they were a pain in the arse. There are many ways to control prisoners without resorting to nicking's. Also, applications in the morning could be chaos, with prisoners crowding around the desk and others leaning over the railings on upper landings.

We decided to tell them that unless they formed an orderly single line in front of the desk we wouldn't take applications; they didn't take to this until we just sat there with our arms folded until they did. If someone shouted from an upper landing for their mate to put in applications for them we wouldn't take them they had to come down themselves and queue up. This might sound harsh but it made life easier for everyone, we had gym lists, phone lists and it meant everyone got a chance instead of a few hogging things.

This would come to a head when Popeye was due a visit, but his visitors never turned up. Popeye thought the P.O had stopped the visit because he didn't like him; Popeye was a cleaner and able to walk between the spurs unsupervised.

Popeye was shouting and swearing about the P.O and the staff that were on the spur just let him walk up to the control bubble where the P.O was. Nobody stopped him and I saw him approaching the bubble threatening the P.O, luckily the gate next to the bubble was closed and so Popeye could not get at the P.O as he wanted to assault him.

I went up to Popeye and pulled him away and took him back to the spur to calm down, a few minutes later after I had contacted visits and found out his visitors had not turned up, I let Popeye use the phone to confirm this.

When he got off the phone he wanted to see the P.O to apologise and so I phoned the bubble to see if the P.O would agree. To give Popeye his due he apologised and shook the P.O's hand but the P.O had been shitting himself and later insisted that Popeye go to the Seg unit. I escorted Popeye there and put him in his cell, once this was done the house block governor turned up and asked what had happened. I explained the events and the governor asked me what I thought, I told him the P.O would not have Popeye back on the house block and because of this the months of work Shep and me, as well as some other staff, had done to bring Popeye into line would be wasted.

It was decided that he should be moved to Dovegate prison which is a therapeutic prison so he could continue dealing with his issues. I said me and Shep would do the escort so as we could keep things as calm as possible, so on the 23rd May 2002 we took him to Dovegate, he was placed in their Seg to start with for an assessment before being moved to a wing, we never did find out how he got on but when we got back me and Shep continued with our 'Spanish practices' and the P.O left the house block soon after.

Soon after all this fuss the S.O who told us what the P.O had said was asked to go to the Seg as S.O as they were pulling most of the staff out because of all the problems the Seg was having.

He asked me and Shep if we would come with him as we had worked there before and he knew we wouldn't take any shit from prisoners or staff.

Shep

14. House Block 3

As you walk onto House Block 3 on the left you have the S.O's office which is also the detail office, then you have 2 rooms, one used as an induction room the other as an inmate holding room, then the treatment room. The other side is a staff room; officers cloakroom, staff toilets, P.O's and Governor's office and probation office. Then you have the wing bubble which is surrounded by Perspex with a gate on either side cutting the wings off from the offices. This is where you report to with all movement of inmates on and off the wing, also if staff leave or enter the wing and also visitors, visiting the HB. This is where the wing roll is kept; it is manned by an officer and sometimes an S.O. From the bubble, you can see onto all 3 Spurs.

You have spur 1 and spur 3 on either side of the bubble and spur 2 straight in front. If you walk under the bubble downstairs you have a couple of storerooms, inmates canteen room, entrance to the exercise yard next to spur 2 with a couple of washing machines in and a dryer, at the end of the HB, the other end to spur 2 is the servery, where inmates collect their meals, the food is brought over on hot plate trolleys and placed in the servery where it is kept hot, the meals are dished out by inmate hot plate workers, supervised by officers. For breakfast, the inmates get breakfast packs that are given out with the evening meal, for them to use the following morning.

The inmates are fed off the bottom landings, 6 at a time from one spur, they walk down to the hot plate collect a tray, get their meal then back to the spur get hot water then banged up. On weekends the inmates have a cooked breakfast, not breakfast packs.

On the Spurs, you have 3 landings, 1s ground floor, 2s middle, 3s top, double cells down one side and singles down the other, 2 recess on each landing one either side, 70 inmates per spur, 210 on house block. Each spur has several cleaners doing different jobs, basically keeping the place clean. Nearly all the inmates we had were on remand. Some came to us on HB 3 straight from court with a sentence, or they were convicted but on a basic regime.

The prison ran 3 regimes, Basic, Standard and Enhanced.

The basic regime was for inmates that didn't conform to prison rules (pains in the arse) if you got 2 warnings from the S.O you ended up on the basic, regime until your attitude changed. We had all the basic regime inmates from around the prison remand or convicted on spur 2, located at the top in single cells, some in doubles. They had to wear prison clothing; they could only spend a small amount of money in the canteen, and had the minimum time on visits, no association, and exercise when we remembered.

The standard regime, everyone who came into the prison started on the standard regime, you could spend more money in the canteen, and have longer on visits than the basics, and you didn't have to wear prison clothing. Most inmates on standard regime were working part-time or taking education and got association.

The enhanced regime was for full-time workers, hot plate workers and cleaners, they could spend the most money in the canteen and got the longest time on visits, and basically out of their cells nearly all day.

For the first couple of weeks, I worked on all 3 Spurs, then the S.O asked me to become an induction officer, which means telling inmates all that they can and can't do and what they need to know in Belmarsh, also sorting out their problems when they first come into prison, spur 2 was the induction spur also the basic spur so that is where I would be based. Spur 2 was known as BEIRUT; the inmates called it that because it had nothing on it, nowhere for them to sit whilst on association, spur TV only turned on at weekends, no pool table. They hated it on there, the induction inmates couldn't wait to be moved to the other 2 Spurs or moved off the house block.

Inmates that are new into the prison all go to HB3, spur 2 (BEIRUT), for induction, whether they are convicted or remand, all new inmates from a court or other prisons have to have an induction, this is where everything is explained to them, how to get visits, basically everything they'll need to know while they are in Belmarsh. They are given clean bedding, towel, toiletries, washing kit, washing bag to put dirty washing in, breakfast pack, and prison clothes if they want them. This they get when they first come on to the HB once they have been processed in reception. The next morning up to the induction room, for induction.

If there are any inmates in the health care we visit them same with the VP's. (vulnerable prisoners) any inmates in the seg, say seg to seg move we would see them as well, so no inmate could say," I never had induction so I don't know." The inmates on induction would be told as soon as we could we would move them off BEIRUT, but if they came back to us on basic "they would get fuck all and plenty of it." Probation would have their say and try and sort out any problems, if the chaplaincy wasn't busy they would come over and chat to the inmates as well, so did some of the PEIs (physical education instructors) to tell them about what was going on in the gym. The only day we didn't do any induction was on Sunday, also no binning off on weekends, the inmates that came on Friday evening and Saturday morning were stuck on BEIRUT for the weekend.

When you say, (Right any problems) "Gov my dog has been left in my flat for 3 days, I've been in police custody, it needs letting out and feeding". "Gov my wife's in Holloway Prison, the mother in law has got the kids, she won't bring them to either prison for me and the wife to see, and I want to see my kids." That one took some sorting out got his wife from Holloway to Belmarsh for a visit and got social services to collect the kids from the mother in law and bring them to Belmarsh for a family visit.

Another inmate on induction was telling all the other inmates he was in for armed robbery, when we looked in his record he was in for stealing 47 tins of tuna fish from the back of a supermarket in Lewisham.

One morning while sorting out the induction inmates on spur2, there was a lot of shouting coming from spur 1 round the corner, then over the radio I heard alarm bell HB3, spur 1 ground floor, me and another officer shot round there, one black inmate was standing there with a pool cue in his hand, 2 other inmates were holding their heads, when he saw the staff running onto the spur, he ran up the stairs onto the middle landing. Me and 2 other officers went after him, we cornered him near the recess, he stood there with the pool cue in his hand as if he was going to hit us.

By this time staff were everywhere, I said to him "give me the cue, and we will walk you down the seg." He stood there for a few seconds and said, "Only if you and the other officer walk me down I don't trust the others. So he gave the cue to the female officer who was with me, I rubbed him down and then we started to walk him off the spur, when another scuffle started, 2 more black inmates started fighting as they were being banged up, so staff restrained them.

We walked our inmate down the seg followed by 2 others under restraint, then in the afternoon 2 black cleaners decided to have a punch up on the ground floor outside one of the storerooms, luckily there were quite a few members of staff around to deal with it, I had a lock on one of the cleaners arms, and down the seg again we went, that was 5 of our inmates in the seg. The next day in the morning meeting our new wing Governor who had become a Governor because he had a degree in something certainly not in being streetwise, said " we are restraining too many black inmates on the house block it has got to stop ".

He was told by staff that they were restrained because they were fighting, and we have a problem on here with black gangs, they are at war with each other that's why they are fighting. He said. "The number of black inmates we are restraining is making us look bad." So I said." Fine the next time a black inmate starts bashing other black inmates with a pool cue, I won't do anything I'll let him carry on." The P.O looked at his watch and said "ok let's get them unlocked".

Down to spur 2 I went, the P.O came onto the spur and said the "The Governor wants to see you in my office, I said." What now?

He said it's not the wing Governor it's the number 1, he was sitting at the back of the room during the meeting you didn't see him. So up I go into the P.O's office. "Hello, Governor ". I said. "Officer Shepherd, "he said, "I listened to what you and the staff had to say in the meeting, I agree with what you all said, but you will restrain any inmate in this prison understood." I said." Yes,

Governor you know I will." "Good." He said." I will speak to your wing Governor about the incident yesterday Ok." "Yes, Governor." I said. "Ok, you can go ". I turned and walked towards the door, I opened it, and he said." Officer Shepherd." I turned around he had a grin on his face. "Wind your fucking neck in." He said. I grinned back. "Yes, Governor," I said. I walked back to the spur grinning. His name was Bill Duff, I had a lot of respect for him, and he was a good governor. We would meet again later.

One Monday morning me and another officer were doing the Binning for a change, we were getting rid of 20 inmates from the induction spur (BEIRUT), and deploying them to other House Blocks, they were all Black inmates; they were all looking forward to getting off (BEIRUT).

We got them all lined up with their kit ready to take them off the House Block, when the wing Governor comes on, we quickly moved them off, when we came back he said to us. "Why are all those inmates you binned off all black?" I said." Because they were the ones the court sent us on Friday, so it's their turn to be binned off, they've been on the induction spur all weekend." I just smiled at him and walked off. A visits officer brought a black inmate back from visits one afternoon, he said I've left the inmate in the holding room, I think he has got something up his arse; we strip-searched him but found nothing. "OK".

We said to the visits officer we'll deal with it, I went and took him out of the holding room and with 2 other officers, we took him along to his cell, unlocked it and he walked in, we shut the door and opened the spy hatch, another officer got out his keys and quietly put them in the door. We looked through the spy hatch, and as soon as the inmate was in his cell he dropped his trousers and started taking something out of his backside. We all put our rubber gloves on and we went in and jumped on him, we got him on the floor and restrained him, then I noticed something sticking out of his backside, I kept one hand on his arm, stretched over and removed the article from his backside.

He started to struggle and was calling us all sorts of names, the S.O. appeared at the cell door "what are you lot up to now." He said. I showed him what we had. He said ". Where did you get that?" I said." I pulled it out of his backside." He said. "Oh god." We took the inmate down the seg in locks as he was calling us all sorts of names. We located him in the seg, when the seg staff unwrapped the article with gloves on, it was £100 all wrapped in a small plastic bag. The inmate got cellular confinement, and closed visits, on the Adjudication and didn't want to come back to our HB when he finished his punishment because he was in debt to someone, so he went to another HB.

Our wing Governor was not amused with us," You can't go around pulling things out of inmates backsides, you could have caused him damage." He said, me and a few other staff on HB3 had worked on visits; we were used to fighting inmates and visitors to get unauthorised articles off them. Anyway, it's not my fault our wing governor didn't have a sense of humour.

One day I was speaking to a couple of black cleaners on spur 2, they had put the spur TV on for a few minutes while having a cup of tea, and the news was on something about the Stephen Lawrence murder, I said to one of the cleaners what do you reckon about this, he said ".

I don't think the murder was racist, I think it was a drug deal gone wrong." He then said." I think both of them black lads or just one of them owed them white kid's money for drugs.

You don't just get off a bus to kill someone for the colour of their skin, I think there is more to it but we will never find out". I thought he should know, he was in on remand for supposedly running all the drugs around the area where Stephen Lawrence was killed.

We were having a few restraints a day sometimes and some governors were saying on Adjudication that the assaults on staff from HB3 were making the prison look bad, well sorry but some days on HB3 were a battlefield, especially when you have all the basics from the prison on one HB. But you mustn't mess up the governor's figures, we were told every month figures came out about assaults on staff in the London prisons and Belmarsh was top of the list for assaults on staff, and we were getting the blame for it on HB3. So some of the governors started investigating our nicking's from HB3.

Myself and another officer were sitting on spur 2 when another officer brought an inmate round from spur 1, he was a Middle Eastern-looking person, the officer said we believe him to be a cell thief, can you keep him around here for a while in case he gets done. We located him on the middle landing in a double cell on his own; all he had was a small bag with a wash kit in it.

A couple of days later a couple of cleaners said they had some canteen missing out of their cells. So when the cleaners left their cells to go to work we locked them, and then we decided to give our suspected cell thief a visit. Me and two other officers went to his cell, I stayed outside his cell by the door, the other two went in. On the inmate's bed was a small plastic bag with some canteen in it, I said to the other officers. "He never had that when he came round here." One officer went to grab the bag and the inmate grabbed the officers arm, that's it game on, I shouted to the S.O who was standing by the bubble, then ran into the cell, we restrained the inmate, the S.O. arrived we cuffed him at took him down the seg. He was searched and left in a holding cell, till the doctor came and saw him which was only minutes, as the doctor arrived he started banging his head on the cell door, this was written down and noted on the Adjudication paperwork by the doctor and a seg officer.

When the inmate was on Adjudication he said he was assaulted by staff, which is how he got a cut on his head and nose. The governor didn't seem to look at the paperwork where the doctor and seg officer wrote that he was banging his head on the cell door. So the governor said I think it is assault I'm sending it to the police, so the three of us who restrained him had a police interview, the inmate was sent to another HB away from us. The POA the (prison officers association) got involved and got us a solicitor, about 10 days later, we had to go to Plumstead police station for the police interview. We met our solicitor there, then we were interviewed by a D.S. and a D.C. we each, in turn, told them our side of the story, and it matched our Adjudication paperwork.

The police said. "We have been to the prison and interviewed the inmate; he can't tell us where he was assaulted, whether it was in his cell, on the way to the seg, or in the seg. So we think he is lying so we are not interested, your governor could have dealt with this, the paperwork from the doctor and seg officer stated that he was banging his head on the cell door. We are sending it back to your governor to deal with. That was that and we thanked the solicitor and went back to the prison.

A couple of days later a seg officer told us that the nicking had been written off the inmate had gone to court in the meantime and had not returned to the prison he had walked from the court. Made a note to myself, never trust that Governor again, he was one of those that got promotion through getting staff in trouble or sacked, not for dealing with inmates.

We had a few more incidents on HB3; one black inmate got nicked and spent a bit of time in the seg for threatening to jug me and another officer (that means throw hot water over you). On evening duty one night, there was an almighty scream from one of the middle landing recesses on spur 1, we ran around there, a black inmate had Chucked a bucket of boiling water he got from the urn over another black inmate in the shower, the boiling water must have had sugar in it, because nearly all his skin on his back came off, the first time I saw a black person go pink.

We were feeding one lunchtime when one inmate was walking back from the servery with his meal when suddenly he just collapsed on the floor, his lunch went everywhere he started to shake violently, he's having a fit I thought I ran over grabbed his head to stop him from banging it on the floor, other officers who hadn't seen what had happened had thought I was restraining him and ran over to grab an arm each. I said, "No it's ok he's having a fit". We got him to his cell and the duty nurse came and saw him, I think he slept for most of the afternoon after his fit.

Another time when we were feeding, we had one cleaner that took his job to heart he had to hand out the tea packs they contained tea bags powdered milk and sugar. Make sure the inmates only take one pack each, "ok Gov" He said. About ten minutes later he has got one inmate round the throat, saying to him. "The officer said one pack, not two." (Priceless). The same cleaner came back from visits one day and came over to me and the other spur 2 officer and said "I think I'm in the shit Gov" "why what have you done." "I'm under suspicion for handing out money on a visit to my girlfriend, she needed the money, they never caught me but they suspected that I did it." Me "did you hand money out" Yes I did Gov "Me "You fucking idiot" Other officer."

Where did you get the money from "Cleaner" I got it in on a visit last week from a mate so I could give it to my girlfriend today on my visit." Me "why didn't you just get your mate to give the money to your girlfriend, it would have been easier." Cleaner "I never thought of that Gov" Me and the other officer looked at each other and both said" Fuck Me" The cleaner just got a warning from the security department, saying they couldn't prove he handed anything out but any more suspicious activity on a visit again he would go on closed visits, plus a right bollocking from me and the other officer.

He was a good cleaner but this was his final warning, at least he was honest with us. He was a convicted inmate but we kept him as he was a good cleaner, and respectful to staff he was only serving a small sentence when he finished his sentence he said thanks for still keeping him on as a cleaner, about a month later another officer on our house block heard he had been stabbed and killed in the street.

Our wing Governor that was not very streetwise was on the move he was going to another prison, so we got another governor, this one came from head office, I thought along with some other staff, not another pencil pusher that ain't streetwise, but actually, he turned out alright.

The health care, was getting overcrowded so we had some of their inmates on the middle landing of spur 2 these were people that should have been in some mental institution but they were all full or closed down, so put them in prison just to get them off the streets seemed to be the order of the day. You couldn't put them on induction because they were not fit mentally, they wouldn't understand what we were saying to them, so the doctor told us. We had about five of these inmates, so we put them on a half-hour watch, I went up to check on them, four were laying on their beds the other one was sitting in his single cell on a chair stark naked and covered himself from head to toe with shaving soap and was just sitting there staring at the wall, our new wing Governor came on and said how're the health care inmates doing.

I said "Have a look" I showed him the inmates when we got to the fifth one." I said this one needs help." When we looked in the inmate had put his chair on his bed and was sitting on top of the chair still covered in shaving soap. The Governor looked at me, I said to him "welcome to spur 2" It took about a fortnight before we could get the inmates back to the health care.

We had a couple of white inmates that came to us from a private prison because they were being pains in the arse.

They were given an induction and put on the middle landing of spur 2, when I was taking them back to their cell, I heard one of them say to the other it won't be long before we run this place really I thought, let's see. I banged them up, about 10 minutes later my spur cleaners came back from the gym they were all big blokes, they were wearing vets and shorts you could literally see cut marks stab wounds and bullet wounds on some.

I said before you jump in the shower can I borrow you for a second, "yeah what's wrong gov" follow me lads, when we got to the two white inmates cell I told the cleaners what they said. So I said to the cleaner's just stand there and let them see what they'll have to take on. I unlocked the door and said "You two come here " they came to the door I said "I heard what you said about running this place before you try it you will have to deal with this lot " One cleaner said " your welcome to try it lads " The colour run from their faces they went white I then said to the two white inmates" enough said " They walked back into their cell I said to the cleaners, " Cheers lads get your shower" one problem nipped in the bud. After that they were really quiet we moved them round to spur 1 a couple of days later.

Just before one Christmas, we were moving some inmates off of the house block; one of them was refusing to move he wanted to stay on the HB with his mate he was a bit of a gobby twat. I said no your moving, he went round complaining to anyone who would listen the number 1 Governor came on (Bill Duff) I suppose he was doing his Christmas rounds, the inmate went up and complained to him saying that he wanted to stay on the house block over Christmas.

He came back and said the governor said I can stay, I said "I don't fucking care what the governor said he's not the binning officer I am." The number one Governor heard what I said, he pulled me to one side and said " I know you're the binning officer but just let him stay on here for Christmas then bin him off I've known this inmate a long time." Ok" said I as I walked past the inmate he said," Told you I could stay" Me "You jammy wanker, your off after Christmas." In January of 1998, I had completed two years on House Block 3; l was asked if I wanted to move to the security department so I did, House Block 3 was a good eye-opener, and I worked with some brilliant staff.

15. Security Department

The security department is situated in a small corridor between the two large secure corridors that everyone uses. The security P.O's, S.O's and Governor's offices are next to the orderly office, also the Cat 'A' office. The security staff had an office around the corner where we would give out the cuffs and keys to the escorting staff. In days gone by the security, staff would be out searching cells around the prison, but we had a DST (Dedicated search team) that only specialised in searching.

So the security department was given another task drug testing, basically taking a sample of urine from an inmate asking him if he is on any medication making a note either yes or no, then sealing the sample in 2 glass test tubes in front of the inmate and sending it off to a laboratory in London for testing, when the results came back from the laboratory by fax we would go through the paperwork to find out the samples the inmates gave were negative or positive. If negative he got a certificate to say he was drug-free, (well till the next test anyway) If it was positive for drugs and the inmate was on medication, we would see the doctor and ask him if any of these substances that were in his urine were to do with his medication, if yes then he didn't get nicked, if not the inmate got nicked.

On the Adjudication, the inmate could ask for another test as we sent off two samples of his urine to the laboratory enough for quite a few tests. If then he still said he didn't take drugs then he would have to pay for another test himself. I think the punishment was up to 35 added days for a positive test. We had to make sure that the inmate had been in prison the right amount of time to nick him for a positive test, cannabis stays in your system for 30 days, some other drugs about 3 to 7 days. If an inmate had been in prison custody say for 10 days and his sample came back positive for cannabis, you couldn't nick him because he would say I was taking it when I wasn't in prison. So all the dates of when they came into custody had to be checked. Our security S.O got a list of random inmates' names off the computer there were about 250, that had to be tested every month. Plus the ones that staff have their suspicions about.

Our office for urine testing was above reception, when we had about 30 samples, we would take them out of the fridge pack them up, phone or fax the laboratory then we would take them over to the gate to be picked up. We would be drug testing Monday to Saturday roughly about 8 inmates a day, we would pick them up from the wings first thing in the morning or first thing in the afternoon and take them down to our office, get them to urinate in a sterile jar then pour it into 2 sample test tubes and seal it.

If the inmate couldn't urinate he was given a small amount of water, not too much or it can dilute the sample. To be able to carry out these tests and become a drug tester we had to do a 3-day course. This was my main job in the security department, when we had finished drug testing we were given other tasks, like helping out on visits and in reception watching that the searches were done properly or wandering around the education classes seeing what the inmates were up to, but drug testing was high up on the prison's list.

Some of us were sent out on escorts if the escort commitment was high, when we went out on escorts we were told by our security S.O to keep an eye on the strip-searching out at court and make sure it was up to standard. One escort was taking some members of the Taliban (supposed to be members) to the Old

Bailey for the start of their trial one of them never stopped moaning from the time we got in reception till the time we got to court. He didn't want staff to search his legal papers but we did, he complained to his brief, his brief said the officers are allowed to, then he moaned about the cuffs being too tight, to which his brief brought it up in court and the judge said "I'm sure your client has been cuffed to Cat 'A' regulations, and I'm sure the prison staff know what they are doing, so I don't want to hear any more about it " thanks judge, what a whining little shit he is.

On the way back he was moaning again even his partners in crime told him to shut up. When we got back to the prison they were all strip searched and legal papers searched again the whiner said he was going to report me to the governor for searching his legal papers. My answer was "go ahead mate " about a week later, my security P.O says I've had a complaint about you searching someone's legal papers," Good lad Crack on, keep it up ."

Another time I was at the Old Bailey with two black inmates that were charged with a series of armed robberies, if they were found guilty they were looking at a long time behind bars. It was the start of their trial and their defence barristers were trying to say that the police were over excessive by shooting their clients 9 times each whilst on the last of their armed robberies, at the lunchtime interval I was in the Cat 'A' cells with a doctor from the defence, counting and marking down where and how many bullet hole scars they each had. Yes, it was 9 each; I couldn't believe it and they were still alive mind you both had difficulty in walking. I was told at the end of their trial they were found guilty and got over 20 years each, and the police got told off for using excessive force.

We had to take this inmate from the health care unit to a psychiatric hospital somewhere in south London, when we got there in the Cat A van, a security guard said you will have to walk with him through that door over there so I get cuffed to him and off we go another security guard came with us and let us through the door, we stepped into a room with loads of people in it suddenly the door behind us locked shut. Over the far side of the room was a Perspex bubble with two staff standing in it staring at us.

Suddenly one of them started waving his arms around and mouthing the words," What the hell are you doing in there; you're not supposed to be in there it's dangerous." All these patients started to stare at us, and then someone opened a side door and said quickly this way. So three officers and one inmate make our way to this side door, then I hear." Hello, Gov remember me from scrubs, I was on D wing remember." I looked over and this inmate came towards us, I said "Yeah I said I remember you, what are you doing here " He said," I had a bad time with drugs when I left Scrubs, the other nick sent me here, drugs done my head in." "Look after yourself. "I said as I was being pulled through the door. We uncuffed the inmate and two other staff took him off us and signed the paperwork.

One of them said "you were really lucky some of them can get violent we stand in the bubble when we give them association" I thought you should have worked on House Block 3 mate then you would have seen what get violent means.

Sometimes we would have to help out in reception in the mornings and evenings if they were busy. In the mornings we would have to pick up some of the inmates from the House Blocks that are going to court, one morning my S.O said could I go onto HB 4 and unlock a couple of Cat A's that are going to court, so myself and a female officer go onto HB4 and unlock a couple of

Cat A's one being Charlie Kray the elder brother of the Kray twins he was going to Woolwich crown court.

I unlocked his door and said ". You're at court this morning." He said," Yes Gov, can you give me a couple of minutes". Other inmates were being unlocked, Charlie Kray came out of his cell, I locked it behind him, and he said, "Hello miss." To the female officer, as he said that, two young black inmates walked past laughing and joking with each other, one of them swore at the other. Charlie Kray said "lads no swearing female on the landing" And pointed at the female officer. The two black inmates said, "sorry Charlie, sorry miss" and off they went.

I thought he still holds some respect, we were helping with searching in reception one evening when this inmate came through to the search room, he was wearing women's clothing makeup and had shoulder-length hair and a large bust. I thought what the fuck? He stood on the mat, and the officer I was with said "you're going to have to give us a strip search". As he started to remove items of clothing that we told him to remove, He said "I think I should be in a women's prison because I have got these," and grabbed his breasts I said "all the time you've got that hanging between your legs (pointing to his penis) you're classed as a man, so you're staying here" I think he was located in the Healthcare, I don't remember seeing him on the House Blocks.

On the 3rd June 1999, Kenneth Noye was remanded to Belmarsh for the road rage killing of Stephen Cameron; he was extradited from Spain where he went on the run. All the news vans were outside the prison, most of the security officers were in reception when he arrived, the phone rang in the security office, I answered it and someone said " I don't know if I've got the right place but, we know you have just received Kenneth Noye in your establishment we would like an up to date photograph of him for our newspaper which is ...., we know you take photographs of inmates when they first come into prison we will offer you a lot of money for the photograph.

   I said ." Sorry, but I can't give you any information about any inmate over the phone " and put the phone down. As I did that the Security Governor came in and said who was that, when I told him about the phone call, he said " how did they get through to this office" I said, " it could have been a hoax call " Just in case it wasn't I had to go down to reception and collect all the spare photographs of Noye and had to make sure the Cat 'A' unit only had one photo of him, also one photo in his Cat A book, and one in his record, and just one in the Cat 'A' office. The rest I had to shred and sign a paper saying to the best of my knowledge all spare photographs of Noye were destroyed. The only time I actually met him was when he was on trial, and I took him to court at the Old Bailey.

   Because of the Good Friday Agreement on 10th April 1998, all the convicted IRA were going to be sent back to Ireland, only those on remand awaiting trial we're staying until their court case was over then they would be sent back as well.

   I remember IRA inmates coming to Belmarsh being put in the unit, then the security staff going over to the unit with about 4 or 5 Cat 'A' vans, searching the IRA and their belongings loading them onto the Cat A vans, and with a police, escort taking them to London City Airport. We drove straight onto the runway and pulled up next to a plane. Armed Police were everywhere, we picked up an IRA inmates property bag and got cuffed to that inmate, I got cuffed to one of the IRA that escaped from Whitemoor, the one who said he would shoot me, but wouldn't kill me. We stood in line on the Cat A van it was our turn to get off next, and then this armed police officer got on the bus looked at me and the person I was cuffed to.

He pointed to me and said," If this arsehole you're cuffed to slips those cuffs you hit the deck I've got 20 armed police out there ready to shoot this piece of shit". They recognised him he was the one who killed the off duty policeman up north. The inmate looked at me and said" Don't worry gov I not going to do anything stupid I'm going home " We took them off the van and onto the plane they were uncuffed from us and cuffed to a police officer on the plane. The one I was cuffed to said" See yah Gov, take care" I said" Yeah and you" When they were all loaded on the plane took off and we had to wait at the airport until the plane was over halfway to Belfast, then we could go.

I remember watching the news on the TV a few months later and seeing a lot of them that went back were being released from prison in Northern Ireland, some of them had got a 25-year sentence and they were being let go.

We had 3 or 4 IRA left in Belmarsh, they were in the unit awaiting trial, I thought what's the point of sending them to court when they go back to Ireland, they're only going to get released after a couple of months like the others did. I had to go over to the unit and help with the legal visits; I picked up one of the IRA inmates with another officer we went over to the visits building, then into the search room to strip search the inmate. I was moaning to another officer about these illegal immigrants that were coming through the tunnel at the time, and disrupting the trains or hiding under them, I said to the IRA inmate." This is all your fault if your lot had blown the tunnel up like everyone thought you were going to we wouldn't have this problem with immigrants coming through." He just laughed when his legal visit was finished we strip-searched him and took him back to his spur. He said to me

"Gov you remember what you said about my lot blowing the tunnel up, well you don't know how near the truth you were" He smiled and walked into his cell.

Me and him had another meeting like this, I picked him up about a week later for another legal visit, I was still moaning about these illegal immigrants coming through the tunnel to Britain he said " I like your anger we could do with someone like you in the IRA, I'll get you an application form ".

Another job I did on security was to go out to a cemetery with another officer a Cat A's family member had died, we had to draw a plan of the whole place, mark, all the exits down and find a place for the Cat A van to park. Then I had to go to the local hospital in Woolwich, with another officer, to draw up a plan of the ward and side room the Cat A inmate would be staying in after he had an operation.

On my set of nights in the security department, the first few hours of the evening is spent working in the gate until 10 pm then the prison is all locked up, the night P.O does a key check, I have to get the Cat 'A' records out and ready for those Cat A's going to court the next day, then wandering around the prison making sure the other night staff are ok. This night the duty governor comes on duty to check up on us, just as we get a call from the Health Care officer, one inmate is trying to hang himself, we all run up there, and as we enter the cell he is hanging from the bars, in we go and cut him down strip him and search him and put him in an anti-suicide cell for his own safety.

We had to deal with other problems in the Health Care during the day as well, we had to get kitted up a few Times to restrain inmates so the doctor could inject them with the medication they refused to take.

We had to go over to the Cat A unit one evening the inmates there were refusing to move to another spur because the one they were on was going to be redecorated. So we had to go in the cells in 3 man teams, remove them and locate them in cells on the Spurs they refused to move to. They didn't put up a fight they were just being awkward.

I upset a probation officer because I wasn't going to clear an inmate for a cleaning job, he was in Britain illegally he was in prison for sexually assaulting two women he was going to be deported when his sentence had finished she was trying to keep him in the country. I said it was dangerous having a cleaner on a normal House Block that is in for a sexual offence he could get assaulted if the others found out what he was in for. Besides I said he should be deported anyway he's an illegal immigrant, she reported me to my governor he said "next time try and word it a bit better".

You will be surprised at what inmates can use to make weapons from; we helped the DST (dedicated search team) search one of the house blocks one afternoon for weapons.

We found a knife made out of the metal skin of a pp9 battery, a toothpaste tube flattened down to make a knife a makeshift gun made out of a bar of soap and shaving soap and a toilet brush handle sharpened to a point. After being in the security department for 2 years, I went to work on House Block 4 with my mate Bob.

16. House Block 4

HB4 is the same layout as HB3, except the servery is closer to the Spurs, and where the servery area is on HB3 it's the Cat 'A' visits area on HB4. Me and Bob were working together on one of the Spurs when this black inmate wanted to move cells, he didn't want to go in with a white inmate. Bob was I/C of the spur and said" No you ain't moving" He started shouting at me and Bob" Take me down the seg then" Bob said," The only way you're going down the seg is if you assault me." All the other inmates just looked it went all quiet. He thought they were going to back him up, then he realised they weren't so he just walked away, me and Bob just looked at each other and laughed.

Also on the same spur, we had an argument with a Russian inmate, me and Bob were talking and he kept butting in. Bob told him to wait as we were talking.

He said "You can't talk to me like that I was in the Russian special forces, I was in 2 wars," Bob said "Yeah and you lost both of them" He then got the hump and said, "I don't talk to people with tattoos" Bob and I both looked at our arms as we both have tattoos and said together "You had better fuck off then" He just looked at us and walked back into his cell.

We had another Russian who could make a good job at smashing up a cell, and he could do it properly. He was standing in the middle of his cell with a lump of copper piping in his hand; he must have pulled it out from the back of the sink or toilet. The cell was flooded with water and pieces of broken porcelain lay all over the cell floor. The Governor we had at the time was not streetwise at all, two 3 man teams were kitted up standing at the door ready to go in, one team was a reserve in case the others got injured on the wet floor and broken porcelain. The Governor came over to see what was happening, and then he said to the inmate through the cell door "People in silly uniforms are going to come into your cell and arrest you" I thought, what the fuck. Then all the staff started laughing the S.O told Bob to take over as he was a C and R instructor. Bob told the inmate to stand at the back of the cell he refused, so the first 3 man team went in they restrained him after a long fight and cuffed him and took him down the seg.

We had another issue with our wing Governor when this black inmate who was about 6 ft. 4ins tall and about 20 stone wanted to move spurs. Bob and I said no, we knew he wanted to get with his mates and cause trouble. Eventually, he got to see our wing Governor, Bob went with him to see the inmate in his cell later Bob said to me "That governor is an idiot, the inmate said he was being bullied that's why he wanted to move". Bob said to the Governor. "It's all bollocks he only wants to move to be with his mates", the governor couldn't see that.

This was the same inmate who said to me and Bob earlier " If I play up you'll have to get the (SPG) Special Patrol Group in from the police to deal with me " We both looked at him and said "Don't worry mate we will deal with you ourselves" he just walked away.

Me and Bob were moved to Spur 2 with other experienced staff, spur 2 was where the Cat 'A's were when HB4 became the Cat 'A' unit for a while a few years earlier. We were told we were getting this inmate called Day (Popeye) he had a history of smash-ups, shit ups, assaults and he suffered from paranoia.

He came to us on spur 2 in E man clothing, we put him in his cell, then about an hour later, we decided to see what he was like, we went to his cell and told him he had to have a strip search he started stripping off and me and Bob just walked out the cell, he started shouting through the door "what was that about " We said "Nothing we were only joking" He started shouting through the door " Nobody has ever done that to me" We shouted back "we have " Later he came down from his cell, stood in front of our desk and started to take his E man's bib and brace off. Bob said, "What are you doing?" He said "I'm going to shit on the floor Bob said "Go ahead we'll just get a cleaner to clean it up," He then said " You pair of fuckers don't give a shit do you " " No," we said, he pulled up his bib and brace and went back to his cell. Eventually, he started to come out of his cell more and the wing Governor said to give him something to do to keep him occupied.

So we made him a cleaner, but you had to keep an eye on him. The staff on the other weekend weren't very happy about it because sometimes he wouldn't do what they said, but he was ok with staff on our weekend.

Once me and Bob were deployed to the Healthcare to help them with exercise when we came back Popeye was still in bed, the other staff said he won't get out of bed me and Bob walked into his cell and tipped him out of bed on to the floor and told him to get dressed and start cleaning, he came out of his cell dressed he looked at the pair of us and said "Fuckers" and started cleaning.

One morning over a weekend we were on duty, I remember Popeye putting rashers of bacon on the bed of a Muslim Terrorist who was a bit of a nutter.

Bob saw him and another cleaner come out of this terrorist's cell and wondered what they were up to, later he told me he had to remove about 20 rashers of bacon off his bed. I remember the

Muslim Terrorist calling Bob a racist and Popeye said "He can't be a racist he hates everyone."

We had a new P.O come to HB4 he knew me and Bob of old, he said to the S.O that he wanted me and Bob to stop our Spanish Practices on the HB. Like stopping inmates from going to the gym if they played up, we run the wing our way. We controlled the inmates without nicking them. Popeye had an argument with our new P.O and was moved to the seg, he was then transferred to another prison, one that dealt with inmates that have issues. Me and Bob took him to this prison and brought another one back with us. We would see Popeye again later when me and Bob worked in the seg unit after HB 4.

We had the dome raiders on spur 2 for a while, they were high-risk Cat A's because of staff shortages in the prison some of the Spurs in the unit were shut down. The dome raiders as they were called tried to steal diamonds from the Dome in Greenwich London where they were on exhibition. The diamonds were fake they were for display only. They got caught in the act, the police were waiting for them they got arrested and ended up with us.

One time on association this father and son who were part of the dome raiders who were Gypsies, seemed to have a problem, the father was moaning at me about something, then Bob said to him "What part of fuck off don't you understand" The whole spur went quiet He said "You can't talk to me like that" Bob then said "Piss off" he walked away, later I saw Bob talking to him I think he apologised to Bob.

We had an E man on the spur a black lad, he and his mates tried to barricade in a cell and refused to come out, Bob was one of the staff that got them out it only took 90 seconds.

One evening I looked into his cell and found him wiring up, he had an electric cable coming out of his light on the ceiling, the cable was going into his radio, some inmates do this so they don't have to use their batteries he must have got another inmate to get the wire from the workshops, it is dangerous to wire up me and another officer went in the cell and took the wire down, the inmate got nicked and the works department put a new cover over his light.

So me and Bob would check his new cover every day to see if he had put holes in it to wire up, so we thought we would play a game with him when he left his cell to get his meals, me and Bob would hang around outside his cell when he came back he would say what are you two up to? We would say I hope you find it before the search team does, we'll contact them now. He would say "You pair of bastards" and run in his cell looking to see if we planted anything in there. We said "Stop wiring up or we will carry on with this" I remember taking this inmate to court for sentencing he got found guilty and his barrister said to the judge "Can I say a few words on behalf of my client," The judge said "Ok if you must if you think it will help, I was going to give him a life sentence anyway" The inmate looked at me I said to him "I don't think he likes you".

We had another inmate come to us on spur 2 from Manchester, he had been causing some problems there, when he came to us he was a right miserable fucker, never smiled always moaning.

One morning we didn't have enough cleaners on our spur they were out at court, so the officer I was with said "Let's see if we can get this miserable fucker to clean he is convicted" So we went to his cell and said fancy doing some cleaning, his answer was " Fuck off." Ok we said this is the deal, you clean for us you can stay out tonight with the rest of the cleaners and you can watch the first half of the Manchester United match, as you are a United fan. He looked at us; I could see him working it out. "Ok," He said so he cleaned the recesses on his landing, swept and mopped his landing and collected the food trays up after meals he did a good job.

When he finished in the evening, I told him to sit with the other cleaners and watch the football, when half time came we turned off the TV the cleaners got their hot water and we banged them up he said to me and the other officer, "Thanks for keeping your word ", we said, "No problem do you want to clean tomorrow?" "Yes," He said later on we had him as a permanent cleaner, his attitude changed completely.

He even said he would help me out if I was getting done over on the spur, I said "Thanks " We had him at Belmarsh for quite a while, then he moved to another prison got involved with a female officer, and ended up back with us for a while.

Spur 1 had been turned into a VP (vulnerable prisoners) spur basically it was called the nonce spur. The spur was sealed off so you could not see onto it. An S.O and me with another officer had to take this black Cat 'A' alleged rapist to court from the nonce spur for the start of his trial. When we got in the dock, the judge was a woman, the prosecuting barrister was a woman, and the jury out of 12 people, 8 were women. He said to me "What do you think of my chances?" I looked around and said "Your fucked" He was he got found guilty, and got a life sentence.

Me and Bob helped out in the seg one morning when they were short of staff as we had both worked there before. We ended up as escorting officers, we sat in the adjudication room next to this inmate, and he was in trouble for threatening an officer on

another HB. We knew this inmate from years before, he was a big
black lad, he said to the Governor, if you put me with these two
officers, I won't cause any problems we have respect for one
another.

At the end of the adjudication, he was found guilty, and the
Governor said ok take him with you his on your spur now so we
had him for a couple of months he went to court and never came
back he was no problem with us.

When I first started on HB4 the Cat A's had their visits on the
House Block, the visits area is where the servery would be on
other house blocks. One black inmate from spur 2 who was on
remand, was always told to sit at a certain table when other
inmates who were having visits sat at different tables each time
they had a visit. He didn't seem to notice or care; I mentioned this
to our S.O on visits he said "Keep this to yourself, this inmate is
on remand for murder but the police can't find the body so when
his brother comes to visit him the police are hoping that they
might talk about where the body is. So he sits at that table all the
time and that camera there can watch his visit and it is recorded
and sent to the police then they will get a lip reader in to watch the
video of the visit, and hopefully, he might be able to tell the police
something. I thought sneaky bastards, but clever. The S.O said,
"Now we will have to get all inmates sitting at the same table or he
will start to get suspicious".

We had Barry George come to us on remand for the murder of
Jill Dando in 2000, he was a Cat A, he suffered from epilepsy and
had a personality disorder, and he was on enough medication to
knock a donkey over. I remember I was working on Cat A visits
on the HB, me and another officer picked George up for a visit and
took him to the strip room, for a strip search before going on his
legal visit, I noticed he had a tattoo of the SAS badge, who dares

wins on his upper arm I asked him why he had that done he said he couldn't talk about it. Me and the other officer stripped him, no problem but when it came to his legal papers I found a copy of Viz magazine among them.

I said to him "Is this to do with your legal visit" He wouldn't answer so I said " I don't think it is so leave it here in the search room you can pick it up after your legal visit " He started moaning and refused to go on his visit so I said "Ok we will sort this out with your legal team " We went to his legal visits room where his solicitor and barrister, was sitting and waiting, when I let him in the room his solicitor moaned how long it took to get him on his visit. I said "Is this Viz magazine part of your client's legal visit? The solicitor said" No" I said, " That's why we are late because he refused to go on his legal visit without this, can you tell your client only to bring his legal papers in future and not comics and perhaps next time we will get on a visit quicker ".

I then looked at George and said "This stays in the search room till your visit is finished" We had a few other little incidents with him, when he went up to the hatch to get his medication he got stroppy with the nurse once so now he had a two staff escort up to the hatch and back.

I took him to court a few times while he was on remand and each time we were told that he could be released from court because the police didn't have a lot on him. When he went for the trial I remember one time at the Old Bailey over lunch period he said he couldn't see because he had gone blind, we still cuffed him and took him to the dock in the court, and suddenly his sight came back. He was found guilty of murder in 2001 and at his retrial in 2008 he was acquitted of murder.

I was walking around the middle landing on spur 2 one evening on association, one of our cleaners was leaning on the railings looking fed up I said "what's up" He said "I've got a problem Gov, I've got the wife living in the house in Spain she's sorted my grandson is in boarding school he's sorted I bought my daughter a nice house in the country, but she's got a bit of a problem and I can't get hold of her.

I can get my solicitor to try and find her or I can get a few mates to look for her" "I said what do you think would be the most effective way to find her?" He then said "Can I use the phone Gov?" I said, "Yes are you going to phone your solicitor?" He said "No I'm going to give my mates a ring and get them to kick a few doors in and try to find her" "OK," I said.

One morning on spur 2 the spur was banged up, we just had the cleaners out cleaning. The spur phone rings I answer it, it's the bubble (movement control). "You've got one coming to your spur, he's a VP inmate," The bubble officer said "I've put him in a single cell on the middle landing," I said "If he's a nonce why isn't he on the nonce spur and what has he done," The bubble officer says " He raped and buggered an 8-year-old girl, he has come to us from HB 3 induction wing he won't go on the nonce spur because he said he can handle it on normal location " "OK," I said send him down about 5 minutes later the cleaning officer brings him on the spur. I took his cell card off him and said "Why didn't you go on the VP spur" he said "I can handle it on here" I said "Ok good luck with that" The other officer wrote down his cell location, I gave him back his cell card the other officer said to the inmate follow me and went off to bang him up.

One of the cleaners on my spur said to me, "what's up Gov", I just smiled the cleaner said "He's a nonce ain't he" I just smiled the cleaner said "what's he in for" I said "He raped and buggered an 8-year-old girl" The cleaner replied with "sick dirty cunt why's he on here ?" I said "He thinks he can handle on here, I don't want him on here I want him off today" "Ok gov we'll sort it," I said let him know that you know what he's in for; if that doesn't work I'll think of something else. "The cleaner said "If he doesn't come and tell you he wants off of here we'll do him," I said "Be careful there are cameras everywhere" when the other officer came back from locating the nonce, he said to me. "What you up to?" I said, "Nothing much the cleaners are going to have a career chat with our nonce while he's banged up".

When lunchtime came it was spur 2's turn to go first for feeding, I unlocked all the middle landing, they went down to get their lunch except our nonce, he came up to me and said "I've got to get off here and go on the VP spur or I'm going to get done" I said "I thought you could handle it on here " He said "Some of the inmates have found out what I'm in for, so I've been warned if I'm still here this afternoon I'm going to get done " He also said "How did they find out so quick " I said " News travels fast " I then told him to get his belongings and follow me.

I took him up to the P.O's office told him the problem and the inmate was then located where he should have been on the nonce spur. When I got back on spur 2 the cleaners said "All sorted gov" I said "yes lads all sorted.

One feeding time this yardie drug dealer we had was causing problems with some of the hot plate workers he was moaning to them about not getting enough food, he was off spur 1 before it became a nonce spur. The S.O and a couple of staff escorted him away from the hot plate without any food, and back to his cell and banged him up.

The S.O Said "Feed him last " So when everyone was fed, I went to this yardies cell and said "Do you want to get your food " He said " Fuck off " I said "I'll take that as a no then " and walked off. About 20 minutes later he is kicking his cell door and shouting "Where is my food" He was told you didn't want any, so he starts kicking the door and threatening to kill staff. So 3 of us go to his door, we open him up he rushes at us and punches one officer on the shoulder now its game on, so he gets restrained cuffed and taken down the seg, with smiles from the hot plate workers.

The inmate gets nicked for assaulting one of the officers, he says we assaulted him first, the typical response from a governor he puts it to an investigation, and so another governor has to investigate the inmate's claims of assault. So while this investigation goes on the inmate stays in the seg because now he is threatening and abusive to seg staff. About a week later a member of the seg staff tells us the nicking has been written off because the inmate has been deported back to Jamaica.

Me and another officer were on the ground floor of spur 2 when our HB probation officer brought around some young would-be probation officers, he was showing them his side of the job from within the prison. They came onto our spur because we were banged up and only had the cleaners out. We were talking to the probation officer and the group when one of our black cleaners called Jelly because he was overweight kept walking in and out of his cell dumping black plastic bags in the spur dust bin. I said, "Jelly what you are doing?" He said "Well I've just killed my cellmate cut him up and I'm dumping parts of his body in the bin that I can't flush down the toilet "You should have seen the look on the group of probation officers faces, it was priceless. The officer I was with said to the group "Don't worry we'll find him another cellmate".

17. Seg (2nd tour for both of us)

On the 14th of July, me and Shep started in the Seg, most of the staff from both weekends had been transferred to other areas because they were burned out and there were so many regimes running down there the prisoners were too comfortable and refused to leave. This sounds stupid but they had a single cell a lot of them had a TV, they showered every day and had phone calls and exercise, all without the pressure of being on a house block.

The seg can be a volatile and violent place; a lot of staff were not suited for it. You don't want the place manned with Gorilla's but you can't have care bears either, there had to be a balance. Soon after starting another governor took over the Seg and made a refusal regime to discourage prisoners from getting too comfortable there. They would only have half an hour of exercise each day on their own, three showers a week, one phone call and they would have to be out of bed by 8.00 am to make their applications, once that was done their bedding was removed to stop them going back to bed and they had to shave every day. It wasn't long before they started reacting; there were several restraints when they refused to comply. Most of August was taken up with dirty protests; a disgruntled prisoner's favourite weapon, at times we had two or three prisoners on protest at the same time.

We got to the stage where we didn't really notice the smell anymore; we just burned joss sticks outside the cells and thought about the extra money we were earning. We put up with conditions like this for weeks on end the dirty protests stopped but that didn't mean the end of my dealings with prisoners' bodily functions.

We had one prisoner on dirty protest who thought he was a bit of an artist; he would pick his shit logs up and throw them up to the ceiling where they would stick and hang down like Stalactites. This made it a bit more difficult for those that had to clean the cells. On the 24th of August, I was Doc's officer doing paperwork in the office when the duty doctor came in to do his rounds. The other staff were busy doing adjudications and other things so I did the doctor a favour and took him around. We had a prisoner by the name of Reilly, he was here from Ireland for some reason but he had been a complete pain and he was in the box (special cell).

I took the doctor to see him and I dropped the flap so the doctor could talk with him, when he had finished I went to close the flap and Reilly had been hiding a cup full of piss by his side and he threw it through the hatch all over me. Luckily for me it never went over my face but hit me from the neck down, my shirt was soaked in piss and dripping.

I went into the adjudication room where the governor was hearing adjudications and just looked at the S.O and said "I've been potted and I'm going home to change". I came home in a tee shirt I had borrowed from the S.O, and showered and changed and went back to work to do the nicking for Reilly.

Reilly was on the E-List and so he had to hand out his clothing at night before being locked up for the night. About a fortnight after being potted Shep and I were on evening duty in the seg and we were doing the rounds with the duty governor, we told Reilly to hand out his clothes and he refused.

The duty governor asked us what we wanted to do about it and we said kit up and go in and take it out. The governor told us to get on with it and left the seg; we phoned the orderly office and let them know what was going to happen and to ask for another member of staff. I went to Reilly's cell and ordered him to remove and bag his clothing but he refused. I went off to get kitted up with Shep and the other member of staff, we got the shield and went down to the cell and I again ordered him to comply but he just lay on his bed, we opened the door and went in. I was on the shield and before he could get off the bed I hit Reilly with the shield and I had a smile on my face as I could see his face squashed against the shield.

I got rid of the shield so we could get locks on but Reilly was still not complying which was good for me because I could give him some pain and some payback. We dragged him out of the cell under restraint and took him to the box as he was still non-compliant, he went in the box and because I was controlling his head I ended up doing the figure of 4 leg lock before coming out of the cell.

I made sure I kept all of my weight on the leg lock so he was in the most pain for as long as possible, we eventually came out and left him in there naked. Reilly was a pain the whole time we had him and would cause problems when he could. In October he decided to go on dirty protest, he thought this would cause us more problems, but as we told him with all the dirty protests we had dealt with in the past it just meant we would get extra pay and give him nothing; it also meant we would take all of his belongings so he had nothing. He wasn't on dirty protest for long as it didn't disrupt us as he thought it would.

On the 12th of December, we had an independent Adjudicator who was a Judge came in to run the adjudication on Reilly for potting me. I was giving my evidence when Reilly kicked off; he overturned a table and began fighting with the escort staff.

The look on the Judge's face was a picture, he obviously wasn't used to seeing violence close up, the alarm bell was pushed and the Judge was even more surprised when the door behind him burst open and half a dozen DST (dedicated search team) staff came running through. Reilly was restrained and put in the box. The Judge laughed about it after and gave his award in Reilly's absence. Seg life progressed as normal until one day two prison officers arrived from the Northern Ireland Prison Service; they came to take Reilly back to Ireland as he had a sentence to serve back there. I couldn't help but laugh as he was clearly scared at the thought of going back.

We got Reilly ready and handed him over, the two officers put the cuffs on him and he was clearly in pain, we laughed at him as he was pleading with the Irish officers to loosen the cuffs but they were having none of it. We asked if the officers could drop him off the ferry halfway across and they promised they would think about it if he played up.

Day to day life went on with the normal round of restraints and dirty protests; this was seg life and carried on as normal for months. The next major pain in the arse was O'Connor a CSC prisoner (closed supervision centre) the most disruptive prisoners in the system, Charlie Bronson being one of them.

O'Connor who came to us to give the CSC system a rest from him, he was constantly making threats and being non-compliant, he was in the double skinned cell (normal outer cell door, with a metal barred gate inside covered in Perspex) so that we didn't have to open him completely to feed him or give him things. O'Connor would end up staying longer than the 56 days we were supposed to have him, unfortunately, Belmarsh seg had a reputation for dealing with disruptive prisoners and generally, their behaviour improved over time.

This was also the case with O'Connor, he went from being a multi unlock and on occasion attacking the shield, to being behaved enough to move into the standard CSC cell.

We had O'Connor for 9 months in the end which was not a big deal; however, when he knew we were getting close to moving him back to one of the CSC centres his behaviour went downhill. He went on the exercise yard one day and refused to come off hoping that if he were seen to be disruptive again he would not be moved. The system for taking someone off the yard is to have enough staff in PPE to cover the width of the yard and then advance until you get close enough to control the prisoner, some Governor decided that we would just have three staff in PPE and we would go on the yard and get him.

Myself and two other officers kitted up and went to the door to give him one more chance to give up and come in, O'Connor refused so we told him if we had to come onto the yard that would be it and he would get hurt; he looked at the three of us and decided to come in. O'Connor would eventually miss going back to a CSC centre because he came to the end of his sentence before we could move him, it is unusual to release a serving CSC prisoner straight onto the street but there was not enough time to put him through the de-selection process.

Day to day life carried on and the months went by, on the 6th April 2003, a prisoner by the name of Wooden tried to commit suicide by jamming the twisted sleeve of his jean jacket in the window frame and tying the other around his neck and sitting down. Shep had by chance checked on him as he was on suicide watch and seen him hanging. I was standing at the door to the main office talking to the SO who was on the phone, Shep came up to me and said 'we have a problem we have a swinger' I said this to the S.O who was still on the phone and he just looked at me and said 'yeah yeah, I got the cut-down scissors and me and Shep went into Wooden's cell. Shep held him up while I untied the noose, I then heaved him on the bed and he let out a big sigh which meant he was breathing.

I told Wooden that he was not going to die on my shift because it was too much paperwork, at this point the S.O came running out of the office running around like a headless chicken, saying 'I thought you were pissing about' we told him to go and ring the healthcare and get a nurse to check Wooden who at this point was moaning about being thrown on the bed. We sat down and wrote our incident reports while the nurse was checking Wooden. The S.O was feeling guilty about not believing us and so he wrote a memo asking for Shep and me to be given a commendation.

15th October 2003 Shep and me were on a rest day and we agreed to work overtime in the care suite a special unit in the lower healthcare especially for high profile prisoners. The prisoner we were going to work with was Ian Huntley. He at the time was on remand for the murder of two 10-year-old girls in Soham Cambridgeshire. Our job was to sit with him and monitor him as his cell was open all day; he was the only prisoner in the unit. We sat with him all day playing cards and scrabble and talking to him.

He was a complete arsehole who thought he was better than anyone else, this was fine because the best way to get people to give information is to let them tell you how clever they are and ask random questions that don't appear to be connected to anything.

Lots of conceited people love to brag about what they have done, and Huntley was the same. What he didn't realise was that whilst he was in the shower we were searching his cell and finding razor blades he had hidden in the toilet.

He had threatened suicide previously, although he didn't confess to us as he was at that point pleading not guilty, we did however get some decent information from him which was passed to security and then the old bill. He would tell us how sorry he felt for the families of the two girls, the arsehole made your skin crawl but we had to pretend we agreed with a lot of what he was saying. We worked three more times with him and at no time did he show any remorse, he was so arrogant and really believed he was better than everyone else.

On the 21st of October, we had just sent a prisoner called Malik back to the house block, about 10 minutes later he had been escorted back for refusing to locate on the house block. Shep me and Colin took him downstairs to locate him in the cell he had just come out of. When we got to the door he refused to go in saying it smelled of paint, I told him he had only just left the cell. At this point Malik ran into the servery which was close by, Shep went in after him followed by me and Colin, Shep was telling him to stop being stupid. Malik grabbed a pen out of a cup the cleaners kept on the side and tried to stab Shep, he had a graze on his hand which I thought was from being stabbed. I hate people who use weapons so I grabbed his head to take him to the floor.

Malik was struggling and at this point, I twisted his head around until he was almost facing backwards, it was like watching a cow being wrangled at a rodeo. How I never hurt his neck I will never know, the red mist had fallen because of the weapon (I hate people who use weapons). We went to the floor and someone had pressed the bell, I wasn't aware of all the staff that had turned up as I had my mouth near his ear and I thought I was talking to him explaining the error of his ways.

So I was told later I was shouting at him calling him all the stupid bastards he was, I was flying so much that I was told later that I had told a Governor to "fuck off big nose" I don't remember that but if I did he never said anything and I was almost dragged off of Malik and someone else took control of his head. I was so wound up it took me an hour sitting down in the office to calm down. Later Shep came up and told me he hadn't been stabbed he had grazed his hand on the metal sink unit. I called him all the bastards under the sun as I had nearly broken this prisoner's neck, I slapped Shep and then we laughed about it.

In 2003 we also had what I would class as the most dangerous prisoner pound for pound I have ever worked with. Kamal Bourgas is a terrorist who was found by accident when the police raided a flat in Manchester for a ricin plot. The police entered the flat and weren't expecting Bourgas to be there and didn't know who he was. At some point, Bourgas had an opportunity to escape but chose to stay and went to the kitchen and got a kitchen knife and stabbed one of the policemen twice in the neck and on both sides of his groin. He also injured four other policemen at the same time; we got him in the seg whilst he was waiting for trial.

He was assessed as an S.O and six in full PPE, stab vests and with two shields. As more information came it turns out that they believed he was an ex-Algerian copper and a self-defence expert, and that we could believe after the way he used the knife to kill the copper.

Me and Shep had spoken and agreed that if he kicked off we would forget C&R and just beat the crap out of him until he could be controlled. Because he is a high public interest prisoner we weren't allowed to have a photo of him in his Cat 'A' movement book, so Shep cut a picture of an Arab riding a pushbike out of a paper and put it in the book.

That was fine until the No1 Governor came down to see how things were going and looked in the book, he looked at the picture of an Arab on a pushbike and said to the S.O who was going bright red 'I think you need to change this' the S.O was really embarrassed and we were just looking on sniggering.

One day the police came to take him to a police station to charge him with trying to stab a Met copper in the eye with a pen when he was in police custody. They sent three of the biggest gorilla's I have ever seen. We all kitted up and moved him out of his cell and downstairs to the rear door to hand him over. The inspector said to the governor how professional we were and then the police took him and literally picked him up and threw him on the floor of their van and sat on him.

The police came back with him the same way and we were waiting all kitted up to put him back in his cell. Bourgass was convicted at the Old Bailey in June 2004 of the murder of DC Oake, the attempted murder of two other officers and the wounding of another. Eventually, Bourgass was moved to another establishment to continue with his sentence, this was a relief not because he was difficult to deal with but spending a long time in riot gear and stab vests was a pain in the arse.

The usual round of prisoners and adjudications carried on and soon another year had gone. It may sound as if the seg was all fights, attempted suicides or dirty protests, but there was at times a lighter side we had a Nigerian officer who worked with us, he always enjoyed a laugh and so one day when we had some visitors from head office or somewhere we were in the office and the S.O was telling the visitors what went on in the seg in his best voice trying to be P.C, I said to the Nigerian officer "have you still got those spears and shield above your mantelpiece" the S.O looked over at me and glared I looked at him with a smile and asked what the problem was. The S.O said I couldn't say things like that; I looked at the Nigerian officer and said have you got spears above your fire at home and he replied yes with a smile on his face. He knew what I was doing and was more than willing to go along with it, the S.O all flustered just turned back to the visitors and carried on. One day not long after this the Nigerian officer was Doc's officer in the office and he had an evidence bag next to him with a bottle of hooch (home brewed alcohol) in it, this can be volatile stuff and then without warning the hooch bottle exploded this homemade alcohol hit the ceiling and came back down, I looked at the Nigerian officer and he was sitting at the desk completely soaked with lumps of foul-smelling bread and orange peel all over him.

Those in the office fell about laughing for ages much to the disgust of the officer it was times like these that helped us keep our morale up.

We had a prisoner called Freeman he was in the double skinned cell because he was unpredictable and would happily attack staff, this day we were going to put him on the exercise yard so we had two teams in PPE. One to bring him out of the cell and one at the bottom of the stairs as the exercise yard was downstairs, Shep me and another officer were the team to bring him out of the cell. As we entered the cell Freeman attacked the shield and grabbed both sides of it and started trying to pull it out of my hands, he was bigger and stronger than me so I knew I wouldn't win a tug of war with him. I let go of the shield (you should never give up your shield) but I knew it would give us the edge, the look of surprise on his face was a picture and at that moment he was wondering how he had the shield, me Shep and the other officer came around the sides of Freeman and grabbed him. Freeman let go of the shield and was fighting with us, somehow he managed to

pull the helmet off the third officer who left the cell leaving Shep
and me fighting with Freeman for a short time before we all went
to the floor and an officer on the downstairs team came in to help
us.

We controlled him and he never got his exercise that day, once
we had him in locks he was saying 'ok I give up because he was in
pain, I told him it was too late to give up and he should consider
the consequences of his actions.

We were running a regime where prisoners could only shave
with electric razors, this was done to stop them from breaking the
old Bic razors apart and using the blades as weapons. We had a
prisoner from the healthcare called Odlum who the healthcare said
was bad, not mad, so he was moved to us as he couldn't cope with
the house blocks. One day we were doing the rounds taking
applications and Odlum asked if he could have a normal wet shave
as electric razors didn't shave him properly, I looked at the S.O as
it was his decision and then he asked me what I thought. I said
well he has been with us for a few weeks now and he seems to be
complying with everything we asked of him so he was given a Bic
razor. We told him we would be back in ten minutes to collect it,
he said that's fine I won't be long.

We carried on with apps and then I went back to Odlums cell
to ask if he was finished, I opened the observation flap and Odlum
was standing in the middle of the cell with part of a torn sheet
around his head like Rambo with little cuts all over his face
shouting 'come on then you fuckers get the MUFTI' I called for
the S.O and said you better have a look at this. He looked in and
by this time Odlum was standing on his table shouting 'come and
get me' the S.O just stood there and said 'fuck' I went back in the
office and started arranging for the staff to kit up and take him out.
Just as I started doing this a doctor from Rampton Psychiatric

hospital turned up and said he wanted to see Odlum to assess him, I told him he couldn't because the staff were kitting up to take him out. He then asked if while we were waiting he could talk to Odlum through the observation flap, I told him he could but not to get in the way of the team when they arrived. He was happy with this but before he went to the cell he asked me what I thought of Odlum? I told him he was as mad as a box of frogs, he smiled and went to the cell. When he came back in the office he looked at me and said 'yep you're right' just then someone from healthcare turned up as they have to whenever there's a restraint, and when they found out it was Odlum they said ' oh fuck we should have had him in healthcare' the team went in and Odlum was restrained and taken to the healthcare.

In early 2005 Shep dropped a bombshell on the group and told us he was leaving the job and going to live in Spain, Shep had served 15yrs in the job starting at Wormwood Scrubs before transferring to Belmarsh.

I first worked with him on the visits group and it wasn't long before we had formed a tight bond and would get into all sorts of trouble, but we got away with it because we were good at what we did. As much as I was pleased for him, I was devastated we had been through so many incidents and I knew there would never be someone who I trusted to have my back as much as him, I always had his back. As normal the job doesn't recognise the service people give and so we presented Shep with a certificate from the lads in the seg.

Shep was always known as a Pikey and so we clubbed together for a leaving present, this was a ceramic Gypsy camp with an old fashioned horse-drawn caravan, with the family sitting around a campfire. We arranged his leaving and I produced a menu for the meal which I had arranged with the staff at the Old Mill to give everyone when we sat down for the meal.

The menu carried on the Pikey theme and went down a storm and Shep took it well even though the joke was on him, the leaving do was a good night with lots of food and booze.

When Shep finally went the seg wasn't the same, an element of trust had gone, I knew I could rely on Shep 100% but now there was just a niggling at the back of my mind that I would have to be careful who was around when things were happening. Nothing bad happened there but sometimes you have to move outside the rule book to get things done and make sure things run smoothly, but when you are outside the rule book you have to be certain you can trust everyone around you.

The number of adjudications was increasing and the evidence cupboard was a nightmare, adjudications were beginning to be lost because the evidence was mislaid and the governors were getting agitated about it.

No one was doing anything about it and so whenever I had spare time on nights or at the weekends I decided to clear the evidence cupboard and design a form to log the evidence presented properly. This was hard work because there was evidence missing and evidence where the adjudications had been finished but the evidence had not been disposed of and so there was no continuity. When I had finally sorted the cupboard out I got down to designing the continuity forms so things can be tracked and signed for.

Surprisingly once all this had been done and the forms and the system had been used for a while the S.O decided I should be recognised for the work I had done and so she wrote a memo to be placed in my personnel file and attached to my SPDR (annual report) this was a shot out of the blue as normally any extra work is not recognised.

Life in the seg was up and down and as we had a relatively new governor in charge and most of us didn't get on with him because he was a complete Pratt. This governor was full of his own piss and importance and caused numerous problems in the seg. He came to us one day and told us we would be getting an ex CSC prisoner in about a week and we should keep one of the drop flap cells available. Drop flap cells have a droppable flap in the door as opposed to an observation hatch; this means the flap can be dropped to put food and other things through so you don't have to open the door on a dangerous prisoner. At lunchtime a few days later the phone went in the office and an officer picked it up and it was obvious it was this governor on the phone, he had called to say the ex CSC prisoner was on his way and that he was shiting up in the van and he would be here soon.

I just said to no one in particular but anyone listening "another fucking stitch-up" the officer on the phone just looked at me and grinned but the governor had heard me and asked for me to be put on the phone, the officer said the governor wanted to speak to me and I just said tell him 'I'm on lunch break I can say and do what I want as I don't get paid for my lunch breaks'. Again he heard me and told the officer to tell me he would come to the seg and speak to me later.

We received the prisoner and put him in the drop flap cell and listened to his whinging. Later that afternoon the governor turned up and asked to see me in the adjudication room, I said that's fine and he asked if I wanted a member of staff to come in as well as a witness. I said I didn't need anyone but he said the S.O would be coming in anyway so we went to the adjudication room. As I sat down he said to me that he didn't appreciate my comments and I said 'I'm sure you didn't he again repeated what he said and again I said "I'm sure you didn't'. He then asked me if I had ever read the code of discipline, I just said to him 'I'm opinionated always have been always will be, get used to it' he just looked at me not knowing what to do and got up and said 'that's the end of it 'and I walked out and went back to work.

In the office the others asked what went on and I said he had tried to threaten me with a disciplinary and I told them what I had said, they all laughed and we just carried on. He would continue to cause problems for the staff and change the regime giving the prisoners more and making it difficult to get them to leave the seg when their punishments were up. The governor would back off from me to some degree but it was blatantly obvious he didn't like being challenged by me, and he would start doing things to annoy the staff.

For months we had been dealing with one CSC prisoner after another and often two at a time. This was draining on the staff one of these prisoners had a wound on his leg that he would infect on purpose and then when he was annoyed about something or couldn't get his way he would scoop some of the puss out of the wound and throw it at staff. Another would break his pen apart and put the ink tube down the eye of his dick so we had to take him to the healthcare.

We were told we would be getting a CSC prisoner to go in the double skinned cell, it turned out to be Lieveld who I had first met at Brixton. During the time he was with us he would be very demanding and disruptive, approaching Christmas he decided he wanted to send some cards.

Normally if this was the case we would get two or three from the canteen and let the prisoner choose, but Lieveld wanted to see all the Christmas cards the canteen had. We tried to say no but he complained and we were told we had to get all the cards and let him pick, we did this and an officer had to sit outside his cell and show him all the cards, if that wasn't enough he wanted to make a maybe pile a no pile and a yes pile. This took hours and he loved every minute of it causing problems.

He would make threats to certain staff who he thought he could intimidate, the problem was this was easy for him as if memory serves me right he had previously thrown boiling oil over an officer in another prison. He would in the future go on to stabbing an officer with a sharpened toilet brush handle. We didn't have him for too long but he did disrupt the seg while he was there.

These were the sort of disruptive prisoners in the CSC system, the governor knew this and the opportunity came up to put a member of staff forward for Prison Officer of the year and he chose a member of staff that had only been working in the seg for a couple of months.

He did this on purpose because he knew it would wind the staff up as we had been dealing with these disruptive prisoners for a couple of years.

He carried on with his efforts to demoralise the staff and get his way, and it came to the point where I decided I had to send a memo directly to the No1 governor to try and get something done. As it turned out sending that memo worked better than I thought, I explained all my concerns and waited for a response, his next bright idea was to say we couldn't have our tea making stuff in the top office, he said it was unprofessional if visitors walked in and the staff sitting in the top office drinking tea. I said to him no one had ever complained before including the No1 or any official visitors.

Anyone that came in would be offered a cup of tea or coffee and it had never been a problem. His response was it's going to happen so that's it, he was doing his best to piss the staff off so they would ask to deploy out of the seg.

Luckily all of us stood together and this had the effect of pissing him off more than he was doing to us. It seemed all I was doing during this time was writing memo's telling the governor about how his seg governor was disrupting the running of the seg and demoralising the staff.

I have to say I was also getting pissed off as everyone was moaning about what was happening but I was the only one trying to do anything about it. Still, this shouldn't have been a surprise as previous SPDR's said I had an outspoken personality.

Extracts from SPDR's

Mr Richards has recently had his time extended within the seg unit, but is looking to move at the next reporting period. He is competent in all areas of the seg routine and is often looked upon as a more experienced member of the team. He has excellent computer skills and is often asked to produce typewritten reports, flow charts and graphs for those who are less confident in computer literacy. Although He can be an outspoken member of the group, he is willing to listen to others opinions and accepts that change within the unit is inevitable. His wealth of experience is beneficial when discussing issues concerning the segregation policy and regime. He keeps well updated with new policies. He is always willing to lend a helping hand when asked and is a valued member of the team who raises the spirits of the others producing a happy and harmonious atmosphere amongst the group. **Seg S.O**

"Mr Richard's has achieved all his targets this year and is set for a re-deployment in September. He will be missed within the group as he offers advice and guidance to new staff. I'm sure where ever he is re-deployed to he will give his full potential within any role he adopts.

His only negative point would be his outspoken personality, however, this can be a strong point as his knowledge and experience of being a prison officer, is valued by both his peers and members of the management team. I wish Bob all the best in his career and hope that we work together again in the future." **Seg Governor**

Although these comments could be seen as negative I actually take these as a compliment, I was told by a governor at Brixton that just because someone is a governor it doesn't mean they have all the best ideas or are always right. I have always worked on this premise and that is why I would often challenge governors because of what was said to me but also because often those governors would come to me because I know what I am talking about or I don't give my opinion. I was seen by many of them as an old dinosaur but when it comes to talking to or dealing with prisoners or difficult situations I am a necessary dinosaur because I deal with the situation and have nothing to prove.

I was proud to have made it to the position of dinosaur and wore the tie pin to show it. I hoped other staff members would see me as someone with experience who they could come to for advice and a truthful answer.

I think this was probably true of most of my time in the prison service, I don't know if someone was looking over me or someone saw something in me but I was working in security at Brixton with eight months in the job, I was a C&R instructor within 2 years of joining and I was acting up to S.O with only months in the job. Back then you had to have years in before you did things like that.

A few days after this latest memo the No1 came down to the seg and walked around the place to see for himself what I was talking about and then he came to the office to speak with me and the staff. He asked me to explain and I pointed out all of the negatives of the current seg governors ideas, and to be fair I thought he would back his governor up. The No1 listened and said he would speak to him, I finished the conversation by saying to him 'I am fifty years old and I refuse to be banished to the bottom office like a naughty school boy' the No1 looked at me with a smile on his face and said 'very succinctly put Mr Richards' he left the seg and he must have been true to his word as our governor backed off.

Thankfully it wasn't too long before he saw he wasn't going to beat us and he transferred to a different prison, this was good news but unfortunately, he left multiple regimes in place as well as all the other crap ideas.

Between October 2005 and February 2006 we had a prisoner called Farhan with us he was another the healthcare had said was bad, not mad, he was about 5'6" and seven stone dripping wet. He would not stop assaulting staff, between the dates above he was restrained 71 times either for spontaneously assaulting staff or for causing damage to his cell.

He smoked but we couldn't let him have a lighter or matches because he would set fire to his bedding, we tried to use a lighter as a bargaining tool to get him to comply but he wouldn't he clearly had some crazy shit going on upstairs but the healthcare said he had no mental health issues. He was a real drain on staff, he had to be a three officer unlock because of all the assaults. In some ways, it was embarrassing because to look at him you would think blow on him and he will fall over. He just didn't care, getting restrained hurts but it just seemed to be a game to him, after numerous complaints to the governors expressing our concern for his safety because of the number of restraints the healthcare were forced to take him. What this demonstrates is you don't need to be the biggest or the meanest to cause problems.

2005 came and went and life carried on as normal with idiots coming down and the normal adjudications. This was interspersed with days at court when I was jobbed and I had started working rest days to earn some extra money, one of these extra days involved taking Abu Hamza to the old Bailey. Abu Hamza is a Muslim cleric who stood on the streets of London preaching hate against Britain and America and was allowed to get away with it. He had both of his hands blown off planting a bomb in another country.

In my opinion, he is a complete arrogant pig who believes he can do and say what he likes and hide behind people's fear of upsetting Muslims. He was always trying to find a reason to complain about anything and everything, he was also a drain on the staff. He had a nurse that had to go everywhere with him to administer his medication and wipe his arse because he couldn't do it with his hooks.

In February of 2006, we were taking apps one morning when we came to one of the cells with a prisoner by the name of Robinson, the S.O dropped the flap and told Robinson to stand back so he could open the door. The S.O opened the door and before he could take his key out of the door Robinson came out of the cell throwing punches, how the S.O managed to get out of the way I have no idea, he has the biggest head in the prison service.

As Robinson came further out of the cell an officer grabbed Robinson. After that we all ended up on the floor struggling with him, there was a big pool of blood spreading out on the floor from his nose which he hit when being taken to the floor. When it had kicked off I threw the clipboard and pen, we had him under restraint and then Oscar 1 turned up and told us to relocate him in his cell. Although this can be done it is not easy to relocate someone under restraint in a normal cell because of all the stuff in there. I said he should be put in the box but Oscar 1 was having none of it.

Shep

Seg 2nd Tour

In July of 2002, me and Bob moved off of HB4 and followed our S.O also from HB4 to the seg unit a second time for me and Bob. There were a few inmates on dirty protest throughout August, but as time goes on you get used to the smell. We had an inmate come to us from one of the House Blocks; his name was Reilly he was from Ireland he was a right pain in the arse. We had him in the special cell as he was playing up, Bob came out of the office to help he opened up the hatch to let the doctor see Reilly. Reilly then threw a cup of piss out of the hatch which hit Bob, it went over his shirt.

Bob then went home to get changed, later Reilly started to calm down a bit and was located into a normal cell in the seg, being an E man he has to hand his kit out of the cell at night, he refused. So Bob called the duty Governor, he came down and said

I'll leave it up to you two to sort it, and he sent another officer down from the orderly office. Bob gave Reilly another chance to hand his kit out and he refused, so the 3 of us got kitted up, we went in Reilly was laying on the bed as he got up Bob hit him with the shield, we restrained him and put him back in the special cell. About a month later he went on dirty protest, it didn't last long he got fed up with it before we did.

Reilly went in front of an independent adjudicator (a judge) that came into the prison for the throwing of urine over Bob. I was not there but apparently, Reilly kicked off in the adjudication room in front of the judge and started fighting with staff. The alarm bell was pushed and the Dedicated Search Teams office is just upstairs so they all piled in. Reilly was restrained and put in the box; I believe the adjudication went ahead in his absence.

Later on, some prison officers came over from Ireland to collect Reilly as he was wanted in Ireland, when they cuffed him he moaned about them being too tight. They said if he carries on moaning they would throw him over the side of the ferry. One of them said to me. "Watch the news tonight, you might hear about a dead body being found on the motorway it'll be him" Pointing at Reilly.

We had an inmate called O'Connor, he was of mixed race, and he was another pain in the arse. He was a CSC prisoner that came to us on a lay down for 56 days but he stayed longer, he was located in the double skinned cell so we didn't have to open him up completely only for showers and exercise. His behaviour improved and he was moved out of the double-skinned cell and into a standard CSC cell. He stayed with us because he was getting near the end of his sentence; I believe he even got some days back that he lost through playing up. He moved onto an HB, then released.

I was patrolling the landings and conducting a check on the inmates by looking through the spy hatches when I saw this inmate by the name of Wooden put his head into a noose that he made that was hanging on the bars. I legged it to the office and said "We've got a swinger" At first I didn't think the S.O believed me, Bob grabbed the cut down scissors and we ran to Wooden's cell.

I grabbed him and held him up and Bob untied the noose from around his neck, then we threw him on the bed and he started breathing.

The S.O came running into the cell and said "I thought you were pissing about" We called a nurse and she checked him over, the S.O. wrote a memo to the Governor asking for me and Bob to be given a commendation. If he had died there would have been a lot of paperwork to fill in.

Ian Huntley arrived at Belmarsh for his trial at the Old Bailey. He tried to commit suicide at the other prison he was at, the Governor wanted him on permanent watch. He must be seen to face trial. The Governor said "You officers guarding him will have to keep him alive" Me and Bob were on a rest day but came in on overtime to the Care Suite a special unit in the lower health care for high profile inmates.

He was on remand for the murder of two ten-year-old girls.

We sat with him all day long till the night staff came on duty; we would watch TV with him and also play cards, when he went for a shower, I kept an eye on him in there while Bob searched his cell. We worked with Huntley quite a few times. One time he said to me and Bob "You two are alright you are quite placid" Bob said "Don't let that fool you, we'll drop you like a stone if we have to" He just looked at us; he did have this arrogant nature about him.

When he was at court his mother came to visit him on Saturdays in the care suite, once when she was leaving I saw her crying. I said to her "Are you ok?" She said "Yes thanks", and then she started to smile. Nice lady too nice to have a son like him.

I took him to court a few times and in the court, I had to sit between him and his girlfriend Maxine Carr I think she was in Holloway prison. I remember her legal team saying to her. "When you get in the court don't even look at Huntley or smile at him if the jury sees it they will think you still have feelings for him and we don't want that". Huntley got life x 2 and later the High Court imposed a minimum term of 40 years. Maxine Carr his girlfriend got 3 and half years for perverting the course of justice because she provided him with a false alibi.

We sent this inmate named Malik back to the House Block after he had finished his punishment; about 20 minutes later he came back he refused to locate on the House Block. So me Bob and another officer took him downstairs to locate him, he refused to go in the cell then suddenly he runs in the servery opposite, quickly followed by me Bob and the other officer.

I told him to stop being stupid, he grabbed a pen from the side of the sink that the seg cleaner was using and tried to stab me with it.

Suddenly Bob grabbed his neck and gets him in a headlock, me and the other officer dive on him I shout out "Fuck it" Bob thinks the inmate has stabbed me so Bob tightens his grip and starts to explain the error of his way to the inmate, me and the other officer get a lock on the inmate drops the pen, I think the seg cleaner pressed the alarm bell, we restrain the inmate and then the Cavalry arrive, and we get Malik in the special cell. After that in the tea room, I tell Bob the inmate never stabbed me, I caught my hand on the sink and grazed it in the struggle.

He said "I thought he stabbed you that's why I nearly took his head off" He gave me a dig and then we had a coffee and a laugh about it. I nicked Malik, he got about 3 Added days for assaulting me. He said afterwards I never assaulted you, I said I know but you were going to.

Another dangerous inmate we had was Kamal Bourgas; he was a terrorist who was in a flat when the Manchester police raided it. Bourgas grabbed a knife from the kitchen and stabbed a police officer to death and injured others. He came to us, so we put him in the double skinned cell he was an S.O and 6 unlock with full PPE and 2 shields. Bob and I said that if he kicks off, fuck C & R we will beat the crap out of him then restrain him.

Because he was of high public interest we were not allowed to have a photo of him in his Cat A movement book. So I cut out a picture from a magazine of an Arab riding a pushbike and stuck that in the Cat A book.

Well they did look similar later on the number 1 Governor comes to visit the seg and looks in the Cat 'A' movement book, he says to our S.O "You had better get rid of this" and shows him the picture, me and Bob sneaked out the office laughing.

Later the S.O said the Governor wasn't pleased. (Typical Governor no sense of humour) Bourgas stayed with us till the end of his trial, he was convicted of murder and attempted murder of two other police officers, when he moved on to another prison, we could finally hang up our PPE equipment and stab vests.

Whilst working in the seg we were given a chance to work overtime that was when me and Bob and a few other officers worked with Huntley, this particular day I finished working in the seg at lunchtime, my overtime was, over to the unit for the afternoon and Oscar 4 in the evening which probably meant running inmates back to their House Blocks from reception after they have been to court.

The afternoon was spent on Cat A visits in the unit, I reported to the Orderly Office in the evening and was told a P.O me and another officer had to go through the tunnel to Woolwich crown court to pick up Abu Hamza. He was arrested for inciting violence; he was an Egyptian Cleric and was the Imam of Finsbury Park Mosque in London where he preached Islamic fundamentalist views. So we go over to the court via the tunnel, we go to the Cat A cells and find Abu Hamza, he is quite a big bloke, good job we were informed before we went to the court that he had no hands, so we took a body belt to put him in. He lost his hands and an eye when making a bomb in Pakistan, the explosives went off while he was holding them.

The P.O put the body belt around him and secured it I was cuffed to the body belt, the other officer had the hooks that he used as hands, and some of his possessions. We walked back through the tunnel to the prison and then on to reception. A male Health Care nurse was waiting for us there, Hamza had to be stripped searched, and then he was told that his hooks were classed as weapons so he would not be able to have them while he was located in the Cat A unit. A male nurse from the Health Care would go over 3 or 4 times a day to help him wash and eat. It took 8 years for him to be extradited to America for terror offences.

One evening I was on duty in the seg with another officer when reception phoned to say they were bringing an inmate down to us, the police had been called to a disturbance at a house, this ex-inmate was drunk and breached his licence by being there also he had a row with his probation officer. So the police brought him straight here, he had been released about a week he came in the seg with 2 officers escorting him more like carrying him he was drunk as a skunk. We put him in one of the cells and I told him to sleep it off till morning, we recognised one another he was a hotplate worker from spur 2 on HB4. He kept saying "I love you, Mr Shepherd, I love you," I said, "Go to sleep". Then when we shut his cell door he started shouting it out. "I love you, Mr Shepherd," I said "Shut up go to sleep" The other officer was in stitches. When the night man came on, I told him just to keep an eye on him. The next morning we woke our ex cleaner up, he didn't know where he was plus he had a hangover.

He told me he had a row with his probation officer, got drunk in the pub then went round to his ex-girlfriend's house which he shouldn't have done, which meant he breached his license. We sent him to a house block, and the probation officer there was going to have a word with him.

I was doing a set of nights in the seg, as I needed the week off afterwards to fly to Spain to see my family they moved out there earlier in the year.

As I was taking over from the day staff one of them told me that an old mate of mine and Bobs was back. When I checked the inmates and the doors I found inmate Popeye from HB4 who me and Bob had taken to Dovegate prison. Basically, he played up there so they put him in the seg, he still played up and finally, they moved him to Belmarsh seg. He was no problem to me on nights, he was ok with Bob on days but not with some of the other staff, and I was told he could be aggressive with them. I finished my nights with no problems, I went to Spain to see my family, came back to the seg Popeye had gone to another prison. I had it in my mind I wanted to be with my Stepdaughters and grandsons in Spain.

We had this inmate come to us in the seg he had spent a couple of months in Broadmoor mental hospital, they sent him to us to see how he would get on back in the prison system he was a lifer, I believe he was a Muslim. He said to us when he starts to get depressed he wants to fight people; it gets all the aggression out of his system. One morning he asked if he could shave, a few of us noticed a slight change in his behaviour; anyway someone had given him a razor and a metal mirror, which I thought was not good.

The next minute he was banging and kicking his cell door, when I pulled the flap back his face was covered in cuts and blood, I noticed the blades from the razor on the cell table covered in blood. I went into the office and told the S.O he went and had a look, by now the inmate was kicking the door and becoming abusive. 3 officers got kitted up, I was told to get the special cell ready.

The team went in and had a massive struggle with him; they restrained him and put him in the box. For a few hours after that, he was kicking the door of the box, then it all went quiet an officer looked in the box he was fast asleep. The next day the nurse came to see him and attended to the cuts on his face.

He was let out of the box and put back in a normal seg cell. We put on his cell door no razor; he was with us for a few weeks then went back to Broadmoor. We had a few inmates like this, Broadmoor would send them to us saying they were cured, within about a month we were sending them back saying no they aint.

In January of 2005, me and my partner decided to move to Spain to be with our family. It was hard telling the lads, especially

Bob I felt I was letting him down, we always watched each other's backs we formed a formidable two-man team. So I gave a month's notice, in February I left the service after 15 years. Bob arranged my leaving do.

We had a sit-down meal and a good drink afterwards, I was presented with a ceramic gipsy camp with an old fashioned horse-drawn caravan, as the lads said I looked like a gipsy also a book on snipers, my sister has the ceramic gipsy camp as she said you can't take it to Spain, but I have the book.

After 16 years in Spain, I am still in contact with Bob and quite a lot of other staff. To all those staff I worked with that have passed away God Bless you all, we will be together one day.

18. SMU

In April 2006 I was deployed with another officer to SMU (sentence management unit) this group was responsible for categorising prisoners as well as doing OASYS reports on them and we ran the education and workshop departments, along with this we controlled what was called free flow where at certain times of the day the prisoners would be sent off to different parts of the prison using the secure corridors. Standing in the corridor watching free flow was like being in the monkey house at the London zoo, there were hundreds of prisoners going where ever and the noise was horrendous shouting and whooping. The majority were black but there was a large proportion of Eastern Europeans and Vietnamese, none of which are the quietest of people.

I never understood why people couldn't go where they are going without shouting or screaming; it would be great if they just talked to each other. Apart from free flow, we were also responsible for supervising the Education department and the Workshops, with education there would be two officers at the door receiving the prisoners.

We had a list of all those that were supposed to attend and what classes they were taking, the problem was that all the Vietnamese have names that sound the same and are unpronounceable they would be going to the ESOL class (English as a second language). Once they are all in they went to their classes and then we had to count how many we had in education as a whole and how many came from each house block and then we called the house block and compared numbers.

When education was over we had to rub down search all the prisoners before they left, there could be between sixty to eighty prisoners to do that's a lot of up and down and it was knackering. The workshops were the same mark them in and count them and confirm numbers with the house block. There were normally eighty prisoners attend the workshops daily, on my first day marking them in there were 120 it was chaos not just because of the numbers but all the names I couldn't pronounce and the accents I couldn't understand.

The daily routine was the same it was either education or workshops and the odd day jobbed off or at court, on the 29th of June three of us went to Newbold Revel for an OASYS course. The day at Newbold was a nice change from the boring days on free-flow or the workshops/education.

When I came back I spent the next couple of weeks back in the seg as the S.O because they were short-staffed. On the 17th of July, we were back at Newbold for a four-day OASYS course. The weather at Newbold was great and so after completing a boring day learning our way around the OASYS document and different cases we went back to our rooms freshened up went to get something to eat and then into the bar.

The evenings were spent drinking taking the piss out of each other and enjoying the sun on the patio and lawn. I always enjoyed going on courses because the job would hire cars for us to travel in and it gave me a chance to drive some cars I couldn't afford. The next few months were spent in education, workshops and the corridor on free flow.

19. OMU

Things were about to change, on the 2nd November myself and three other officers were called into the Activities Governor's office, we were looking at each other trying to think what we had done wrong. We sat down and he told us there was a new initiative called OMU (Offender Management Unit) rolling out across the Prison Service, he told us head office had run a tabletop exercise to see the viability of the idea.

He went on to tell us that Belmarsh would be getting an OMU department and he asked if we wanted to start it up, he went through each of us and told us why he had chosen us. When it came to my turn he told me he had chosen me because others would load the gun and I would fire it, what he meant by this is that if something needs saying I will say it. He went on to say there will be resistance to the idea of an OMU, by staff and governors alike and the group would need someone to challenge them and not be scared to speak their mind.

We all looked at each other again and all agreed to take it on, he then told us it was so new we had to start the group from scratch as there were no official forms or paperwork and so we would have to design our own.

Because we would be 'Ring fenced' which meant the National Offender Management Service would be funding us, we would also have to come up with our own shift pattern as we would now work Monday to Friday only. We went back to the SMU office and people were keen to find out if we had been called into the governor's office because we were in trouble. When we told them we had been chosen to start a new group that was separately funded and we would work our own shift pattern a lot of them were not happy.

On the 5th November OMU officially started, over time the resentment from staff members who did their best to do as little as possible got worse as they thought we were getting an easy ride. Throughout my career there has been a lot of staff who do jack shit and then complain because they think you are getting a cushy number, they forget people like me work their nuts off and help anyone they can while the others sit on their arses only thinking of themselves. You could see the resentment on their faces increasing when they were told that because we were separately funded we couldn't get involved with the day to day tasks SMU officers did such as rub down searching the prisoners returning to the house blocks from the workshops.

The next few weeks were taken up with meetings and the start of the training we would need concerning Probation risk assessments. We were busy sorting out ways of communicating with the police, probation and any other service we needed to, the task of designing forms to assist us with the various processes began. If the police came into the prison it was usually for a legal visit to see a prisoner, but we would be having face to face meetings with the police and so we had to set up a better and quicker way to get them into the prison so they could come to our offices and the same with probation.

So we came up with a way to bring these visitors in through the staff entrance and not legal visits, this would be the first of the forms to be designed. Then came the task of designing forms to identify police officers in the case for IPP/Life Sentenced prisoners, so they could be invited to the 'MARAP' (multi-agency risk assessment panel) these were to discuss the case and ascertain any risk factors we needed to be aware of.

We were using files for the prisoner's paperwork that were not fit for our purpose so we had to decide what needed to be contained in the prisoner's files and design a file to fit our needs. Another officer and me did this and we found a print firm who could manufacture them for us.

These files contained sections for Pre-Cons, Warrants, Medical reports, Case summaries, Parole reports and several others. We ordered 5000 of these and we ran out about a year before I was medically retired so we had worked as a group with over 5000 in scope prisoners in 7/8 years.

The work would turn out to be very interesting having to work with other agencies like the police and probation, as we progressed we would also work with the Anti-terrorist units. We were all allocated a personal caseload and we would all work with our prisoners on this caseload.

It started with identifying those convicted as in scope (posing a high risk of harm to the public) and then we would interview them and start the process of sentence planning and deciding how to manage their sentences. Through doing this we built up good working relationships with lots of Probation officers at the various offices they worked at. We had to work with Probation teams from all over the country as not all of the prisoners were London based, to assist in doing this we had to set up video link and conference calling facilities, as the OM's (offender managers) couldn't always attend our offices. On the 6th of December, the whole group went to Exeter prison as they were supposed to be one of the first prisons to trial Offender Management, we went to see what we could learn from them and the trip was an overnighter.

On the way down everyone was starving and we were looking for somewhere to stop for breakfast, as we were discussing this I remembered that just up the road there was a caravan that was converted to a greasy spoon café. I knew it was there because I had passed it loads of times when Carol, me and the family had come to Devon for short breaks; we stopped and had a massive full English breakfast to set us up for the day.

We arrived at 10.00 am and were in the local pub by 12.00, we spent a couple of hours there and then went to find our digs, and we freshened up and then went into Exeter on the piss. We returned to the hotel and carried on drinking, by the end of the evening we were all legless. It was a relatively quick four-hour journey going but coming back took us over six hours as there was an accident on the M25, I was so glad when we finally got home. It now fell to the four supervisors on the group to catch up with the outstanding OASys that had been ignored before the OMU came into being, there were 210 outstanding and we had 3 months to complete them before they were overdue.

We had an evil little witch as admin assist allocating them to us but because she didn't like us because she was a lazy backstabbing little bitch, and we wouldn't put up with her crap she did all she could to make us fail.

We could only do the OASys on overtime, lunchtimes and evenings, but because this was out of our normal hours we got paid quite well for the work. Much to her disgust and her efforts to make us fail we completed 230 in the 3 months allotted. Although it was a lot of work doing 230 OASys we used to have a laugh in the evenings when we were doing them, there had been a probation meeting one afternoon and food had been supplied for the guests.

That evening there were sandwiches and Profiteroles left over so we decided to play cricket using the profiteroles as cricket balls, by the time we had finished there were lumps of profiterole and cream all over the walls and ceiling in the office. It took us ages to clean it all up but it was a great laugh and we were finding bits of profiterole for ages that we had missed.

Our caseloads were building up and we were getting into the swing of having sentence planning boards and meetings with the police and probation for those in-scope of offender management. Because the group was still in its infancy the No1 governor said we should take advantage and visit other prisons to see how they did things. We didn't need to be told twice and so we arranged a visit to Manchester (Strangeways) and on the 2nd April 2007, we got the train to Manchester.

This time we were in the prison a lot longer than 2 hours, our P.O was determined that we would spend the time finding things out and not just go to the pub. Eventually, we got out and that evening we went into town for a drink and a meal, we had a Brooke Bond monkey as our department mascot and he came on tour with us.

When we returned to the hotel we all went to our rooms, about five in the morning I was woken by an extremely loud claxon. I was looking around wondering where the sound was coming from and then I noticed it on the ceiling, I tried to get up there and turn it off not realising it was a fire alarm.

The whole hotel was evacuating but I just got washed and dressed and gathered my wallet, phone and train ticket and then wandered outside, the rest of the crew and the other residents were either in pyjamas or various stages of undress and I was fully clothed.

They were all looking at me and I said to one of the others the rest of my stuff can burn if it's real but I was not going to stand around outside undressed and have my money and ticket burn. Eventually, after the fire brigade had gone they let us back in and I finished packing for the journey home. When we returned to work we decided that Manchester's way of working was not what we wanted for our unit so we carried on with the way things were.

On the 24th of April the reason the governor who started OMU chose me came into use, I received a phone call from Oscar 1 the P.O in charge of the prison asking for one of the offender supervisors to report to CRS (central resourcing) to be cross deployed as another area was short of staff.

Remembering what the governor had said about not letting ourselves be cross deployed, I said to the P.O that we didn't have any S.O's on duty. He told me I would have to send someone I informed him that as an officer of equal rank I couldn't order another officer to stop what they were doing and go somewhere else.

After some orders to just do it I again refused and he said he would have to contact the duty governor, so I told him to do what he had to. I then received a call from the duty governor telling me just to comply with what I had been asked to do; I then told him as someone of equal rank I could not order an officer. He then started getting quite agitated; I explained I was just doing what I had been told about not allowing our staff to be cross deployed by our governor.

He again told me to do it in a very agitated manner and so I said to him that I was speaking to him calmly and respectfully while explaining why I couldn't comply and that I did not appreciate his aggressive and bullying manner in speaking to me. I then went on to say that if he gave me the order in writing I would comply, he replied fine and put the phone down but a few minutes later I received an e-mail from him giving me a written order to deploy someone.

I did this as I could not go myself as I had a meeting arranged, and then I contacted our governor to inform him of what had happened. I found out later that the duty governor had spoken to our governor complaining about me but had been told I was doing as instructed.

Our caseloads continued to grow with in scope prisoners and we continued with numerous meetings and training days. We had a Ukrainian civilian who worked for probation in the prison and he came onto the group as an offender supervisor, up until then all the supervisors had been uniformed officers. One day we were told all of us had to attend a meeting with probation and civil service staff in London at G.O.L (government offices for London) so the following day off we all trotted to the venue which was on the bank of the Thames directly opposite the MI6 building.

We were on the top floor and had a clear view of the MI6 building, we were all sat around a table and I looked at our pet Ukrainian and said if anyone sees a red dot appear on his forehead they should shout duck as it will be MI6 taking out our Ukrainian. Everyone but our Ukrainian friend found this funny and we would tease him about it for ages.

In January 2008 one of the more interesting cases I worked on was allocated to me, Roger Coutts who was part of a gang that carried out a 53 million pound raid on a Securitas depot in Kent. The depot manager and his wife and child were taken hostage as part of the plan, in all seven gang members heavily armed entered the depot and used cable ties to secure the 14 staff working at the time. It took them just over an hour to steal the £53 million; they left £154 million behind because they couldn't fit it into the seven and a half tonne truck they were using.

As part of the investigations and arrest of members of the team £20 million of the 53 million had been recovered and the other £33 million was outstanding at the time of the arrests. Coutts was sentenced to an IPP sentence with a minimum tariff of 15 years, after the raid, all the employees as well as the depot manager and his wife and son were locked in the cages used to carry the money.

They only escaped when the manager's son squeezed through the cage and released them. The investigations to track down the outstanding money continues to this day, and the police are working to get other gang members extradited to this country from Morocco so they can also stand trial for their part in the crime.

I would carry on working with those who were deemed a high risk to the public, most of which received a standard sentence and had a set release date. Those that had committed three or more violent offences were in fear of receiving an IPP sentence. The IPP sentence meant that they would serve a minimum tariff before being considered for parole and this was a good deterrent. At the start, though these sentences caused some problems as Judges didn't understand the implications of the sentence and tariff's as low as 28 days were given.

The whole point of the tariff was that prisoners had to serve that tariff and complete offending behaviour programmes before they were released, and with a 28-day tariff, this was impossible.

In the end, Judges were told if they imposed an IPP sentence the minimum tariff had to be at least two years, so we could get prisoners through offending behaviour programmes. Basically, after a public outcry, the IPP sentence was introduced because prisoners who posed a high risk of harm to the public were being released.

Having not completed any offending behaviour courses which would help reduce their reoffending and committed a further crime. The system could not force them to take part in these courses, and so these prisoners would sit out the custodial part of their sentence, knowing they had a definite release date. The government response to this was the introduction of the IPP sentence, this meant the sentence did not have a definite end date and those sentenced to IPP would have to engage in offending behaviour programs or risk not being released as they are subject to the parole system and this would not be granted if they had not engaged.

I had a VP (vulnerable prisoner) on my caseload called Bristow, he was not a sex offender as most VP's are but he was an inadequate who couldn't survive on normal location. He was a drug user and a prolific thief, he stole to feed his habit and he was always in and out of prison and whenever he came into Belmarsh he would ask if I could be his supervisor. I would see him regularly and try and help with his issues, and I would end up sticking my neck out a bit to try and get him a ROTL (release on temporary licence) so he could attend a drug rehab near Reading. After a lot of discussions with probation and the drug rehab, I finally managed to arrange it.

I decided I wouldn't be the one to escort him in case he did a runner, so I arranged for an officer who was not part of OMU to take him. This officer took him there so he could speak with the rehab staff and see if they could help him, and I was relieved when he came back with him. It was arranged that Bristow would go to the rehab when released as part of his licence conditions. Bristow was a determinate sentence prisoner but assessed as a high risk to the public. Most of the prisoners I worked with complied because they had to, but the odd one would appreciate the work you did for them and Bristow was one of these, to show this he wrote to the head of OMU praising the help I had given him.

In June 2008 I was allocated a prisoner called Hussain who was serving 18 years that had been transferred to us and he was not happy about this as he said he was being messed about by other prisons. When I first interviewed him I thought he was going to be a pain in the arse because he kept saying how various prisons had promised him things and then transferred him out. This meant his belongings hadn't caught up with him and he thought the whole of the prison service was pissing him around.

He made claims that all he had done was help two prison officers who were in danger of being assaulted. I checked out his claim about helping staff and found that it was true and so I decided to try and sort his problems, this was not easy because he had been moved so often it was difficult to trace his property. On top of this, I had to try and find out what his sentence plan was and arrange to get him to somewhere he could complete it as Belmarsh offered very little in the way of offending behaviour programmes at that time.

I contacted his previous prisons to try and find his OMU file which should follow him where ever he goes, but I just kept getting told it must have gotten lost with all his transfers, this didn't help me because I had to make up a file from scratch with virtually no info and he was already six years into an eighteen-year sentence.

Well I obviously did something right because out of the blue I was called by the head of OMU to tell me Hussain had written to him about me, I was surprised because he had been so anti when I first spoke to him and a lot of long-termers believe they are entitled by the length of sentence they are serving, and cause no end of problems.

We were beginning to get more terrorist cases allocated as there were more and more arrests. When the word terrorism is used everyone thinks of the twin towers on 911 or the London tube bombings, but terror charges come on all levels. I had a prisoner called Al Figari on my caseload who was accused of attending terrorist training camps in England. Mohammed Zakariyya Al-Figari, 44, of Tottenham, was born Roger Michael Figaro in Trinidad. Al-Figari is a trained pharmacist who converted to Islam in 2004. He lived with his wife in Tottenham and once worked as a clerical assistant at University College Hospital, in London.

Al-Figari was accused of attending several camps in Hampshire and Berkshire in June 2006, this may come as a surprise having terrorist training camps in Britain but it was disguised as a paintballing venue.

When police raided his home they also claimed to find a series of terrorist documents, including some on jihad and al-Qa'ida. Al-Figari was sentenced to 4 years 2 months for his offences.

Abdul Sherif was the brother of bomber Hussain Osman and his role was mainly in assisting him to escape to Italy after the failed attacks of 21 July 2005. Osman fled initially to Brighton but then headed back to London, equipped with his brother's passport.

Because of the close facial similarity between the brothers, Osman was able to board a Eurostar train to Paris and from there he travelled to Italy, where he was eventually captured and extradited to Britain. Sherif had also made numerous phone calls to Italy to arrange a safe house for his brother in Rome. Sherif was sentenced to 6 years 9 months for his offences.

Shahid Ali and Shabir Mohammed these men, from Birmingham, had admitted at the Old Bailey supplying equipment such as computer parts, mobile phones and camping gear. Mohammed Nadim, 29, (not on my caseload) Shabir Mohammed, 30, and Shahid Ali, 34, were arrested last October and charged under the Terrorism Act 2006. Nadim was sentenced to three years while Mohammed and Ali received two years and three months.

A fourth Birmingham man, Abdul Ishaq Raheem, 32, (not on my caseload) was jailed for failing to disclose information about an act of terrorism.

All four were members of a cell run by Parviz Khan, a British and Pakistani passport holder jailed for a minimum of 14 years in February 2008 for plotting to kidnap and behead a Muslim soldier in the British army.

They helped Khan send four shipments containing 86 boxes of supplies between April 2006 and February 2007. Nadim, Ali and Mohammed were said to have known nothing of Khan's murder plot. Raheem knew about the shipments but failed to tip off the police. Prosecutor Duncan Atkinson said the items were sent to be used against British, American and Pakistani forces. These cases go to show that there are many levels to terrorist offences, but that does not mean that just because these people didn't shoot, stab or bomb anyone they all played an important part in terrorist offences. They did this by training, supplying and knowingly assisting front line terrorists, the same way paedophiles who watch child abuse films on the internet perpetuate child abuse.

All our caseloads continued to build and as we went into 2009 I would be dealing with a lot more IPP's, Lifers and terrorists although we still had our run of the mill offenders who were a high risk to the public but received determinate sentences. My caseload would also become more challenging because I would get a lot of sex offenders and hard to manage disruptive prisoners.

I don't know if this was done on purpose by those allocating the cases who had been upset by me on a few occasions as we had moved to the main admin block and all of the case admins had changed, and those that took over were very cliquey and some thought they were the dog's bollocks.

Unfortunately, this was not the case and I had to write an idiots guide on how to Case Admin for OMU. Lots of them didn't like this, so I had upset them by pointing out they didn't know it all.

Unfortunately, these case admins had become almost untouchable as their boss had managed to wrap most of the governors around her little finger and so the staff thought they could do and say as they pleased, they would bully anyone they could and often picked on the weaker ones in their own group. That was not the way we worked on OMU we said it as it was so no one could get the wrong end of the stick. It was not unusual for one of the admins to go running to her boss crying when she thought she could challenge us and lost. One who had previously tried to prevent us from completing the OASYS was an evil backstabbing Weeble; the only difference was she didn't fall down.

Now we were in the main admin block we were a target for people to try and ruin the good work we had been doing, we had a couple of changes of management and they had no idea what it was we did, and so they tried to change everything to make themselves look good at our detriment, they kept giving the supervisors different case admin and I always seemed to get the worst of the bunch and so I would end up doing most of their work as I couldn't rely on them.

In April 2009 I was allocated a VP called Samir Daya he was a rapist but all through his trial and after he refused to admit his guilt. (Taken from a Newspaper article) A rapist who viciously attacked two women has been told he may never be freed from prison. Samir Daya, 23, must serve a minimum of almost seven years and will only be released if a parole board considers him safe near women.

This looked like it was going to be a difficult one for me to progress, when we had the Marap the police officer in the case said that Daya refused to admit the offences all the way through. I saw Daya every day for at least two weeks trying to find out why he wouldn't admit he had done it, the more I spoke to him the more I realised he was in denial because of his parents who were both doctors and were well known and well-liked in his area.

He was afraid that if he admitted it, it would have an adverse effect on his parents standing in the community as well as him being afraid his parents would disown him. After just over two weeks of speaking with him and explaining that it was him who was serving a sentence and not his parents and that if he continued to deny it he could not progress through his sentence and as he was on an indeterminate sentence he would never reach his parole point.

Eventually, one day when speaking with him he admitted to carrying out the rapes. I asked him if he was going to stand by this confession as I recorded all meetings with him and I would be writing this on his contact sheet. He assured me he would as he didn't want to stay in prison forever, when I got back to the office I contacted his offender manager and the police officer in the case, both of them couldn't believe I had got him to confess and comply with the terms of the SOTP (sex offender treatment programme) so he could be moved on and work through his sentence plan.

Yet again I was allocated a couple of terrorists who had been cleared of helping with the London bombings on the 7th July 2005. Two British Muslims cleared of helping the 7 July bombers choose their targets were today sentenced to seven years in jail each for planning to attend a terrorist training camp.

Waheed Ali, 25, and Mohammed Shakil, 32, were yesterday found not guilty at Kingston crown court of conspiring to cause explosions with the four men who carried out the attacks that killed 52 people in 2005. The pair, who were arrested as they were about to board a flight to Pakistan in 2007, were found guilty of conspiracy to attend a terrorist training camp.

They have already spent two years in jail on remand. The trial heard that an estimated 1,000 young Muslims from the UK visited training camps in Pakistan between 1998 and 2003. The judge said: "It must be made entirely clear, if necessary through sentences of an appropriate length, that such conduct is unacceptable." The head of Scotland Yard's counter-terrorism command, Deputy Assistant Commissioner John McDowall, said Ali and Shakil shared the same extremist beliefs as the London bombers, with whom they had grown up in Beeston, Leeds.

It always amazes me with these terrorists how easily they are indoctrinated, they are for the most part intelligent men but their thought processes are warped. Waheed Ali was born in this country he went to school and university here and had white friends throughout his life. All he could go on about was how the west is killing his brothers across the Middle East, and he will do what he can to fight for them.

He does not come from a radical family but when I asked about his parents he just said they didn't understand. They were both sentenced to 6 years 10 months, and both will be released in 2010 on licence but at the very latest 2014 when their sentence expires.

As with all terrorists that are released they will be restricted as to what Mosques they can attend and they will be observed by the anti-terrorist branch at least until the funding runs out.

I also picked up another terrorist but this time he was not anti the west but was a Tamil Tiger fighting against the Sri Lankan government. The head of the Tamil Tigers in Britain was found guilty today of supplying bomb-making equipment for the Sri Lankan terrorist organisation. Arunachalam Chrishanthakumar, 52, known as Shanthan, coordinated the supply of materials for the Liberation Tigers of Tamil Eelam (LTTE), also known as the Tamil Tigers. Despite warnings to stop his activities, Chrishanthakumar, described as a "very prominent figure" in the UK's Tamil community, continued supplying electrical components for the LTTE, some of which had "an obvious terrorist purpose". He was also found guilty of receiving documents for the purpose of terrorism. He was sentenced to two years.

Most of the offenders I had on my caseload were relatively young if they were connected to violent crimes, but I was allocated a 72 year who had committed murder. Byrne was an alcoholic who strangled a landlady days after she had taken him into her home out of pity.

Byrne was told by an Old Bailey judge he still posed a danger and was given an indeterminate sentence for public protection. He attacked Grandmother Khalifa Ali, 68, in her home in

Leytonstone, east London; Byrne pleaded guilty to manslaughter due to his alcoholism and must serve a minimum of three-and-a-half years. The court was told Mrs Ali had taken him in temporarily as a favour to a friend but she was killed nine days later.

Although there are those that you can look at and think "he's a wrong un" you can just never tell what people are capable of, and although working in OMU gave me an insight into the lives and the crimes of those I worked with, that as a landing officer you never got. That insight never excused what they had done, no matter how hard and rough their lives were they still had the choice of whether to commit their crimes or not.

I would get a little insight into the gang culture in London with my next allocation, teenage gangster who shot dead a student as he shopped for a pint of milk was jailed for at least 32 years today.

Ashley Bucknor, 20, had been released early from a prison term for committing a stabbing when he blasted 18-year-old Ryan Bravo in a drive-by shooting. His five-strong gang had been aiming for two rivals who had fled into the Costcutter supermarket in Walworth.

The victim's brothers and cousin were left to try to save the teenager, but he died from his wounds. Bucknor, 19 at the time of the killing in August last year, was convicted of murder at Woolwich crown court and jailed for life, with a minimum of 32 years. As the sentence was passed, the killer smirked and strutted down to the cells. Bucknor had been released early from jail after stabbing a 40-year-old man who tried to confront a group of youths.

He had been sentenced to six years but the term was reduced to four-and-a-half by the Court of Appeal. Sentencing him today, Judge Charles Byers said: "Ryan Bravo was by all accounts a nice, intelligent young man who had nothing to do with crime or gangs. He had a lot to offer, he had his whole life before him. But you were part of a gang of young men that night who took his life, and the grief left in your wake is inestimable.

Ashley Bucknor points a gun in a CCTV image of attack "You must realise, as must all young people, that when those involved in this type of crime are caught and convicted, they must be punished severely.

" The judge stressed that the supermarket was full of shoppers and "the number of shots fired could have meant more victims". He added: "I am quite satisfied you knew exactly what you were doing.

You have shown no remorse. You have protected others who could have been brought to justice. I don't accept for a moment that your involvement with gangs is finished. "You are a dangerous young man who will stop at nothing to pursue your own selfish purposes." "On that evening, Ryan Bravo was with his brothers Alex and Perry and his cousin Daniel. Daniel wanted to buy some milk. He intended to go to the local garage, but changed his mind and, to save 20p, he decided to go to Costcutter on Camberwell Road." The teenager was shot in the back. He died of internal bleeding and the collapse of his right lung. Police spotted five youths running away but none of the other gunmen has been arrested. Outside court, Detective Inspector Tim Carter, of Operation Trident, said: "Bucknor was part of a group who targeted two young men as part of retaliation for an incident earlier in the day. "It was a warm evening in one of the busiest streets. They paid no regard to any innocent members of the public.

Bucknor was only caught because the area had been flooded with police and two police officers in a car had seen Bucknor walking through an estate carrying a crash helmet, they thought this was suspicious and they knew the gang had ridden off on scooters. They stopped Bucknor and searched him and found the gun in a bag he was carrying.

When I first spoke to Bucknor he denied the offence even though he had been caught with the gun, he also had a bad attitude because he was part of a gang and thought he could intimidate people. Unfortunately for him, I told him his attitude didn't impress me and he would be an old man when he got out. Bucknor had his 32-year tariff reduced to 24 years on appeal.

And then we come to George Maben who was in his mid-40's when he was allocated to me, he was a weasel of a man and although he sort of accepted that he had murdered his girlfriend's mum he always tried to blame the mother. He was given a life sentence but with a very low tariff of 13 years, life normally started at 15 years but Maben told me the judge had taken his mitigation into account and said Maben was a caring man. The police thought the sentence was too low and were considering appealing the sentence.

Maben thought he could get the sentence reduced further and decided to appeal. I warned him appeals can go both ways. I was in reception the night he came back from the appeal hearing and he was devastated.

He had been given an extra 5 years taking his tariff up to 18 years and he was gutted, I tried not to smile and just said "I told you appeals can go both ways" I was happy this had happened as he was a thing who had murdered a defenceless old woman, and he was always trying to ingratiate himself with the staff.

When we had the MARAP on him it was quite clever and lucky the way the police had built their case, they had tracked his route to and from his girlfriend's mums house using CCTV from the buses he took. The lucky part was that he had been wearing a brand new jacket which he had dumped in an alleyway; a man had found it and was wearing it when he used a cash point. The police had pictures from the cashpoint timed and dated from when Maben would have been in that area, the police tracked the man from his card info and he had the jacket hanging up in his flat. The police managed to get Maben's DNA from the jacket to prove it was him wearing it in the bus CCTV, all the time Maben was at Belmarsh he continued to play the victim, and I was glad when he transferred.

It was also the first MARAP I had done where the crime scene photos were computer-generated with real photos of the wounds superimposed on the graphics. The police said this was to make them less graphic and not show a real dead body lying on the floor.

In 2010 I would pick up another 16 murderers serving life sentences; this was apart from all the other IPP's and other in-scope offenders. The first two murders would be classed as domestic by the police as the victims were known to the murderer.

IRSHAD WALI, A 52-year-old man who bludgeoned his flatmate to death then dumped his burning body beside a motorway has been found guilty of murder. Afghan immigrant Irshad Wali faces a life sentence for killing 60-year-old businessman Sher Khan, with who he shared his home in Plaistow, east London. The charred remains of Mr Khan were found on the M45 motorway near Rugby, Warwickshire, on 30 December 2008. A jury at the Old Bailey took just an hour to reach their verdict, they rejected Wali's claim that a mystery man killed the father of seven before forcing him to dispose of the body. Mr Khan's brother Raj said in a victim impact statement that the way his body was disposed of was a "humiliation".

Jurors heard that Wali killed Mr Khan by striking him repeatedly in the hallway of the home they shared before wrapping his body in a sheet and driving it north. Later Wali attempted to clean up the murder scene and "set about a deception that the dead man was in fact still alive and well" by withdrawing £300 from the victim's bank accounts.

"If the body was not identified and if the victim had not been reported missing, because people thought he was alive and well, then this defendant would quite literally have got away with murder," said Jeremy Donne QC, prosecuting.

"Unfortunately for him a thorough and painstaking police investigation did uncover the identity of the dead man and uncover the evidence that points conclusively to the defendant's guilt." The silver Toyota Carina used to transport the body was traced to Mr Khan. It led police to the address in Plaistow where they arrested Wali. CCTV from a Texaco service station showed the defendant filling a plastic container with petrol before the fire, Mr Donne told the jury. Petrol found around the body was later identified as having come from Texaco. A witness had seen a man she later said was Wali standing in front of a silver vehicle on the hard shoulder of the motorway, while another described a "whoosh of flame" as the fire was lit, the court heard. Wali, who was also convicted of perverting the course of justice, will be sentenced on Friday. Wali was sentenced to life imprisonment. This murder was classed as domestic because they had shared a flat; the next was domestic because the couple were husband and wife.

A bullying husband who stabbed his wife to death in a High Street clothes shop was facing a life sentence at the Old Bailey today. Thaker Ramanlal, 48, was bitter and angry that Vasha Champaclal had taken out a court order banning him from seeing her and their daughters. She had foreseen her own death when she made a statement saying: "Without an order, I'm certain that mine and my daughters' lives are in danger and our next encounter with him will, for sure, be our death. Six months later, armed with a knife, her husband followed her to work at Peacocks in Mitcham and was caught on CCTV lurking around the counters waiting for his chance to strike.

Finally, he followed her to the staff room and cut her throat and stabbed her through the heart. He then fled through the fire exit before confessing to the police the following day. Ramanlal, a call centre worker, admitted to killing his wife but pleaded not guilty to murder on the grounds of diminished responsibility due to an abnormality of mind. The jury heard that Ramanlal and Ms Champaclal, 43, had been married for 20 years, during which he subjected her to "bullying, abusive and controlling behaviour."

The couple had split up in August the previous year when he had chased her out of their Kingston home with a hammer.

She obtained a court non-molestation order against him which made him "bitter, angry, tearful and self-pitying", the court heard. "She, no doubt, felt safe surrounded by her colleagues and members of the public going about their ordinary business," said Mr Finnegan. "He bided his time in the store until she went to the staff area at the rear of the premises where he followed her, confronted her and used the knife to cut her throat and stab her in the heart." Ramanlal was sentenced to life with an 18-year tariff.

These cases were interspersed with the normal day to day issues of the OMU department, like being cross deployed to cover other areas in the prison. This would lead to rows with management about how this affected our ability to manage our caseloads and the meetings with outside agencies we had to have. At the end of March 2010, four of us had a bit of a break as we spent 3 days on an anti-terrorism course in London, this was run by probation and had guest speakers who talked about anti-radicalisation programmes they were running. As much as probation liked to preach about how good they were at managing offenders, we came up with some ideas as we saw offenders from a different perspective, and the course tutors said they would have to look at how they presented their courses as they had never thought about things the way we do as prison officers.

After this short break, it was back to the grind but my next case would have a bit of a twist, in May 2010 I was allocated a murderer by the name of McFadden, I went to the house block to interview him and found him in his cell. He was a cleaner and so his cell was open, I asked him to come downstairs as I didn't carry out interviews in prisoner's cells. He told me he was suffering from gout, I asked him if he could make it downstairs and he said he could so he hobbled downstairs and we got on with the interview. When I finished I went off to another house block and didn't think anything of it. When I returned to the office sometime later everyone started to take the piss calling me doctor death, I was confused but eventually, someone told me that about an hour after I interviewed McFadden he had been found dead in his cell. Everyone knew about me being involved in a death in custody at Brixton which I haven't mentioned for the sake of the prisoners family, hence the doctor death reference. I answered the questions that the governors asked me and told them he was alive and well when I left him apart from his gout. I knew in the future this would land me in Coroners court again, and so I just got back to doing what I did.

The next case had a twist to it as it was a Saudi Prince who had murdered his servant. A Saudi prince who beat and strangled his servant to death at the culmination of a campaign of "sadistic" abuse is facing a life sentence after being convicted of murder. Saud Abdulaziz bin Nasser al Saud, a grandson of the billionaire king of Saudi Arabia, was found guilty at the Old Bailey of killing Bandar Abdulaziz at their five-star hotel suite in central London. Saud had been drinking champagne and cocktails when he bit the 32-year-old hard on both cheeks during the attack in February.

The pair had just returned from a Valentine's night out. The 34-year-old prince was found guilty of murder today after the jury had deliberated for an hour and 35 minutes. He showed no reaction as the verdict was returned. The court had heard that the murder of Abdulaziz was the final act in a "deeply abusive" master-servant relationship in which the prince carried out frequent attacks on his aide "for his own personal gratification".

Jurors were told that by the early hours of 15 February, Abdulaziz was so worn down and injured having suffered a "cauliflower" ear and swollen eye from previous assaults that he let Saud kill him without a fight. The prince then spent hours on the phone to a mysterious contact in Saudi Arabia trying to decide how to cover up what he had done.

He ordered two glasses of milk and bottled water on room service as he set about dragging the body into the bed and trying to clean up the blood. It was only about 12 hours later after a chauffeur had received a call from Saudi Arabia telling him to go to the £259-a-night Landmark hotel, that the body was discovered in room 312.

The prince claimed he had woken in the afternoon to find he could not revive his friend – by then stiff with rigour Mortis – and explained his injuries by saying he had been attacked and robbed of €3,000 in London's Edgware Road a few weeks before. Detectives took him to the area to try to retrace the route, but as they did so, other officers who were reviewing CCTV at the hotel found footage of Saud mercilessly attacking his aide in a lift on 22 January. When he was then taken to Paddington Green police station and arrested, Saudi officials tried to claim he had diplomatic immunity, but this was scotched by a check of Foreign Office records. Saud tried to cover up the true nature of his relationship with his servant, claiming they were "friends and equals", but a porter at the Marylebone hotel where they had stayed said Abdulaziz was treated "like a slave".

The prince also claimed he was heterosexual and had a girlfriend in Saudi Arabia, but he had booked appointments with at least two male escorts and one gay masseur and looked at hundreds of images of men on gay websites. Photographs of Abdulaziz in "compromising" positions were found on his phone. Saud had denied killing his servant until shortly before the trial, before finally admitting that he had caused his death. Jurors rejected a claim by his barrister, John Kelsey-Fry QC, that Saud was guilty only of manslaughter. The prince was convicted of murder and a second count of grievous bodily harm with intent relating to the attack in the lift. Sources said detectives in the case had received little help after requests for information were sent through Interpol to their Saudi colleagues. Saud's lawyers also failed in a last-ditch attempt to stop details of his encounters with male escorts from being revealed during the trial. In a sign of the anxiety about his sexuality becoming public, the prince's lawyers had initially argued that the legal argument about the escorts should be held behind closed doors. Kelsey-Fry said Saud had already faced abuse from Islamic fundamentalists being held alongside him at Belmarsh prison. The court heard that homosexuality remains a capital offence in Saudi Arabia, and the country in which the acts take place has little relevance to prosecution under the country's sharia law.

Outside court, Detective Chief Inspector John McFarlane said: "The defendant used his position of power, money and authority over his victim Bandar to abuse him over an extended period of time.

CCTV recovered clearly shows Bandar was subjected to assaults in the hotel. The injuries which were noted by the pathologist clearly show Bandar was the victim of many more assaults over an extended period. This verdict clearly shows no-one, regardless of their position, is above the law."

In March 2013 he was flown back to Saudi Arabia to serve the rest of his sentence there. The prince did not stay at Belmarsh for long before being transferred to another prison, there were lots of things going on in the background because he was a prince and although the agreement between the Saudi's and us is that he will serve the rest of his sentence but I doubt that.

In July I was asked by one of the security S.O's if I would go with him to the Treasury Solicitors office in London, to give a talk on IPP sentences. I prepared myself with handouts and information for them and then gave them a talk. They seemed to enjoy it from the feedback. As usual, things were busy with meetings and compiling parole reports and the usual cross deployments.

Amongst my many murderers was a hitman who had been living in Thailand. A Guinness world record holder turned hitman is likely to spend the rest of his life behind bars after being found guilty of strangling a disabled woman in her home. Paul Cryne, 62, turned to jurors who had convicted him and said: "Innocent man," before being led away to begin his life sentence. The court at the Old Bailey heard how Cryne, who had fallen on hard times in Thailand, flew back to Britain in 2007 to kill 52-year-old Sharon Birchwood at her bungalow in Ashtead, Surrey. Birchwood, who suffered from ME, was strangled and left "cruelly trussed-up" with parcel tape and an electrical cord. Cryne, originally from Manchester, was hired to carry out the murder for £30,000 by Sharon Birchwood's ex-husband, Graham "George" Birchwood, 54 who stood to gain £475,000 on her death.

Cryne and Birchwood, who planned to share the insurance payout, had met in Thailand through the expatriate community. Judge Jeremy Roberts QC jailed Cryne for life but reduced his minimum term from 32 years to 28 and a half years because he had already spent time in a Thai prison. He said: "The victim, Sharon Birchwood, was a vulnerable lady who was devoted to George and hero-worshipped him despite his callous behaviour; George repaid that trust by paying for her to be murdered by you.

"Sharon was murdered in a particularly unpleasant and personal way in what should have been the safety and security of her own home. You had either crept into her home or lain in wait for her in the house. One can only imagine the mental and physical suffering she must have undergone in the last few moments of her life." An electrical cord had been wound around her head and the small handle of a magnifying glass had been used to tighten it like a garrotte.

Cryne, who still holds the Guinness world record for swimming the longest distance underwater in 24 hours, lived the high life in Thailand in the 1990s thanks to a £500,000 insurance payout following an accident involving a boat in the Maldives. He turned hitman after squandering the money, running up debts of £11,000 by 2007. He was on bail, suspected of carrying out another contract killing in 2003, when he flew to the UK to kill Sharon Birchwood in December 2007. Sharon Birchwood allowed her ex-husband to stay overnight regularly and in 2001 made him the sole beneficiary to her will. She suffered from ME and bouts of depression and was often housebound. Cryne was caught out because of a crime he had committed more than 30 years earlier.

His DNA from the earlier crime scene matched that found on a cup at the house of Birchwood's mother, on which there was also a set of fingerprints. The prints were linked to Cryne's 1972 conviction for holding his girlfriend hostage, for which he was jailed for seven years. Detectives tracked him to the island of Koh Chang in Thailand and he was extradited. Cryne was another one who was full of his own piss and importance because of his World record for swimming underwater. Even after conviction he would still tell me he was innocent, and I would tell him he better start taking responsibility or he would spend the rest of his life in prison as he wouldn't be able to complete offending behaviour programmes if he didn't admit to his crime.

As time progressed I would have people who committed all types of crimes for any of a hundred reasons, my next murderer had his wife killed and they treated it as an Honour killing. These crimes are quite commonplace in Asian and Indian communities; they are usually down to some perceived slight on the family bringing dishonour to the family. The victim is nearly always the wife but not always, sometimes a daughter may be the victim. Often they are carried out by a mother who believes their son's wife has dishonoured him, the attacks range from throwing boiling oil over them to murder.

Shortly after 6.15 pm on 16 November last year Geeta Aulakh left her office for the routine trip she made almost every evening. After a brief bus ride, she set off on foot down a series of tree-lined, suburban roads towards her childminder's 1930s semi-detached house in Greenford, west London. She never arrived. Sometime close to 7 pm, on a quiet corner only a couple of hundred metres from where her two sons, then eight and 10, awaited their mother after school, two men approached Aulakh out of the early winter dark. One of them, a teenager called Sher Singh, produced a 14in machete and hacked at her repeatedly, with extreme force. Aulakh, then 28, suffered appalling injuries to her head and body and died soon after arriving at the hospital. Her right hand was severed completely as she sought to shield herself from the blows. An already horrific crime took on a still more disturbing outlook as police uncovered her husband had recruited the attackers and sent them out that night: Detectives soon found that while the couple had spent almost 10 years together they could not have been more different. Geeta Aulakh, every friend and colleague agreed, was selfless, hardworking, uncomplaining and devoted to her children.

Although her husband could be charismatic – notably when he first wooed Geeta – he was ultimately, to use the private words of one detective on the case, "a shit of biblical proportions". During the marriage, Harpreet Aulakh routinely put down his wife in public while developing an apparent infatuation for her sister, Anita. When Geeta finally left him he became obsessed with the idea she was seeing another man, confronting male colleagues, hacking into her Facebook account and going to her flat to pore over receipts, seeking evidence of a new attachment.

When Geeta began formal divorce proceedings, the 32-year-old planned her death. The prospect of divorce was, police say, a humiliation too far for a man immersed in a shallow, narcissistic machismo, a product of both his male-dominated Punjabi Indian upbringing and his self-styled image as a gangster, involved in minor drug and immigration scams. You have a hard-working young woman who dotes on her two children and only wants the best possible life for them. Then you have someone like him," said Detective Inspector John Finch, of the Metropolitan Police, who led the investigation. Police have treated the murder as an "honour killing", although not everyone agrees with this definition.

What everyone agrees on is that when she ignored her parents' opposition and eloped to Europe with Harpreet Aulakh, Geeta Shinh, as she was before the wedding, made the biggest mistake of her life. She was the adored, English-born daughter of Hindu parents who had come to London and set up a jewellery business, establishing themselves at the heart of respectable life in the Indian-dominated suburb of Southall. Harpreet, in contrast, from a poorer Sikh family, was suspected by Indian police of involvement in a series of violent crimes even before he entered the UK illegally in his early twenties. Convinced he was a skilled criminal, Aulakh planned a murder he was believed could never be traced back to him.

He recruited a friend, 30-year-old Jaswant Singh Dhillon, and Sher Singh 19, to ambush his wife while he drank in a pub under the watch of the CCTV cameras he knew were there. Police believe Sher Singh, who had entered the UK four months before on a student visa obtained by Aulakh, was chosen to wield the machete as a stand-in for the younger family member usually picked for an "honour" crime, perhaps because his family home in the Punjab was close to Aulakh's.

He carried out the murder, it seems, simply because he was asked to. "Sher Singh was young and impressionable, just a teenager," said Finch.

"This man had got him into the country and helped him find a job and a place to live. He looked up to him. He probably felt he owed him." The plan fell apart when Dhillon approached police, initially claiming to be an innocent witness. He led them to the canal in Slough, Berkshire, where the gang dumped the machete and Sher Singh's jacket. The key breakthrough came when officers discovered the rare, Brazilian-made weapon was stocked by a shop just half a mile from Aulakh's home in Hounslow, west London. CCTV footage showed three people buying such a machete. Two were tracked down and still had them at home; the third was Aulakh. Despite such compelling evidence he insisted on his innocence throughout the trial, calling Geeta his "first love". The dead woman's family were appalled to see him occasionally look up to the public gallery and offer them a sardonic wink, probably aimed at Anita. Harpreet Aulakh was jailed at the Old Bailey today for life and ordered to serve at least 28 years. Sher Singh, who wielded the machete, and Jaswant Dhillon, who acted as a lookout, were also jailed for life and given minimum sentences of 22 years.

On the 1st March 2011, I was 55 and this was my official retirement age as I was Pre-Fresh start. Instead of retiring, I went to working a three day week.

There was an obvious advantage for me, but there was an advantage for OMU as it meant they would keep some experience on the group and I had agreed to run a full caseload like the full-timers. This upset some of the less proactive supervisors because if I could manage a full caseload working three days a week and constantly beholding MARAP's and sentence planning meetings what were they up to.

Although I didn't have to do free flow (prisoner movement) anymore I was still subject to being cross deployed and so some of the others were made to look even worse. I have previously mentioned I seemed to end up with all the problematic offenders; I had three in particular who took up an awful lot of my time. Their House block would ring me all the time telling me they were causing problems, this came to a head when two of my little cherubs were put on the same spur and ended up fighting each other. Once they had finished their time in the seg they were sent to different house blocks and I carried on sorting their problems. Holt was a licence recall, but because of his previous violent behaviour, I had to get him on whatever offending behaviour programme I could.

Belmarsh had just started the Thinking Skills Programme (TSP) and so I got him on that as it was designed to teach offenders how to identify what triggers them into whatever offending they do, it also gives the coping strategies to try and prevent them from offending. Pohl on the other hand was an IPP sentenced offender who was violent and didn't care, I don't know why but I always seemed to get on with the violent ones. Maybe it was because they could never intimidate me, and a lot of them thrived on people being scared of them. That's not to say that at times I wasn't scared myself but they would never know it.

One with who I built up a relationship was Scott Hayes, I first came across him when I worked in the seg and he was going through the selection process for the CSC system. This is where they put the worst of the worst, he was only a skinny thing but prone to violence. I have stood in his way many times in the seg when he was threatening Governors or someone else who said something he didn't like. He would look at me and say "don't you're old and I don't want to hurt you" and I would just look at him and say don't be stupid.

He left Belmarsh eventually but would return sometime later serving an IPP sentence and end up on my caseload.

One day after I had put myself in the firing line, by backing him when he had a dispute with the health care over his medication. He said to me I was like a dad to him because I wouldn't give it Charlie large and would just talk with him about the possible consequences of his actions, and I didn't judge him.

Because of these types of offenders I became well known to the psychology department as they too were involved with the problematic offenders in Belmarsh. The cases kept coming and I would be allocated Clinton Bailey who had disposed of a woman's body in a suitcase. An IT worker who killed a woman he met on the internet before emptying her bank account and dumping her body in a suitcase was jailed for life today. Clinton Bailey, 36, was told he must serve at least 30 years in jail after being convicted of the murder of Leah Questin. Bailey used his victim's money to buy bottles of champagne for another girlfriend days after the killing, inviting her round to drink it while Questin's body was still stored in his garage last September.

Bailey had posed as a BBC executive and offered gifts to seduce women he met on the internet. He had no steady job and struggled to make ends meet, and was described as a "conman" who "lied through his teeth" by a source close to the case.

The South African, from Lewisham, south-east London, swore and called jurors "stupid" after being convicted of murder at the Old Bailey, before storming out of the dock. After hearing that he faced a minimum term of 30 years because the killing was done for gain, he shouted: "Fuck me, I didn't kill her. Are you people stupid or something?' Look at the pathology how the hell?' Bailey's victim, a 37-year-old care assistant, had told him she loved him but he was more interested in the £3,000 she had saved up over years of hard work.

He killed her, thinking she would not be missed, before clearing out her account and continuing to look for women on the internet. Questin's naked remains were later found dumped near a dried-up pond in the countryside near Cliffe, Kent, and were identified by fingerprint records. Her 4ft 11in body was discovered by a passer-by, stuffed into a padlocked and bulging suitcase, along with several air fresheners. It was too decomposed to find a cause of death.

Judge Gerald Gordon said: "What he did with her body was dreadful but pales into insignificance compared with the fact that he murdered her, that murder was done for gain.

Bailey later admitted getting rid of Questin's body but his barrister, Bernard Richmond QC, said that while his client was "prone to dishonesty and deception"; it could not be proved he killed her, Jurors rejected this. The victim's sister, Alda Magdalena Questin-Esta, said: "She didn't deserve the grim and tragic circumstances that led to her death.

She became the unfortunate victim of a mad and senseless killer." Peter Wright QC, prosecuting, told the court that at the time Bailey met Questin, he had "serious money problems", with his bank account heavily overdrawn and his credit card cancelled. He had a steady girlfriend, Debra Jooste, but told friends he was sexually frustrated and placed an advert on the Gumtree website last August. Bailey described himself as a "very intelligent 33-year-old" – with an email address starting "hi. iq.146" – looking for a woman from the Philippines. Questin, of Cricklewood, northwest London responded the same day and was soon regularly visiting Bailey's one-bedroom flat.

"Leah Questin was searching for affection, a relationship, and possibly marriage," said Wright. Soon she was texting him that she loved him, and he persuaded her to withdraw £900 from her bank account so he could pay the rent. On September 12, Oyster card records showed her travelling to his home. Hours later she was dead, jurors were told.

Later that evening Bailey used her bank card to withdraw £180, and over the next nine days her bank account was "systematically drained", leaving a final balance of £4.96, the court heard. Bailey sent text messages to and from her phone to cover his tracks and used her Oyster card to go shopping for a large suitcase. Wright said: "He placed her body in that suitcase and then waited for the opportunity to dispose of it. Firstly, he emptied her bank account on an almost daily basis." On 18 September, Bailey invited another woman he had met on the internet to his home while Questin's body was still stored in the case in his garage. Five days later he dumped it in Kent, and it was discovered the next day. The court heard there were no obvious signs of trauma but that suffocation, asphyxiation or strangling could not be ruled out. A small amount of Questin's blood was found on Bailey's bed.

A source close to the case said that because Questin had no family in the country, the killer thought "she wouldn't be missed that much". "She did have a couple of thousand pounds in her account and she was vulnerable. She wanted to meet someone and marry someone and have kids. "During the MARAP the police told us that Bailey had kept the body in the suitcase in his garage with about 8 air fresheners to disguise the smell, he would also go out to the garage to visit the body and say "good night".

The crime scene photos showed the body bent in an unnatural position in the case, it was difficult to see what part was what as maggots had eaten a lot of the flesh.

I would pick up another murderer John Sweeney was known to me before he was convicted of two murders; he was on house block 4 when I worked there between 1997 and the early 2000s. He was a difficult and disruptive prisoner, but he was never a real problem to me. I can only think this again was down to me not being intimidated and just telling him how it was and what he would do.

He had a fascination with the Occult and was always drawing weird pictures.

The police believed there were clues to other possible murders contained within his drawings. News article: Life sentence without parole for a double murderer who killed girlfriends and left dismembered body parts in canals. A carpenter who murdered and dismembered two former girlfriends before dumping their remains in canals in Rotterdam and London has been told he will die in prison.

John Sweeney, 54, from Liverpool, was given a whole life tariff at the Old Bailey after being convicted on Monday of murdering Melissa Halstead, 33, a former model from Ohio in the US, and Paula Fields, 31, a mother-of-three living in north London. The women's remains were found a decade apart, and detectives fear three other women known to Sweeney may also be victims.

Sweeney already serving a life sentence for the attempted murder of a third girlfriend whom he attacked with an axe and a knife, refused to leave his prison cell at Belmarsh prison to hear his sentence. Judge Mr Justice Saunders, sentencing him in his absence, said the gravity of the offences was exceptional and only a whole life term was appropriate. "These were terrible, wicked crimes. The heads of the victims having been removed, it is impossible to be certain how they were killed.

The mutilation of the bodies is a serious aggravating feature of the murders. "Not only does it reveal the cold-blooded nature of the killer, but it has added greatly to the distress of the families to know that parts of their loved ones have never been recovered." The remains of Halstead, whose head and hands were missing, were found in the Westersingel canal in Rotterdam after she vanished from her Amsterdam flat in 1990.

She was only identified in 2008 after Dutch detectives carried out a cold case review and matched familial DNA. A freelance photographer, she met Sweeney in London and embarked on a tempestuous relationship, with him following her to Europe when she was deported from the UK for overstaying her work visa. Fields, originally from Liverpool, a crack cocaine user leading a chaotic life in north London that involved working as a prostitute, met him in 2000. She vanished three months later and 10 body parts were found in six holdalls in the Regent's Canal near King's Cross in February 2001.

Her head, hands and feet were missing. Saunders said the killings had been planned. "The method of disposal of the bodies demonstrates that there was a substantial amount of planning. "Why the killings occurred, I cannot be sure, but I am satisfied that this defendant is controlling in his relationships with women and, chillingly, that control extends to deciding whether they should

live or die." The jobbing carpenter, who worked under assumed
names on construction sites around mainland Europe and southeast
England, had denied both murders. But the jury heard he had a
hatred of women and turned violent when they tried to reject him.
In 1994 he went on the run living under assumed aliases following
the attack in Camden on Delia Balmer, a nurse, with whom he had
a relationship.

He was finally arrested six years later at a central London
building site after the discovery of Fields's remains. Police then
realised there was a connection. The identification of Halstead
then allowed them to place crucial pieces in a gruesome jigsaw
they fear may not yet be complete. Clues to Sweeney's visceral
hatred of women were found in a hoard of more than 300 violent
and lurid paintings and poems found at his home, with one,
entitled the Scalp Hunter, depicting a female victim and a bloody
axe.

On the back of a scratch card he had written a poem: "Poor old
Melissa, chopped her up in bits, food to feed the fish, Am*dam
was the pits." They also found a calendar on the back of a minicab
receipt with 16 December 2000 circled and then "9 1/2 Weeks"
and the letter "P" written under it which within three days was the
period before Paula's body was discovered on 19 February 2001.

The jury heard that while on the run Sweeney had told his best
friend that he found Melissa in bed with two German men and had
killed them all. He also told his former wife, with whom he has
two children, that the police were looking for him and he had
"done something really bad which would make her hair stand on
end". At the MARAP the crime scene photos from the Regents
Park canal were shown and if you didn't know what they were you
could almost believe they were joints of meat in a butcher's
window.

Sweeney had dismembered the body at the ankle, knee, hip, wrist, elbow and shoulder. The bags might not have been discovered if it wasn't for two boys who saw a bag in the water which was unusually shallow at the time because the hot weather had caused the water level in the canal to recede.

Sweeney would revert to being difficult and obstructive because he had received a whole life sentence, so as he said what incentive was there for him to comply with anything we wanted him to do. There was nothing we could do to him, even if he was adjudicated for something and lost so many days canteen; it didn't matter to him as he had very little money to buy things with. The best thing we could do was get a sentence plan done and move him to a long term prison. The problem was he wouldn't comply with a sentence plan because he knew we couldn't make him comply. Myself and his offender manager did a very basic sentence plan and I informed him what was on it, he showed no interest and so I told him we would move as soon as possible, and he just said whatever.

The day to day work continued and I kept going with the problematic offenders, up to this point I had dealt with murderers, rapists, armed robbers, paedophiles, the next murderer would baffle me because I couldn't understand how a father could kill his own children.

A father who slit his son and daughter's throats to spite his estranged wife was today told he will die behind bars as he was jailed for at least 30 years. Jean Say, 62, murdered Regina, eight, and her brother Rolls, ten, while they were staying with him for the weekend.

He then phoned his wife Adjoua, 44, and told her: 'Come and get the bodies'. Say turned on his children after finding out he was to lose his three-bedroom flat because Mrs Say, who was also known as Antoinette, and the children had moved out. He also told a 999 operator his wife had accused him of being a 'raper' on Facebook, adding: 'She kill my dignity. I warn her.' Say who is originally from the Ivory Coast, was due to stand trial at the Old Bailey but admitted the murder of both children last week.

Today he was given a life sentence and told he will serve a minimum of 30 years before he can be considered for release. The judge, Mr Justice Cooke, told him: 'You decided to take revenge on your wife, whom you blamed for the misfortune you had brought about and you murdered two vulnerable children whom you and your wife had brought into the world.

Say knifed the children while they were 'defenceless' in the early hours of February 13, said Edward Brown QC prosecuting. 'Each of the children likely tried to fend off the attack upon them before they were each quickly overwhelmed and killed by him,' he said.

'The defendant's acts were as brutal as they were determined. 'The dreadful fact is that the defendant took a knife and cut the throat of each child as they lay where they had been sleeping. 'The killings came at the culmination of long-standing marital difficulties born from the violent, jealous and possessive behaviour of the defendant and from the consequences that the departure of his wife and children from the home was likely to have on his situation.' Police and ambulance crews raced to Say's flat in Southwark, south London, just after 8 am after he made a 999 call in which he confessed: 'I kill my children.' Moments earlier he had spoken to Mrs Say on the phone and told her: 'I have killed your children. I have called the police and am waiting for them. 'He rang her back immediately after the 999 call and told her simply: 'Come and get the bodies.' When detectives arrived they found the shaven-headed father sitting calmly beside the bodies of his two children. They had been dead for several hours.

A post-mortem found Regina had been stabbed three times and Rolls five. Rolls, who had been sleeping in the living room and was later dragged into the flat's bedroom, had also suffered serious head injuries.

As he was led away from the scene in handcuffs, Say gestured towards a pile of documents and told officers: 'This paper is evidence of why I did it.' Mr Brown said: 'Those documents, it transpired, related to the defendant's forthcoming eviction from the flat in which his children lay dead. 'His estranged wife and children had moved out of the property. As a result of his wife moving he was no longer entitled to the former family home, a three-bedroom flat. A letter from his solicitors - believed to have been received the day before his children's bodies were discovered - advised Say he had no grounds to stop his eviction from the Southern Housing property.

Mr Brown added: 'On three occasions, once not long before the events of February 13, he had told either his wife or others that he would one day do something dreadful and that would shock 'the whole world' and would get into the papers and onto the television. CCTV footage from the housing association block showed Say leaving shortly before 8 am with a plastic carrier bag, which detectives believe contained his bloodstained clothes.

They have never been recovered. Rolls' blood was also found on furniture in the living room, as well as on a kitchen knife and the killer's trainers. The couple had been estranged since November 2008 and Mrs Say was living in Holloway, north London, with the children at the time of the killing.

Mrs Say had previously been hospitalised by her husband, who had accused her of being a 'witch' and an adulterer and had reported him to the police. But she was unwilling to press charges, though she had taken out an injunction to stop him threatening her.

The court was also told he had been violent towards other women, punching a previous girlfriend in France so hard in the stomach that she lost her baby. She later had a daughter but fled from Say after being repeatedly beaten and raped, but he allegedly tracked her down and threatened his daughter at knifepoint. Say also kept secret two children he had with two separate women in France when he met Antoinette in 1997. Tim Moloney, defending, said Say did not accept the allegations about his previous conduct but admitted the murders had been 'horrific crimes'.

The murderers kept coming thick and fast, apart from the others I was dealing with. By the end of 2010, I had done 16 MARAP's, 29 Sentence Planning boards and 18 other various meetings.

That was 63 meetings in that year, more than one a week and I was only working three days a week. I can see why some of the other supervisors were not happy because this put pressure on them as they were working five days a week.

The MARAP's are only carried out on those who receive a Life sentence or IPP, which means they had committed murder, Manslaughter or serious sexual offences. The news was full of politicians saying violent crime had fallen, but this was lies any of us at work could see violent crime was going up. Admittedly this was not all gang-related but there was a good percentage of gang-related offenders coming into Belmarsh.

My next murder was a gang-related shooting in which an innocent girl buying fried chicken was killed. Two gangsters who murdered an innocent 16-year-old girl with a submachine gun in a drive-by shooting are both facing life sentences today. Leon Dunkley and Mohammed Smoured, both 22, shot Agnes Sina-Inakoju in the neck as they casually cycled past a chicken takeaway in Hoxton.

They were both senior figures in the notorious London Fields Boys gang, Detectives believe they carried out the shooting of Agnes Sina-Inakoju in revenge after a senior figure in the 'LF' was beaten up by rivals from Hoxton. Tragically Agnes just happened to be in the Hoxton Chicken and Pizza shop that the gang chose for their reprisal. She died two days later in hospital. A witness later told how Smoured joked: 'It was funny the way she dropped'.

Both Dunkley, the gunman, and Smoured, the lookout, were convicted of murder after a trial at the Old Bailey. Dwayne Wisdom, just 16 at the time of the murder, and a boy then aged 15 who cannot be named, were convicted of firearms charges relating to a stash of guns kept by the London Fields Boys. They included the murder weapon, an Agram 2000 9mm submachine gun used by Croatian special forces, and four other guns, including a Mac 10 submachine gun, stored under a nine-year-old boy's bed.

The Mac 10 is capable of firings 9mm rounds at a blistering 1100 rounds per minute. The Agram 2000 had been used in six previous incidents including an attempted murder in September 2009. The Mac 10 had been used four times since 2007 and had been discharged in Fellows Court, Hoxton, two days before the murder.

Members of the London Fields gang promoted their love of gangs, guns and violence on Facebook and their mobile phones. Dunkley, known by the street name as 'Bacon', was well known to police and had stood trial for a courthouse brawl a year earlier but was acquitted.

Smoured came to the UK from Algeria at the age of six and failed to get any qualifications or a job. In 2009 he was released from prison after serving a sentence for supplying class "A" drugs.

Smoured accepted he was a member of the gang and had posted pictures of himself making 'L' shapes on the social networking site. Both he and Wisdom, now 17, used the name 'Fields' in their Facebook profile names. The younger boy had also uploaded a picture of guns to the site and had a custom-made t-shirt with the letters 'LF' and 'E8' on the chest. The trial was based on the evidence of a 16-year-old former member of the London Fields gang who went to the police for help after being threatened to keep quiet. He told the jury that there had been a history of trouble between his gang and the Hoxton Boys. On April 11, 2010, a senior member of the gang had been beaten up in Crondall Street, Hoxton. Three days later on April 14, the 16-year-old witness overheard Dunkley and Smoured receiving a call on a mobile phone.

We know he has told the truth about that in the sense the police found [the gang member] had been beaten up at that time, just around the corner of the Chicken and Pizza shop. 'Given the gang warfare that had been ongoing, could a beating up be allowed to go without an immediate response?' Jurors heard Agnes lived with her family in Hoxton and was popular and successful at the local Haggerston School. At around 7.15 pm she and her friends went to the Hoxton Chicken and Pizza Shop in Hoxton Road to order a pizza. She was standing inside next to the window when Dunkley and Smoured rode past.

Prosecutor Simon Denison QC said: 'Two young men on bicycles wearing hoodies cycled up to that window. 'One of them calmly took out a gun, pointed it towards the window where Agnes and her friends were and fired.

'It was very quick. He didn't even stop his bicycle. He didn't pause to see who was in the shop or to aim at anyone in particular. 'The bullet hit Agnes in the neck and she collapsed immediately.' He added: 'It was as callous and cold-blooded as it could be, carried out in broad daylight in a busy street in Hoxton. Agnes Sina-Inakoju appears to have been the innocent victim of an ongoing rivalry between gangs in that part of London.

'The gun that was used to kill her was one of several guns that lay in the hands of a gang that were rivals of a gang in Hoxton.' Fortunately, one passer-by was later able to identify Dunkley as the gunman thanks to his acne-scarred face. The murder weapon was recovered a week later when a police officer spotted Wisdom, then aged 16, running away from him with a rucksack. In the chase, the bag was thrown over a wall into a garden. It contained both the 9mm sub-machine gun and a converted Umarex Walther P99 self-loading pistol with ammunition. His phone contained pictures of a London Field's street sign, the letters 'L' and 'F' made out of money, diamond-encrusted weapons and a chilling photograph of the 'LF' sign taken at a graveyard.

The prosecution key witness was arrested for drugs offences after police received a tip-off. He later told officers how Dunkley dropped off his jacket after the shooting. Tests revealed the presence of gunshot residue. His information also led to the recovery of weapons from the home of a 15-year-old member of the gang, under a bunk bed he shared with his nine-year-old brother.

They included a loaded Mac 10 sub-machine gun, a loaded shotgun with ammunition and a loaded .38 revolver. Dunkley, of Kenninghall Road, Hackney, and Smoured, of Hopwood Walk, Hackney, both denied murder and possession of a firearm with intent to endanger life and were convicted of both charges.

Wisdom, now 17, Graham Road, Hackney, was convicted of possession of a 9mm submachine gun with intent to endanger life, possession of a prohibited firearm, possession of an imitation firearm in a public place and assisting an offender by moving the firearm involved in the murder.

The 16-year-old boy, also from Hackney, was cleared of possession of a firearm with intent to endanger life, relating to the 9mmm sub-machine gun and three counts of possession of a prohibited firearm, the converted Mac 10, a BBM Olympic .38 revolver and a 9mm pistol, and possession of a shotgun without a certificate.

He was convicted of the possession of a prohibited weapon relating to the 9mm submachine gun. Whatever the reason the murders and other serious offences were committed, I had to adjust how I dealt with them.

Some like the black gang members were always arrogant and cocky and thought nothing could happen to them.

With these, I would try to get through to them that just because they put a gun in their hands they weren't hard men, and they didn't have the protection of other gang members in prison. I would also remind them that I could transfer them anywhere I wanted and prisoners in the northern prisons weren't impressed by little London plastic gangsters. Some would blame drink and or drugs for their offences and try to distance themselves from what they had done. These I would work on trying to get them to take responsibility for the offences, and that it was them who had committed the offence, not a bottle of booze or a bag of drugs. On rare occasions, some would just put their hands up and say they had no excuse, and on occasion show genuine remorse.

Some would wallow in self-pity and become whinging bastards, others would accept they had a sentence to do and use the time constructively, attending education or learning a trade to try and better themselves for when they were finally released.

An example of the "it was because I was on drink and drugs was a prisoner called Langland.

A Winchmore Hill pensioner's family has been torn apart after she was stabbed to death by her grandson. Doris Langland's was murdered by 27-year-old Jack Langland's as she stood preparing food in the kitchen of her home in Green Dragon Lane. Langland's attacked the 83-year-old in a booze and drugs-fuelled rage after years of alcohol and cocaine abuse, and was today convicted of murder. Mrs Langland's' son Jeffrey, in a statement at the Old Bailey, told of the devastating impact of the murder, on Easter Saturday last year, on his family, placing blame not just on the killer but on Langlands' parents Malcolm and Irene for not helping their son tackle his problems. He said: "The family is in deep shock with the way she died, and no one except Jack's direct family knew what was happening.

Doris Langlands accepted her grandson into her home in November 2009, but the court heard evidence that Langlands was verbally abusing his grandmother and that he had been carted off by police in January last year after ripping her phone off the wall. Langlands would regularly sink ten pints of lager a day and snort up to two grams of cocaine, and sponged around £30,000 off his grandmother over nine years to feed that habit. On the night of the murder, he carried out a "brutal and frenzied attack" that meant Mrs Langlands' family could not see her body one last time because of the horrendous injuries she had sustained.

Jeffrey Langlands said: "You have to question what makes a man do a thing like that to his own grandmother. He accused Jack's parents of putting Mrs Langlands in danger, and added: "We will never forgive Jack for what he has done, or the fact Malcolm and Irene knew what he was like and did nothing about it." Judge Paul Worsley, sentencing, said to Langlands:

"Your grandmother was a generous and loving lady, and you sponged off her. "When you needed it, she provided a roof over your head, when you wanted it, she gave you money. Over nine years before her death, you sponged off her some £30,000 to feed your alcohol and cocaine addiction."

The judge was satisfied Langlands was taking drugs and drinking large amounts of alcohol around the time of the murder and said: "The ferocity of the attack on her was considerable." Judge Worsley said Langlands was suffering from paranoid psychosis at the time of the killing, but added he has since shown no remorse for what he did.

He said: "I hope that a time may come when members of the family may be able to come together and share the grief which they undoubtedly feel." Langlands was unanimously found guilty of murder by a jury and was ordered to serve a minimum of 22 years behind bars.

Psychiatric experts told the court Langlands is at "high risk" of lapsing into alcohol and drug abuse in the future and warned his mental health would need to be closely monitored for the protection of others.

2011 finished off with yet another murderer who had previously killed another man but had only been given an 8-year sentence for Manslaughter; there would be uproar if the public knew how many killers receive such low sentences.

Pensioner Michael Zubrot, 67, was found stabbed to death at his home on September 9, 2010. Police went to his house in Buckingham Avenue, Perivale, west London after concerns were raised about his welfare.

Mr Zubrot, a retired classical music retailer, had bled to death from multiple knife wounds to his neck.

The police investigation revealed that the victim had last been seen on August 30. That day he was captured on CCTV in Ealing Town Centre before taking a 297 to Perivale with 37-year-old Mohammed Khaleel. Khaleel, of Ealing west London, was charged with murder and went on trial at the Old Bailey on November 21, 2011. The court heard Khaleel was already a convicted killer and had been sentenced to eight years in 2003 for the manslaughter of 35-year-old David Sheehan in Hanwell, west London.

He was released in April 2010 and was living in a probation hostel when he met Mr Zubrot. On December 19, 2011, Khaleel was convicted of murder and jailed for life with a minimum of 33 years before parole. The sentence was reduced to 28 years by the Court of Appeal in October 2012.

As we entered 2012 we were as busy as ever, a slight break from this came on the 11th of January when there was a full staff meeting in the chapel. This turned into a presentation for staff who had served 25 years and we would receive our long service and good conduct medal. This was the last of the three medals I was entitled to, the Queens Golden Jubilee, Queens Diamond Jubilee and the long service medals.

Officers especially from the northern prisons had been fighting for years to have a long service medal cast, as the other emergency services were awarded one for long service but the prison service only gave out tie pins if they were requested. This was just another example of the prison service being the forgotten service; we were always the ones nobody spoke about in government or the media unless it was to highlight any failings we may have had. To finally get a long service medal was a big deal, but even now there is no pomp or ceremony attached to it and a lot of staff receive it through the post or are given it by a member of a prisons admin staff.

Brief respite and show of respect over, on the 25th January I had another gang-related MARAP. Two men have been jailed for 28 years each after murdering the wrong man in a roadside execution. Michael Ofori was shot shortly after midnight on June 23 last year in Oslac Road, Catford, as he sat in the driver's seat of his car talking to his estranged wife. As they chatted, a man approached the car on foot and fired three times, Michael was shot once in the head and once in the arm. The gunman left the scene in a white van which was driven by Nicholas Allon-McVytie, aged 23, of Vanguard Street, Deptford, who had earlier purchased it using a false name.

Today Allon-McVytie and Sahid Sule, aged 23, of no fixed address, who coordinated the operation via his phone, were both sentenced to life imprisonment and ordered to serve a minimum of 28 years. During their Old Bailey trial, jurors heard the intended victim of the shooting was in fact another person, who had been lured to the area that night. The court was told of a rivalry between the defendants and their intended target which led to several shooting incidents in Sydenham and Brockley.

Following Mr Ofori's murder, detectives from Trident trawled through hours of CCTV and analysed huge amounts of telephone data, allowing them to piece together the movements of the defendants.

Detective Inspector Andy Muir of Trident said: "These men lived their lives according to their criminal activities which regularly led them to be involved in violent disputes with other criminals.

"Their activities blighted local communities and on this occasion led them to the decision to plan and commit murder. "Tragically, they murdered Michael Ofori who was not their associate and was in the wrong place at the wrong time. "Michael's friends and family have been left devastated by his death and his young daughter has been left without her father.

A jury was unable to reach a verdict on Nathaniel Valton, aged 23, of Adolphus Street, Deptford, who was accused of being the gunman. The jury could also not reach a verdict on 25-year-old Jules Brown of Newham, who was also accused of murder.

In April I had yet another MARAP for an "it was because of the drink and drugs" murderer.

Life for a man who bludgeoned Gipsy Hill woman to death 13 February 2012, a man has been jailed for life for killing a woman whose body lay undiscovered in her flat for three weeks after he beat her to death. Stephen Foad, 42, had denied murdering Siobhan Kelly, 39, but changed his plea three days after his trial started. Foad, of Foxhill Lane, Gipsy Hill, south London, was given a minimum term of 13 years. Miss Kelly may have taken up to 15 hours to die, the Old Bailey jury heard.

Prosecutor Duncan Atkinson said Miss Kelly was the victim of a "sustained and savage" attack after being bludgeoned on the head, punched and stamped on. Police forced their way into her flat in Tudor Road, Gipsy Hill, on 7 February last year. They found her decomposing body wrapped in a duvet on the bed and blood spatter marks in the bedroom and living room.

Mr Atkinson said she had been attacked at different times in both rooms. There was evidence that she had been struck with a red candle in the living room, which may have knocked her unconscious for a while. She had later crawled into the bedroom where she was attacked again. A bedside lamp was thought to have been used to strike her several times.

Miss Kelly also had fractured ribs and boot marks on her clothing. She was last seen alive on 15 January when Foad, with whom she had a causal relationship, was the last person to see her alive. Palm prints in blood in both rooms matched heavy drinker Foad, as did the bloody boot prints. Mr Atkinson said: "It was this defendant who unleashed a sustained and savage attack on Siobhan Kelly. "Miss Kelly had been beaten to death; there were several heavy blows to her head and blows to her body and arms."

During the MARAP the severity of the attack was revealed and listening to the evidence you would not put the crime and the offender together. Foad is about five feet and a fag paper, and 7 stone dripping wet. Although I don't subscribe to the "it was because of the drink or drugs" brigade, this case did show just how violent even the smallest of people can be when they lose control for whatever reason. To be fair to Foad he did show what I think was genuine remorse, and he accepted his role in the murder.

He was on the VP (vulnerable prisoner) spur not because he was a sex offender but because he was inadequate and had been bullied on other spurs and house blocks.

He was very meek and mild and would always say yes sir no sir which would normally wind me up, but I think he was just trying to be respectful because of the assistance I was giving him with getting on courses and ultimately a transfer to where he could progress and learn a trade.

Most of my cases on the VP spur were either paedophiles, most of which were concerned with graphic images of children, some had thousands of images of children being abused; these were graded by the police from 1-5 level 5 being the most graphic. A lot of my other VP's were historic paedophiles; this was where children who had now grown up had made allegations against a person from their childhood. These people were usually family members father, brother "etc" or uncles or friends of the family. The victims were usually girls but sometimes they were boys, usually the wives and partners of these offenders would say they had no idea the abuse had been going on, but every now and again wives or partners would also be charged as they were either aware or actually participated in the abuse.

It was rare for me to get someone who had just been convicted of rape but I picked up a case in May 2012. The offender was a young Muslim who believed he was teaching the women a lesson, as he had no respect for women who went out at night or did not follow the Muslim way.

News item: A man who raped women to "teach them a lesson" for being out at night was jailed indefinitely yesterday.

After Islam's arrest, his DNA was linked with three other attacks near his home in Barking Sunny Islam, 23, dragged his victims, including a 15-year-old, at knifepoint, then bound and assaulted them. Police fear that Islam, who raped four women over three months in east London, may have attacked many more.

At Woolwich Crown Court, Judge Patricia Lees sentenced Islam to a minimum sentence of 11 years before he is considered for parole. She told him: "The nature and extent of these offences drive me to the conclusion that you represent an extreme and continuing danger to women, particularly those out at night." Islam was traced through the number plate of his girlfriend's car after he kidnapped and raped the 15-year-old in September 2010.

He grabbed her from behind as she walked home with a friend, and then drove her to a secluded spot where he raped her twice.

In a victim impact statement read to the court, the teenager said: "No one will ever understand the flashbacks, they are so real, at night I lay in my bed and it is like I am there. "It is like a screen in my mind forcing me to relive that night again and again.

People will say time will heal, but I think the time has helped me accept the truth — that I will never escape what happened." Judge Lees said: "You told her you were going to 'teach her a lesson'.

Those words are a chilling indictment of your very troubling attitude towards all of these victims. You seem to observe women out at night as not deserving respect or protection." After Islam's arrest, his DNA was linked with three other attacks near his home in Barking, said Sara Lawson, prosecuting.

On July 8, 2010, Islam raped a 20-year-old prostitute twice, then six days later attacked a 28-year-old, dragging her into his car where he forced her to perform a sex act. She managed to escape by kicking out the back window. The fourth victim, a 30-year-old, who was also attacked in September, did not come forward until police identified her blood in the back of the car. Islam, who told the jury he was a practising Muslim, was convicted of seven charges of rape, one of sexual assault and one of kidnap.

Islam received an IPP sentence and unless his attitude changes completely he will struggle to be released at his parole point. He has a distorted attitude when it comes to women, especially western women, which can only be due to his Islamic roots and their thoughts about how women should be treated.

Around May time the deputy governor of Belmarsh came up with a plan to deal with an excess of S.O's in the prison. She decided that she would move all of us offender supervisors out of OMU back onto the house blocks and replace us with the excess S.O's. Obviously, we were not happy, we had been doing the job for nearly six years and had all our contacts and processes. None of the S.O's knew how to do our job and the department would have gone to rat shit.

Part of the OMU model was for a seamless end to end process with continuity for the offenders in scope and the probation and other agencies concerned. This would have been lost and a very good department would have been ruined, luckily none of the S.O's wanted to do the job so they never applied. This shot the Dep in the foot and so my belief is out of retaliation we all had to apply for our own jobs within OMU. I had words with our governor and told him this was bollocks for all of us, but for me, I was the only original OMU team member left and I told him it was farcical that I started the group and now I have to apply for my job.

This didn't go down too well but he said that's how it was. To add insult to injury we would have to submit a CV and do core competencies. I had until that point never had to do a CV and didn't have a clue, I took some advice and set about producing my first ever CV.

I had several goes before settling on one I would put forward with my job application, I was not confident but I had no option if I wanted to stay in OMU. Once we had submitted the CV and core competencies we would then have to be interviewed for the job, none of us were happy as this was a complete load of bollocks.

With this done they then told us we would have to complete a pass or fail Offender Supervisors course at Newbold Revel. So on 24th June four of us went on the course. As with all courses at Newbold, we treated it as a piss up as we would be in the bar every night after class. There were staff there from other prisons but the thing that stood out was they didn't have a clue about Offender Management. What was even worse was that we were asking questions of the tutor and he couldn't give us an answer, we ended up telling him how different things should happen.

The course for us was a waste of time and we ended up giving the other course members more answers than the tutor. We returned and almost as soon as we did our Pratt of a governor told us to enlist on a diploma course, as the service was changing the rank structure and we would be Band 4's instead of S.O's.

Straight away I had to put him right and told him I wouldn't do the diploma as all I wanted was to be a band 4 Specialist, not a band 4 supervisor where I would be used to run house blocks and other areas, apart from which I was part-time so there was no point. This went down like a sack of shit, but there wasn't a lot he could do or so I thought.

I carried on with my caseload but the governor started messing around with who had which case admin, this mattered a lot to me as I worked three days a week I needed a good case admin I could rely on to book meetings and contact agencies when I wasn't there. It was okay to start with but as time went on the admin staff would be moved around and I ended up with some less than satisfactory ones.

The result of this meant instead of me dealing with my caseload I would have to start doing more and more of the admin work booking meetings and the like. This took its toll as I was still running a full caseload like the full-timers, so now I couldn't just concentrate on the offenders I had to lose time doing admin work. Add to this the cross deployments and it was getting really difficult to keep up with my caseload.

I began to feel that the admin moves were aimed at making my life difficult, this idea was supported when we were all told that we would be changing desks and admin again. I had to go out and see some of my caseload but the CM (custodial Manager, a new name for a P.O) told me that nothing had been finalised yet and wouldn't be until the afternoon when we would all be told together. I said to him whatever you do, don't put me with an admin I have previously described as a weeble, as I disliked her with a vengeance and she hated me. I went to see my prisoners and as soon as I walked through the door the weeble came waddling up to me saying, "guess who your new admin is" this was still in the morning and no one was supposed to know who was going where until the afternoon.

I spoke with the CM and told him to expect her to come to him in floods of tears very soon saying I had been horrible to her. A bit later she came up to me and said "I know I can be a bit loud at times, but if I annoy you just tell me" I told her not to worry because if she annoyed me I would tell her to shut the fuck up.

This must have had the desired effect because that afternoon I didn't move and I didn't get the weeble I got another admin, she was a nice enough woman but she worked part-time and she worked the days opposite to me.

This was no good for me as I would have to carry on doing my own admin work. After speaking again with the CM and our governor nothing changed which just confirmed my suspicions, I had upset the admins boss and our governor because they didn't like being told the truth and shown they had no idea about what OMU did. This just made me more determined to show I could manage a full caseload, so I carried on.

In September I was allocated a lifer who had transferred to us for some unknown reason, he had been convicted of murder in 2007 at Winchester Crown Court. We were not a long term prison and so I couldn't understand why he came to us.

Miss Colpus was violently stabbed in the stomach by 22-year-old Kieron Simei, who can be seen standing outside the door, wearing the black-and-white jacket he later discarded in panic. During the five-day murder trial, jurors were shown a DVD of the footage depicting Miss Colpus' last moments. Simei, who appeared in the dock and the witness box smartly dressed and cleanly shaven, bowed his head while it was played to the court. Home Office pathologist Dr Hugh White said that Miss Colpus' life may have been saved if she had received urgent medical assistance.

But in his evidence, Simei said he had seen an ambulance when he ran off and presumed it was for Miss Colpus it wasn't. Dr White said: "She would have bled heavily after the stab wound, then felt unwell, collapsed and become unconscious, and subsequently would have died." The pathologist added it was "impossible" to estimate how long it would have taken for Miss Colpus to die. "People sometimes survive for a surprisingly long time," he said. CCTV images show that Miss Colpus opened the door to Simei at 11.51 pm on June 3. Prosecutor Stuart Jones QC told the jury: "Jolene opens the main door to the flats. Two figures appear to close together. There is no time for any meaningful conversation.

"Kieron Simei swiftly stabs her; you can see that from her movement backwards. She bends forwards, clutching herself she staggers back, turns and runs making for her flat where sometime afterwards, she dies from the wound." Simei told the court he tried to telephone Miss Colpus a couple of days later to see if she was all right but got no response. The court heard that he was arrested on drugs charges at Basingstoke police station only three days after stabbing Miss Colpus. Her body had not yet been discovered and no one knew of her death. At the time, Basingstoke magistrates were told he had wraps of heroin hidden in his body.

The case was adjourned and he was remanded in custody. After an extensive investigation, Simei was arrested on suspicion of murder, while he was in Winchester Prison, and interviewed at Alton police station.

He then made his chilling confession to stabbing the 19-year-old but maintained that he did not mean for her to die. A 17-year-old youth from Basingstoke and a 16-year-old from London were also arrested but were released on bail and police took no further action.

Speaking after the guilty verdict, Detective Superintendent Andy Stewart, who led the investigation, said: "This was a very tragic incident where a 19-year-old girl was stabbed to death in her own home. "There is absolutely no excuse for the vicious and violent attack that was carried out on this defenceless young girl."

Det Supt Stewart branded Simei an "exceptionally dangerous man" and thanked the members of the public who dared to come forward and assist the police in their prosecution.

The officer also praised those involved in the investigation for their "high standard of work" which led to Simei's conviction. He added: "I would like to send my condolences to the family and friends of Jolene who have been extremely brave throughout the investigation.

Simei was a bit of a wide boy and thought he was a player, he was always into something but I ended up getting on okay with him because I didn't take any notice of the crap he would come out with. I would tell him he needed to wind his neck in and instead of playing the gangster, he needed to start thinking about his future because he would still be relatively young when he was due parole.

He had anger issues and I got him on the CALM course (controlling anger and learning to manage it) and he did quite well. I also told him if he wanted a move to another prison where he could progress he needed to show he was worth it.

In October I was notified I would have to attend the McFadden inquest, the prisoner who had died an hour after I interviewed him. This would take place at Southwark Coroners Court, so once again I was in the witness box giving evidence to an inquest. This time though I wasn't accused of murder, although the piss-taking from people at work was the same. I was there for a couple of days before the coroner said I was no longer needed.

To finish the year I had a MARAP for yet another murderer, this time it would be evidence from a Sat Nav that would help to convict him.

A man who kidnapped and murdered his ex-wife and buried her body in Poland has been jailed for life. Vitalija Baliutaviciene, 29, had come to Peterborough only to escape the "obsessed" and "jealous" Rimas Venclovas, the Old Bailey heard. Lithuanian migrant worker Venclovas, 47, abducted her in August 2011. Her body was found in a shallow grave two months later.

He had denied kidnap and murder and will serve a minimum of 20 years, Miss Baliutaviciene was last seen on CCTV being abducted on her way to work in Peterborough, at 05:15 BST on 12 August last year. At about 11:50 BST, Venclovas's van was caught on CCTV boarding a ferry at Dover. Lithuania-born Miss Baliutaviciene's naked body was found in a field in western Poland on 30 October last year, but it took a further four months for it to be formally identified. The court heard Venclovas had twice been arrested by police in Peterborough for attacking her. However, after being granted bail he absconded to his native Lithuania each time, before returning to the city. During the trial, he said he and Miss Baliutaviciene had been "getting on well" at the time he kidnapped and murdered her.

As he passed the sentence, Mr Justice Fulford said: "This was a coldly and carefully executed murder. "The judge said he had no doubt Venclovas did not kill Miss Baliutaviciene immediately but tortured her by holding her throat and "keeping her between life and death". Miss Baliutaviciene's mother, Vanda Cerneckaite, 64, and her brother, Audrius Sreberis, 30, said in a statement: "For six months after she disappeared we had to live with the anguish of not knowing what had happened to her".

Our lives stopped the day she disappeared and they will never be the same again. "Rimas is an evil man who went to great lengths to kidnap and kill our beloved Vitalija.

Her son clung to the glimmer of hope that she was still alive and would come back to him. "Rimas had the power to end that pain and uncertainty and allow his own son to start to grieve.

"He selfishly chose not to do this, however, and has continued to prolong that suffering through his lies and denial as he sought to save his own skin. "There can be no justification for the level of violence he used against such a kind and gentle woman who posed no threat to him." Venclovas never showed any remorse and tried to play the system by pretending he spoke very little English and pretending he couldn't understand what I was saying to him.

My way around this was to ask our Ukrainian offender supervisor to come with me and speak to him, and whenever we had an Eastern European prisoner we would use him as most of the Eastern European languages are similar. Venclovas was not interested in engaging at all, he would spend most of his time in the gym and didn't appear to be bothered about being in prison.

2013 started pretty much as 2012 finished caseloads were as high as ever, I was still doing the majority of my own admin and all bar a couple, the admins were as manipulating and whinging as ever. One of the new admins had become close with the weeble and this was not a good thing, I had tried to help her explaining what went on with OMU and giving her a 'How to' guide for case admins. She ignored this and was part of the weeble's clique, one day she and the weeble were giving one of the new supervisor's grief because they thought it was funny.

I said something and the new girl said I couldn't do her job as I wasn't intelligent enough, I told her I wouldn't do her job because only monkeys get paid peanuts and I was paid over twice what she earned. She didn't appreciate this and never spoke to me for a few days which was fine with me.

Over the next couple of months, I had a relatively quiet time as far as meetings went, but I was jobbed quite a bit and covered a few parole boards.

Things returned to normal and I attended several course reviews for different offenders on my caseload. In June I would have to go to HMP Holloway for a MARAP on one of my offenders as his co-defendant was in Holloway.

The day would turn out to be a nightmare; I set off for the station as I was meeting another offender supervisor at Victoria station as he had another of the co-defendants on his caseload. We were also meeting a case admin who had never done a MARAP and asked if she could come along and take the notes for us. We were taken into the prison and the MARAP started, I have to say I don't think it was as professional or friendly as MARAP's at Belmarsh. Psychopathic monster James Danby was desperate to satisfy his urge to carry out a gruesome killing. He found his excuse when a teenage girl falsely accused his slightly built neighbour Luke Harwood of rape. Danby, 27, seized on the bogus claim and used it to justify inflicting extraordinary brutality. He beat and kicked Luke, 18, before taking him to a field where he and Tony O'Toole jumped on his head until it popped like a marshmallow.

Danby then dumped the body in a stream and spent the following day bragging about how the young father's brains had spurted all over his jeans.

He even boasted the killing had promoted him to the 'A-Team' of crime and planned to slice off Luke's fingers and pull out his teeth to prevent his body from being identified.

But he was arrested on the journey to the body with a pair of pliers and three kitchen knives after Luke's housemate, babyfaced Emma Hall called the police. She had egged the others on as they set about their victim but decided she could stand the violence no longer.

Police believe Danby, who had never had a job and had racked up a string of low-level convictions, was looking for any excuse to kill. One officer said: 'There is only one word you can use to describe James Danby – psychopath.' Luke, who was 5ft 7ins tall and weighed just seven stone, was one of a family of six children and had a son who was eight months old when his father died. He had been living with his girlfriend and son but asked to be re-housed by the council when they began quarrelling. On the night he died he moved to the room at the council bungalow in Crow Lane, Romford, Essex, where Danby and the others lived. The house had been divided into seven bedsit rooms with five on the ground floor and two more in the loft.

Behind the house were two more buildings not controlled by the council. By chance, an 18-year-old girl visiting the house that evening saw Luke and claimed he had bestially raped her two years before.

Her complaint had been dropped after she was interviewed by police, who found her accusation were untrue. But when the girl repeated her claims, Hall vowed: 'I'm going to fucking kill him.' Luke was so skinny that he wore jogging bottoms under his jeans, and on the day he died was wearing pyjamas as well. Danby took a photograph on his mobile and showed it to the girl to confirm it was the man she claimed had raped her before he launched his ferocious two-hour assault.

Luke was repeatedly punched in the face in his bedroom as well as in a shower room, spraying blood over the walls and floor. The girl told the court: 'His nose was bent and there was blood everywhere. It was awful. He was so badly beaten that Hall said he looked like 'The Elephant Man' as he was bundled into her blue Fiat Punto. Luke was repeatedly elbowed in the face by sadistic Danby on a journey to playing fields in Broad mead Road, Woodford Green. Hall was driving and O'Toole was also in the car as Danby held a knife to the teenager's neck and said he was going to 'slit his throat.' Luke was 'finished off' on the bank of the stream with repeated stamps and kicks.

'His murder was quite extraordinarily callous and violent and brutal,' said prosecutor Simon Denison. 'His facial skeleton was crushed. 'They then concealed his body by covering it with a mattress and other items.

According to O'Toole, Danby suddenly tried to strangle Luke by putting him in a 'sleeper hold' before repeatedly stamping on his head. O'Toole said he was so shocked by the attack he vomited near a fence. 'It's something a monster would do,' he said. When Danby returned to the car he had blood spattered all over his jeans, top and hands and confessed to Hall: 'I killed him, treacle.' Hall told jurors: 'He said he stamped on Luke's head 20 times until it popped, 'He said it went like a marshmallow and brains spurted everywhere and that he had pumpkin on his jeans.'

They went back to Crow Lane and Hall then drove Danby, O'Toole and another housemate, Billy Duggan, to Hou Hatch in South Weald, Essex where Luke's belongings and Danby's clothes were doused with petrol and burnt.

The following day when Hall announced she had killed a spider with her shoe, Danby replied: 'Oi, you fucking murderer, you're just like me.' And when O'Toole complained he had hurt his foot playing football, Danby said: 'My fucking foot is hurt after stamping on that cunt's head.' Danby then insisted on Hall, O'Toole and Duggan going back to see the body.

At the scene, Danby pointed out a large patch of blood and laughed: 'that's where I stamped on that cunt's head.' Danby rolled the body into the stream and put the mattress on top of it.

Back at the house the group mopped and scoured Luke's bloodstains from the house as attempts were made to 'remove all trace of him.' But Hall tipped off the police on the evening of May 28 after Danby announced he was going to return to the body for a second time to remove the hands and teeth. 'He was laughing and joking about cutting Luke's head off,' Duggan recalled. Hall said she had been so sickened by the violence and Danby's horrific boasts she had to shop him, 'I just thought "I have got to do it,' she said.

Hall called police from a phone box and said she wanted to 'report a dead body.' She gave the location of the stream and said she would be there in twenty minutes. Officers lay in wait at the scene and arrested the group as they returned with the knives and a pair of wire cutters. The killers tried to blame each other, with O'Toole claiming Danby was a 'monster' who had destroyed all their lives. But he, Danby and Hall were all convicted of murder. The horrific death so incensed friends and family that a team of police officers from the Territorial Support Group was brought into the Old Bailey to keep them apart from supporters of the killers during the three-month trial.

Danby refused to leave his cell for the sentencing hearing, where he was jailed for life with a minimum term of 25 years.

Judge Paul Worsley said: 'James Danby is a controlling, manipulative and dangerous individual who manipulated others in the dock to support him in these dreadful events. 'He has shown no sign of remorse but only contempt for these proceedings.'

Hall received a life sentence with a 15-year minimum term, while O'Toole was jailed for at least 17 years. Duggan, 21, who was convicted of perverting the course of justice for helping with the clean-up operation, was handed a suspended sentence. Danby was a thing and found the whole situation amusing, he would do very little to engage with the process of managing his sentence and so I transferred him as soon as I could after carrying out all I needed to do.

The cross deployments continued for all of us and on the 13th August I was cross deployed to the HSU (High Secure Unit) seg to help give the Lee Rigby killers their applications for showers, exercise "etc". There were four of us there as they had previously been non-compliant and not long before fought with other staff. The result of this was one of the prisoners losing two teeth and five members of staff being suspended because the prisoners had made allegations of being beaten up.

They were less than co-operative and had real attitudes, Even though there was a nurse there to dress their wounds, they were still obstructive and had to be told several times what to do. One of them had lost part of his thumb when he was shot by police and if I remember they both had wounds to their bodies which had to be dressed.

2013 was the year I would be allocated two brothers who were part of a large gang from Oxford, who groomed and sexually assaulted young girls as well as selling their services to other men from different areas. The seven men, including two sets of brothers, had been found guilty of a catalogue of offences including rape, trafficking and organising prostitution. Sentencing the men at the Old Bailey Judge Peter Rook said: "These were sexual crimes of the utmost gravity. The depravity was extreme; each victim was groomed, coerced and intimidated." Judge Rook jailed brothers Akhtar Dogar, 32, and Anjum Dogar, 31, for a minimum of 17 years telling them they had been found guilty of "exceptionally grave crimes".

Mohammed Karrar, 38, of Kames Close, Oxford, will serve at least 20 years after being convicted of 18 offences including child rape and trafficking. Bassam Karrar, 34, of Hundred Acres Close, Oxford, will serve at least 15 years. Co-defendant Kamar Jamil, 27, was jailed for life with a minimum term of 12 years. Assad Hussain, 32, of Ashurst Way, Oxford, and Zeeshan Ahmed, 28, of Palmer Road, were both jailed for seven years after they were found guilty of two counts of sexual activity with a child.

Among their victims were girls as young as 11, several of whom were in the care of social services. One victim was even returned to the gang by the manager of the care home where she lived after she returned by cab one evening without money to pay the fare. He was subsequently sacked and the home, in Henley-on-Thames, closed. But both Oxfordshire social services and Thames Valley police were criticised for failing to act sooner to help the girls, despite their plight being brought to their attention on more than one occasion.

Judge Rook said each of the six victims had shown "enormous courage" in giving evidence during the trial. He said they had come "knowing that they would be accused of lying, knowing they would have to relive their ordeals, knowing that they have not been believed in the past".

They groomed them into believing they were in love and then exploited them, injecting them with heroin and forcing them into prostitution. One girl was even branded one of them with an electronic cigarette lighter. Most of the six girls who were abused were too scared to face their abusers in court and gave their evidence from behind a curtain. But one, who was repeatedly raped and sold for sex between 2004, when she was just 12, and 2007, faced down her attackers and told the court: "I am here to tell my story and see the people who abused me found guilty." One of the most harrowing accounts during the five-month trial came from a girl who was groomed from the age of 11. At the age of 12, she was forced to have an illegal abortion on the living room floor of a house in Reading.

Another girl told how she was told she would be shot if she did not have sex with one of the men when she was 14 and how she rang the police after being taken to a flat and realising she was with 11 men who wanted to have sex with her. Yet another victim told how she was plied with drugs and forced to have sex with strangers while being filmed at the age of 13.

One of the girls, who had reported her treatment to the police on several occasions, told the jury at the trial: "Any self-respecting police officer would have seen something was wrong. "If you pick up a child who is covered in cigarette burns and bruises, something is fundamentally wrong. Adults should be doing their jobs; it's not down to a child."

Up until I was allocated this case I had found it relatively easy to put what I had seen and heard throughout my service in little boxes in my mind and close the lid. This case would challenge my ability to do this because of the level of abuse to these girls. Without going into too much detail these young girls suffered multiple rapes and sexual assaults, they had cigarettes stubbed out on them, one was branded with a lighter, one was raped with the handle of a baseball bat and just about all of them were rented out to other men from different parts of the country.

Although I did manage to store away the information supplied in the MARAP it was one of the hardest cases I have ever had on OMU, especially as the offender's attitude was that they had done nothing wrong and they were so arrogant. The year ended the way many before had ended with me working Christmas day, this was spent on house block two and I was bored shitless.

2014 started with a MARAP for another murderer Rakesh Bhyani. He was known as the "mad Indian gambler" who rolled the dice and invariably lost. With mounting debts and dozens of failed scams behind him, conman Rakesh Bhayani murdered a lonely escort to secure her assets in a desperate attempt to pay off his gambling losses and save his crumbling marriage. Bhayani, 41, plunged a knife into the neck of his former lover Carole Waugh, 49, in her £600,000 central London flat in April last year, and planned to sell her home, empty her bank accounts and steal her shares, an Old Bailey jury heard on Wednesday.

Ms Waugh's body was stuffed into a holdall, dumped in the boot of a car and left in a south London lock-up after Bhayani recruited Nicholas Kutner, 48, a career conman, to join his plot. While Ms Waugh's family appealed for help to find the former accounts executive, the men recruited women to pretend to be Ms Waugh and siphoned money from her accounts and cards. Her body was finally found three and a half months later – but by then the two men had already been arrested for fraud. After a life of using charm to ensnare their victims, the pair of conmen turned on each other. In a final desperate gamble, Bhayani and Kutner accused each other of killing Ms Waugh.

But Bhayani faced life in prison on Wednesday night after a jury found him guilty of the murder. Kutner, a swindler who specialised in stealing jewellery and fine wine, was cleared of murder but found guilty of perverting the course of justice over the disposal of Ms Waugh's body. He had earlier admitted fraud.

The scam was just the latest in a long list for the two men, who between them have racked up 27 court appearances and nearly 200 offences. Bhayani, who has a young daughter, groomed Ms Waugh after making contact online; she had been operating under the name "poshtottyfun" and using the name Sarah. She had returned to live in London from Libya where she had worked for an oil company but lived on the proceeds of her sex work. They embarked on an affair and the conman was so successful at making her believe he was "one of the good guys" that she lent him large sums and supported him even when he was sent to prison. When Ms Waugh demanded her loans back and threatened to expose his double life to his family, his crimes tipped into murderous action. In the last of a series of stories to explain his role in her death, Bhayani claimed that Kutner was alone in Ms Waugh's flat when she was killed.

Meanwhile, Kutner claimed that an unnamed "Prisoner X" had witnessed Bhayani re-enacting the killing of Ms Waugh while he was held at Wandsworth jail.

Bhayani had a long history of scams dating back 20 years and claimed that he started gambling from the age of eight, using slot machines at fairgrounds. He was forced to quit his job at a firm of accountants when he was caught fiddling his expenses. Twice he mortgaged his parents' home and spent the proceeds on gambling.

In the grip of a hopeless obsession, he bought a petrol station and started gambling the proceeds until he had no petrol to sell and "the game was up", he told the court. It can also be revealed today that police and prosecutors are set to review evidence raised in the case after Bhayani claimed that two Barclays Bank employees colluded in a plan to trick Ms Waugh into believing that he was repaying tens of thousands of pounds that he borrowed from her.

Bhayani claimed at his trial that two men at the bank's Kingsland branch in east London were involved in a complicated money-swapping and fake documents scam. Detective Chief Inspector Justin Davies, of Scotland Yard, said: "Carole Waugh's murder was the senseless killing of a woman who put her trust in people she thought were her friends. Both men are compulsive liars who have deceived and defrauded their own families, friends and acquaintances throughout their entire adult lives; they went to extreme lengths to defraud Carole".

It never fails to amaze me that most people think of murderers as hard thuggish looking people who have a history of violent crime. The reality is that quite a few of them are weedy insignificant-looking people that eventually turn to murder.

Bhayani was one of these, he was an insignificant weed to look at, but he was also a perpetual manipulator who used his meek appearance to his advantage. Even when convicted he blamed his co-defendant for the murder, to play the victim.

In March I would have yet another murderer to hold a MARAP on this time it was another domestic murder that came about because two young female cousins argued. Liam Hamilton, 32, was stabbed to death in Poplar, east London, on 26 July 2013. Police were called to the junction of Simpsons Road and Poplar High Street at around 10.10 pm. Mr Hamilton, a painter and decorator from Walthamstow, died in hospital at 11.41 pm. A post-mortem gave the cause of death as a stab wound to the chest. Detectives launched a murder investigation and arrested four men on suspicion of murder. On 29 July police charged three of Liam's cousins with murder: Noel Hamilton, 35, of Manchester Road, Poplar, Thomas Hamilton, 36 of Poplar High Street, Poplar, and Paul Hamilton, 29, of Woodstock Terrace, Poplar.

A fourth cousin, James Hamilton, was charged with violent disorder. They went on trial on 14 January 2014. The prosecution claim that Paul Hamilton stabbed his cousin Liam Hamilton in the back with a kitchen knife during a mass brawl involving nine members of the same family. Jurors heard the dispute began as a falling out between two eight-year-old girls, the daughter of Thomas Hamilton and the niece of Liam Hamilton. It culminated with a 'standoff' between Liam and four of his brothers on one side and Thomas and his brothers Noel, Paul and James. Mobile phone footage of the fight, filmed by a local resident, shows Paul inflicting the fatal blow in the doorway of a block of flats, the court heard. Three knives including the murder weapon were found at the scene. Jurors were told two were wielded by Liam's brothers.

On 13 February Paul Hamilton was convicted of murder. Noel, Thomas and James were cleared of all charges. Paul Hamilton was sentenced to life imprisonment with a minimum of 26 years before parole. Judge Paul Worsley QC said: 'This is in every sense a tragic case and the whole Hamilton family has been blighted by the events of that night. 'The victim was your cousin, not a stranger, he was only 32 and his partner will have his unborn child on her own. That child will never know its father. 'The stabbing arose from a petty squabble between two children; it was allowed to escalate into violence.

'Threats were made; weapons were produced culminating with you arming yourself with a terrifying knife. 'At one stage your brothers told you to put that knife away but when Liam arrived on the scene completely unarmed, he never had a weapon in his hand, within moments you had rearmed yourself and followed your brothers into the street to where he was. 'Liam presented no threat to you at that time; you could have gone and called the police. 'What you did was to arm yourself, run around the corner, went straight to Liam and, with your brothers around you, you drove that knife into his back six inches. The knife penetrated his ribs and heart. 'Your violence is incomprehensible and totally out of character. You are hard-working and have a partner and two young children.' Detective Sergeant Martin Head from the Metropolitan Police's Homicide and Major Crime Command said: "What started as a seemingly minor family row escalated into a senseless murder, which will have a long-lasting impact on all members of the family.

"This is a tragedy for all involved and it is right that Paul Hamilton should spend a long time behind bars for his actions." Liam's partner Abbie Unwin, who is now heavily pregnant with his child, said in a statement: 'All the time in the world can never take away the heartache of losing the love of my life and father of my unborn child.

The issue of stopping knife and gun crime on our streets will never be solved until we as a society regain the morals we once held, and parents start teaching their children the morals around community and society as a whole.

In some ways, I can understand knife and gun crime between gangs because they believe they have something to prove, but the lack of morals that allowed family members to kill each other over a child's argument is beyond belief. Through March, April and

May there were lots of cross deployments that had quite an effect on my work.

In May I had a MARAP for a four-handed murder, all four offenders were on my caseload.

Sixteen-year-old Peter Hagan was stabbed to death at a party in Wandsworth on 17 February 2013. He was found injured in the ground floor stairwell of the Albon House block of flats in Neville Gill Close at around 1.30 am. Peter was pronounced dead at the scene. A post-mortem found he died of a stab wound to the left leg which severed the femoral artery. He had also been stabbed in the hip, neck, back and buttock. On February 20 police charged Romell Martin, 21 of Fairgreen Road, Thornton Heath, with murder. A second suspect Jermaal Ferguson, 22, of no fixed address, was charged with murder on April 4.

Two more were charged on 20 June: Malki Ferguson, 21 of Albon House, Neville Gill Close, and Dean Harmes, 26 of Wentworth Court, Garrett Lane, Wandsworth. They went on trial at the Old Bailey on 19 November 2013. The court heard the party was held at the Ferguson family flat in Albon House to celebrate the 19th birthday of their sister Jamelia Ferguson.

Jurors were told a fight broke out soon after Peter Hagan and his group of friends arrived at the party at 1 am. Harmes sprayed CS gas in the living room and the other three defendants armed themselves with knives and a hammer. Prosecutor William Boyce QC told the court: "Peter Hagan went out onto the balcony to escape the fumes. "Members of the older group confronted them and began to attack them. Peter Hagan was stabbed several times before he fell to the floor." Peter was also kicked and hit with a bottle before he managed to escape the flat. He collapsed at the bottom of the stairwell and bled to death. CCTV footage appeared to show Harmes leaving the block with a knife and heading towards a park. On 17 December 2013, the jury convicted all four suspects of murder. They were jailed for life the following day. Jamaal Ferguson was told he would serve at least 21 years before parole.

Harmes, Martin and Malki Ferguson were told they would serve at least 17 years. Judge Peter Rook, QC, told the killers: 'All four of you were involved in a joint attack on partygoers at a 19th birthday party.

'They were not gate crashers and had been invited to the party. The four of you turned a celebration into the scene of a murderous knife attack. 'You used various weapons including a kitchen knife, a bottle of CS gas and a hammer - it would have terrified all those present. 'It was a grotesque and disproportionate attack and was unprovoked. All he did was go to the party to celebrate the birthday. You took away his most precious possession - life itself.

'There were stab wounds to the back, thigh, upper left arm and there was a score mark to the neck. The knife was seen going all over the place and significantly he had no self-defence marks. 'He was kicked and struck while on the floor and that spoke volumes about the nature of the attack. 'Jamaal Ferguson I do not doubt that you were the prime mover and in my view, you are a very dangerous young man. Romell Martin, you lent yourself to assisting this violent attack.

Dean Harmes you discharged the CS canister and you joined in the attack after he had been stabbed, kicking him and hitting him with a bottle. 'Malki Ferguson you fetched a claw hammer from your bedroom and I reject your case that you only had the hammer when the attack was over.' Investigating officer Detective Inspector Simon Pickford, from the Homicide and Major Crime

Command, said: "The level of violence used was extreme and there was little or no provocation to spark the violence. "These four men attended a teenager's birthday party and whilst there armed themselves with an array of weapons including a knife, CS spray and a hammer. They were prepared to kill or seriously injure anyone who crossed them; this has been a brutal and shocking case.

I would like to pay tribute to the victim's family who have conducted themselves with dignity throughout the investigation and court case. I would also like to thank the many other guests at the party who supported the police investigation." With these four it again demonstrates the gang mentality and the lack of morals that life can mean so little, they were all plastic gangsters but Harmes was an especially arrogant piece of shit.

In May I would also pick up a life-sentenced prisoner who had absconded from open prison and committed another armed robbery. An armed robber nicknamed the "Skull Cracker" has been jailed for life for raiding a Surrey building society while on the run from an open prison. Michael Wheatley, 55, pleaded guilty to the £18,350 raid at Chelsea Building Society in Sunbury on 7 May. He also admitted possessing a firearm and being unlawfully at large. Judge Christopher Critchlow at Guildford Crown Court ordered him to serve a minimum of 10 years. Wheatley appeared via video link from prison. The court heard he previously robbed the same building society branch 13 years earlier and staff had been told to be on their guard following his disappearance. Judge Critchlow said this was a "special case" because of Wheatley's prolific record of violent armed robberies and committing offences after being released from prison. "It is clear the public must be protected from you for a long time," he said. The court heard Wheatley had 23 previous convictions for robbery, two for attempted robbery and 18 for related firearms offences. He was serving a life sentence at Standford Hill prison on the Isle of Sheppey in Kent, when he was granted day release and failed to return on 3 May.

He was arrested in Tower Hamlets, east London, after being on the run for five days following the Sunbury raid. In 2002 he was given 13 life sentences for raids on banks and building societies. Wheatley earned his nickname for using an imitation handgun as a blunt weapon to hit people - including a 73-year-old woman - during his robberies. He had gone on the run twice in the past and each time staged a series of violent robberies before being caught and re-jailed. Wheatley was a grumpy old git but I got on alright with him, I would start the process with him but I wouldn't finish all that I would normally do because I would end up being off sick a lot during this year.

20. Medical Retirement

In January 2015, I was called in for a work capability meeting, as I was approaching half pay and the new No1 governor was determined to get rid of staff on long term sick. It was agreed that if I finished on the day of the interview, he would pay me 13 weeks at full pay as severance. It was agreed that the 23rd January 2015 would be my last day in the prison service; he also agreed that pending the outcome of the "Atos" investigation into my medical condition he would alter the record to show I had been granted medical retirement, and not dismissed for medical inefficiency.

I left the prison after the meeting; and handed in my baton, my warrant card, keys and key tallies. I walked out never to return, eventually, my final pay came through and it was about two thousand pounds less than I was expecting. I phoned shared services to check what was happening, they told me the governor didn't have the power to pay me 13 weeks at full pay when I was due to go on half-pay. I wrote a snotty letter of complaint to the governor but his response was Oh sorry I didn't realise, the problem is there was nothing I could do about it, and so I just had to get on with it.

In March I had confirmation that I had been granted medical retirement, and so I had some satisfaction because I had worked my bollocks off throughout my service. The thought of being dismissed for inefficiency was my worst nightmare. The effect of leaving the service when I didn't want to was devastating; it was a job I loved.

Throughout my service, the basics of the job remained the same, Custody, Control and Security. As my service progressed this changed depending on the department I worked in.

On the house block, I would have to add a counsellor and dogsbody running around sorting out prisoners problems. In the seg, fighter was added as it was a volatile place to work, when I moved onto OMU the three basics remained but now I would be overseeing the sentences of those on my caseload. This would include liaising with multiple agencies, so I could complete sentence plans and move the offenders on to other prisons so they could complete the offending behaviour course that had been identified for them. Day to day most prison officers have no idea what a prisoner is in for unless they are on the VP (vulnerable prisoner) spur, During my last nine years in the job working on the Offender Management Unit I got to speak with them in-depth about their crimes. That could mean listening to why terrorists do what they do, listening to the details from a murderer, rapist or paedophile.

This brings a whole new perspective to the job and in reality, most officers shouldn't know these details, I consider myself lucky that I can put what I have seen and heard in little boxes in my mind and close the lid. Recently PTSD has become a thing in the service, and while I am not saying what I have seen, heard and done has not affected me I don't believe I suffer from PTSD as some do.

I believe that you have to be a certain type of person to do the job, if you don't like violence, the sight of blood, verbal abuse or can't deal with someone who has attempted or succeeded in taking their own life it's not the job for you.

Acknowledgements

The Chair

I could not have lived this life and written this book without the help of a few special people along the way. I have to thank my wife Carol and my kids Shelley and Sam, for putting up with me when I came home from work after a bad day. I must apologise for the stress I caused them at times throughout my career, they were always there for me. I must also acknowledge the staff that helped me do the job to the best of my ability, but I have to thank Shep especially for always having my back no matter what situations we got ourselves into, I did and do trust him with my life and we remain good friends.

Shep

This book is dedicated to my partner Pauline, who has always been there for me, my two stepdaughters, Amanda and Kelly, also my two grandsons who are my world. Also to Bob who I wrote the book with, who always had my back and who I trusted with my life on the landings and is still now a great friend. And to all the staff I worked with I wish you luck in life. To those who have passed on R.I.P., I'm sure we will meet again.

Printed in Great Britain
by Amazon